Lecture Notes in Computer Science   6266

Commenced Publication in 1973
Founding and Former Series Editors:
Gerhard Goos, Juris Hartmanis, and Jan van Leeuwen

Editorial Board

Sami Khuri   Lenka Lhotská
Nadia Pisanti (Eds.)

Information Technology in Bio- and Medical Informatics, ITBAM 2010

First International Conference
Bilbao, Spain, September 1-2, 2010
Proceedings

 Springer

Volume Editors

Sami Khuri
San José State University
Department of Computer Science
One Washington Square
San José, CA 95192-0249, USA.
E-mail: khuri@cs.sjsu.edu

Lenka Lhotská
Czech Technical University
Faculty of Electrical Engineering
Department of Cybernetics, Technicka 2
166 27 Prague 6, Czech Republic
E-mail: lhotska@fel.cvut.cz

Nadia Pisanti
University of Pisa
Dipartimento di Informatica
Largo Pontecorvo 3
56127 Pisa, Italy
E-mail: pisanti@di.unipi.it

Library of Congress Control Number: 2010931841

CR Subject Classification (1998): H.3, H.5.2, I.4, H.4, H.5, J.1

LNCS Sublibrary: SL 3 – Information Systems and Application, incl. Internet/Web and HCI

ISSN	0302-9743
ISBN-10	3-642-15019-5 Springer Berlin Heidelberg New York
ISBN-13	978-3-642-15019-7 Springer Berlin Heidelberg New York

springer.com

© Springer-Verlag Berlin Heidelberg 2010
Printed in Germany

Typesetting: Camera-ready by author, data conversion by Scientific Publishing Services, Chennai, India
Printed on acid-free paper   06/3180

Preface

Biomedical engineering and medical informatics are challenging and rapidly growing areas. Applications of information technology in these areas are of paramount importance. The aim of the first ITBAM conference was to bring together scientists, researchers and practitioners from different disciplines (mathematics, bioinformatics, biology, medicine, biomedical engineering and computer science) having such common interests. We hope that ITBAM conferences will provide opportunities for fruitful discussions between all attendees and provide a platform where participants can exchange their most recent results, identify future directions and challenges, initiate possible collaborative research and system development, and develop common languages for solving problems in the realm of biomedical engineering, bioinformatics and medical informatics. The importance of computer-aided diagnosis and therapy has drawn more and more attention worldwide and laid the foundation for modern medicine with excellent potential for promising applications such as telemedicine, Web-based healthcare and analysis of genetic information.

For this conference, after a peer-review process, we finally selected 13 long papers and 8 short papers that are now published in this volume. They are divided in to the following groups: workflow management and database; decision support and data management in biomedicine; medical data modelling and information retrieval; data mining in bioinformatics; knowledge representation and data management in bioinformatics; biological data and signal processing. The papers show how broad the spectrum of topics in applications of information technology to biomedical engineering and medical informatics is.

The editors would like to thank all the participants for their high-quality contributions and Springer for publishing the proceedings of this conference. Our special thanks go to Gabriela Wagner for her hard work on various aspects of this event.

June 2010

Lenka Lhotska
Nadia Pisanti
Sami Khuri

Organization

Honorary Chair

Rudolf Freund   Technical University Vienna, Austria
Marie-France Sagot   INRIA, France
Anna Tramontano   University of Rome „La Sapienza", Italy

General Chair

Roland R. Wagner   University of Linz, Austria

Conference Program Chair

Sami Khuri   San José State University, USA
Lenka Lhotska   Czech Technical University Prague, Czech Republic
Nadia Pisanti   University of Pisa, Italy

Poster Session Chair

Vaclav Chudacek   Czech Technical University in Prague,
      Czech Republic
Roland Wagner   University of Linz, Austria

Program Committee

Werner Aigner   FAW, Austria
Fuat Akal   Functional Genomics Center Zurich, Switzerland
Tatsuya Akutsu   Kyoto University, Japan
Andreas Albrecht   Queen's University Belfast, UK
Lijo Anto   University of Kerala, India
Rubén Armañanzas
    Arnedillo   University of the Basque Country, Spain
Peter Baumann   Jacobs University Bremen, Germany
Balaram Bhattacharyya   Visva-Bharati University, India
Christian Blaschke   Bioalma Madrid, Spain
Veselka Boeva   Technical University of Plovdiv, Bulgaria
Gianluca Bontempi   Université Libre de Bruxelles, Belgium
Roberta Bosotti   Nerviano Medical Science s.r.l., Italy
Rita Casadio   University of Bologna, Italy

Sònia Casillas   Universitat Autonoma de Barcelona, Spain
Silvana Castano   Universita' degli Studi di Milano, Italy
Carlo Cattani   Difarma, Università di Salerno, Italy
Kun-Mao Chao   National Taiwan University, Taiwan
Vaclav Chudacek   Czech Technical University in Prague,
                               Czech Republic
Bin Cui   Peking University, China
Coral del Val Muñoz   University of Granada, Spain
Qiwen Dong   Harbin Institute of Technology, China
Béatrice Duval   University of Angers, France
Hans-Dieter Ehrich   Technical University of Braunschweig, Germany
Mourad Elloumi   University of Tunis, Tunisia
Maria Federico   University of Modena and Reggio Emilia, Italy
Pedro Fernandes   Inst.Gulbenkian de Ciência, Portugal
Rudolf Freund   European Molecular Computing Consortium, Austria
Christoph M. Friedrich   Fraunhofer SCAI, Germany
Xiangchao Gan   University of Oxford, UK
Alejandro Giorgetti   University of Verona, Italy
Alireza Hadj Khodabakhshi   Simon Fraser University, Canada
Volker Heun   Ludwig-Maximilians-Universität München, Germany
Chun-Hsi Huang   University of Connecticut, USA
Lars Kaderali   University of Heidelberg, Germany
Alastair Kerr   University of Edinburgh, UK
Sami Khuri   San Jose State University, USA
Erich Peter Klement   University of Linz, Austria
Michal Krátký   Technical University of Ostrava, Czech Republic
Josef Küng   University of Linz, Austria
Gorka Lasso-Cabrera   CICbioGUNE, Spain
Reinhard Laubenbacher   Virginia Tech, USA
Marc F. Lensink   SCMBB, Belgium
Lenka Lhotska   Czech Technical University, Czech Republic
Roger Marshall   Plymouth Ystate University, USA
Elio Masciari   ICAR-CNR, Università della Calabria, Italy
Henning Mersch   RWTH Aachen University, Germany
Silvia Miksch   Danube University Krems, Austria
Aleksandar Milosavljevic   Baylor College of Medicine, USA
Jean-Christophe Nebel   Kingston University, UK
See Kiong Ng   Institute for Infocomm Research, Singapore
Vit Novacek   National University of Ireland, Galway, Ireland
Philipp Pagel   Technische Universität München, Germany
Francisco Pinto   ITQB, University of Lisbon, Portugal
Nadia Pisanti   University of Pisa, Italy
Cinzia Pizzi   Universita' degli Studi di Padova, Italy
Clara Pizzuti   ICA-CNR, Italy
Meikel Poess   Oracle Corporation, USA
Nicole Radde   Universität Stuttgart, Germany

Dietrich	
Rebholz-Schuhmann	European Bioinformatics Institute, UK
Cristina Rubio-Escudero	University of Seville, Spain
Victor Sabbia	Universidad de la República, Uruguay
Hershel Safer	Weizmann Institute of Science, Israel
Nick Sahinidis	Carnegie Mellon University, USA
Francisca Sánchez Jiménez	University of Málaga, Spain
Roberto Santana	University of the Basque Country, Spain
Kenji Satou	Kanazawa University, Japan
Kristan Schneider	University of Vienna, Austria
Kathleen Steinhofel	King's College London, UK
Ralf Tautenhahn	The Scripps Research Institute, USA
A. Min Tjoa	Vienna University of Technology, Austria
Thodoros Topaloglou	University of Toronto, Canada
Paul van der Vet	University of Twente, The Netherlands
Jano van Hemert	University of Edinburgh, UK
Roland R. Wagner	University of Linz, Austria
Viacheslav Wolfengagen	JurInfoR-MSU Institute for Contemporary Education, Russia
Borys Wrobel	Polish Academy of Sciences, Poland
Filip Zavoral	Charles University in Prague, Czech Republic
Filip Zelezny	Czech Technical University, Czech Republic
Songmao Zhang	Chinese Academy of Sciences, China
Qiang Zhu	The University of Michigan, USA
Frank Gerrit Zoellner	University of Heidelberg, Germany

External Reviewers

Francisco Martínez-Álvarez
Olivier Caelen
Abhilash Miranda
Qian Gang
Chao Zhu
Manish Singh
Shen Xu

Ben Liu
Yi Guo
Zhe Xu
Rung-Ren Lin
Leonidas Kapsokalivas
Abu Z. Dayem Ullah

Table of Contents

Workflow Management and Database

e-BioFlow: Improving Practical Use of Workflow Systems in
Bioinformatics 1
    Ingo Wassink, Matthijs Ooms, Pieter Neerincx,
    Gerrit van der Veer, Han Rauwerda, Jack A.M. Leunissen,
    Timo M. Breit, Anton Nijholt, and Paul van der Vet

MEDCollector: Multisource Epidemic Data Collector 16
    João Zamite, Fabrício A.B. Silva, Francisco Couto, and
    Mário J. Silva

Epidemic Marketplace: An Information Management System for
Epidemiological Data 31
    Luis F. Lopes, Fabrício A.B. Silva, Francisco Couto, João Zamite,
    Hugo Ferreira, Carla Sousa, and Mário J. Silva

Decision Support and Data Management in Biomedicine

DCM Data Management Framework: A Data Warehousing Approach ... 45
    Shehla Khalid, Claire Surr, and Daniel Neagu

Automatic Classification of Intrapartal Fetal Heart-Rate
Recordings – Can It Compete with Experts? 57
    Václav Chudáček, Jiří Spilka, Michal Huptych, George Georgoulas,
    Petr Janků, Michal Koucký, Chrysostomos Stylios, and
    Lenka Lhotská

Clinical Informatics to Diagnose Cardiac Diseases Based on Data
Mining 67
    Sung Ho Ha and Zhen Yu Zhang

Decision Support in Biomedicine (Short Papers)

The Case-Based Software System for Physician's Decision Support 78
    Leonid Karpov and Valery Yudin

SASAgent: An Agent Based Architecture for Search, Retrieval and
Composition of e-Science Models and Tools 86
    Luiz Felipe Mendes, Regina Braga, and Fernanda Campos

Clustering of Protein Substructures for Discovery of a Novel Class of
Sequence-Structure Fragments   94
    Ivana Rudolfova, Jaroslav Zendulka, and Matej Lexa

A Comorbidity Network Approach to Predict Disease Risk   102
    Francesco Folino, Clara Pizzuti, and Maria Ventura

Mining and Post-Processing of Association Rules in the Atherosclerosis
Risk Domain   110
    Petr Berka and Jan Rauch

Medical Data Modeling and Information Retrieval

Optimized Column-Oriented Model: A Storage and Search Efficient
Representation of Medical Data   118
    Razan Paul and Abu Sayed Md. Latiful Hoque

A Semantic Query Interface for the OGO Platform   128
    José Antonio Miñarro-Giménez, Mikel Egaña Aranguren,
    Francisco García-Sánchez, and Jesualdo Tomás Fernández-Breis

BioMedical Information Retrieval: The BioTracer Approach   143
    Heri Ramampiaro

Data Mining in Bioinformatics

A Self-Organizing State Space Approach to Inferring Time-Varying
Causalities between Regulatory Proteins   158
    Osamu Hirose and Kentaro Shimizu

Knowledge Representation and Data Management in Bioinformatics

Retrieving Samples from Biobanks   172
    Claus Dabringer and Johann Eder

Logical Knowledge Representation of Regulatory Relations in
Biomedical Pathways   186
    Sine Zambach and Jens Ulrik Hansen

Smooth Introduction of Semantic Tagging in Genotyping Procedures . . .   201
    Alessio Bechini, Jacopo Viotto, and Riccardo Giannini

Biological Data and Signal Processing

Laboratory Kit for Oscillometry Measurement of Blood Pressure   215
    Jan Dvořák and Jan Havlík

Initial Analysis of the EEG Signal Processing Methods for Studying
Correlations between Muscle and Brain Activity 220
    Helena Valentová and Jan Havlík

Highlighting the Current Issues with Pride Suggestions for Improving
the Performance of Real Time Cardiac Health Monitoring 226
    Mohamed Ezzeldin A. Bashir, Dong Gyu Lee,
    Makki Akasha, Gyeong Min Yi, Eun-jong Cha, Jang-whan Bae,
    Myeong Chan Cho, and Keun Ho Ryu

Author Index 235

e-BioFlow: Improving Practical Use of Workflow Systems in Bioinformatics

Ingo Wassink[1,6], Matthijs Ooms[1,6], Pieter Neerincx[2,6],
Gerrit van der Veer[1,3,6], Han Rauwerda[4,6], Jack A.M. Leunissen[5,6],
Timo M. Breit[4,6], Anton Nijholt[1,6], and Paul van der Vet[1,6]

[1] Human Media Interaction Group, University of Twente, The Netherlands
[2] Biomolecular Mass Spectrometry and Proteomics Group, Utrecht University,
The Netherlands
[3] Open University, Heerlen, The Netherlands
[4] Microarray Department and Integrative Bioinformatics Unit,
University of Amsterdam, The Netherlands
[5] Laboratory of Bioinformatics, Wageningen University and Research,
The Netherlands
[6] Netherlands Bioinformatics Centre, Nijmegen, The Netherlands

Abstract. Workflow management systems (WfMSs) are useful tools for bioinformaticians. As experiences with using WfMSs accumulate, shortcomings of current systems become apparent. In this paper, we focus on practical issues that hinder WfMS users and that arise in the design and execution of workflows, and in access of web services. We present e-BioFlow, a workflow engine that demonstrates in which way a number of these problems can be solved. e-BioFlow offers an improved user interface, can deal with large data volumes, stores all provenance, and has a powerful provenance browser. e-BioFlow also offers the possibility to design and run workflows step by step, allowing its users an explorative research style.

1 Introduction

Today, workflow management systems (WfMSs) are recognised as useful tools for chaining computational tasks [1,2] and in particular for orchestrating web services [3,4]. Open-source WfMSs for scientific computation (e.g., Kepler [5] and Triana [6]) and specifically for bioinformatics (e.g., Taverna [7]) enjoy worldwide use. Several companies also sell proprietary WfMSs, but the bioinformatics community tends to standardise on open-source systems.

In the course of developing several bioinformatics workflows, including a workflow for demonstrating the use of R in Taverna [8] and OligoRAP (to be discussed below), we have run against a number of issues that stand in the way of smooth use of WfMSs in daily practice. Our experiences complement those of [2] and [4]. To demonstrate that many of the problems we found can be solved, we designed and built our own workflow system called *e-BioFlow* [9]. e-BioFlow pays particular attention to user interaction and provenance. e-BioFlow moreover enables

S. Khuri, L. Lhotská, and N. Pisanti (Eds.): ITBAM 2010, LNCS 6266, pp. 1–15, 2010.

the user to build and run workflows step by step. Bioinformaticians can experiment with their workflows until they are satisfied and only then store them. The combination of the ability to handle large data volumes, improved user interaction, and the feature of designing a workflow in an ad-hoc fashion, inspecting all data at all times, is, we believe, unique. e-BioFlow is based on an open-source workflow engine that has proven its worth in practice, YAWL [10]. e-BioFlow is itself an open-source experimentation platform.

Summarising our experiences, we found user interaction provided by existing tools cumbersome, in design, in execution, and afterwards when provenance has to be accessed. We also found it necessary to take extra measures to handle gigabytes of data flowing through the system. Running times can be long for bioinformatics workflows; most of the workflows we ran take hours to complete. This makes working with most current workflow tools laborious. One has to re-run the entire workflow when one wants to change parts of the workflow or when an unexpected termination occurs, for example the system crashes or an essential external resource proves to be unavailable. We realised that we can solve the latter problems by building an elaborate mechanism for storing and retrieving provenance, which in itself is a necessary component of any workflow system for bioinformatics. We avoided many problems associated with web services by using only BioMoby [11] services on databases that were mirrored in-house. Nevertheless, we know that web services pose problems of their own and we therefore address such problems in this paper as well. Finally, we wanted to profit from the wealth of experience with workflows in the business administration community.

A typical example of the kind of bioinformatics workflows we address in this paper is OligoRAP, used for automatic re-annotation of transcriptomics probe libraries [12,13]. A high-quality oligonucleotide probe library is an essential component of genome-wide microarray-based gene-expression experiments. In order to maintain the quality of the information associated with the probes, this information has to be updated when new sequence or annotation data is released. An OligoRAP client orchestrates BioMoby web services to automatically check the target specificity of the oligonucleotide probes and update their annotations. The client calls nucleotide alignment search tools such as BLAT [14] and BLAST [15], fetches annotations provided by the Ensembl [16] project and performs a quality assessment. An OligoRAP run is not wholly linear; for example, the BLAT service is iteratively polled for output and the BLAST service is only called under certain conditions. The result of an OligoRAP run consists of XML files that provide detailed information per probe and a quality assessment of the whole library.

2   Definitions

We will first lay down our terminology. A *workflow* is a representation of a coherent collection of several *tasks* to execute a procedure. At the lowest level, tasks (Taverna says "processors") are executed in a predefined order and with a preset data exchange. This may not be obvious at a higher level, as when, for example, tasks are executed in a parallel interleaved routing scheme. In such a scheme, it would appear that a task t_i is executed repeatedly with a different set of data, while the next task t_{i+1} starts for each set of data output by t_i. Under the hood, however, t_i is not a single task: it is copied as many times as needed to process all data sets and every copy is executed in a predefined order.

A *workflow management system* (WfMS) is a software environment to design and run workflows. When the workflow is run or (as jargon has it) *enacted*, a concrete instance of the workflow is created and executed. Design of a workflow and enactment can in principle be done by different WfMSs as long as both systems understand the language used to represent the workflow. In practice, design and enactment are almost always done within the same WfMS. If we want to interleave design and execution, using the same WfMS for both is of course the only practical solution. A *data pipeline* is a type of workflow in which the flow of data is emphasised, and besides the control imposed by the data flow, there is little or no other control. *Workflow patterns* [17] are generalizations of often-occurring combinations of tasks and how they are executed in relation to each other in a workflow.

Each task in a workflow can be *composite* or *atomic*. If a task is composite, it is a workflow itself. By using composite tasks, the workflow designer can ease the design and interpretation of a workflow. Such workflows are also known as *hierarchic workflows*. Tasks can invoke *resources*, which are by definition extraneous to the workflow. Examples of such resources are: scripts, web services, and programs that govern user interaction.

A workflow can be offered to others for use as such or with some modification. In this way, the bioinformatics community can share and mutually assess their workflows. This concept is promising, as the success of the myExperiment (www.myexperiment.org, [18]) shows.

3   Workflow Use in Other Domains

The use of WfMSs in business administration [19] predates that in bioinformatics by at least a decade and there is a wealth of practical experience with such systems. Business administration WfMSs are used to (partly) automate fixed administrative procedures like that of approval of an application for a bank account. The emphasis is on control. In this tradition, the need for formal models underlying WfMSs has been stressed [20] and a repertoire of workflow patterns has been compiled [17] to assess the expressivity of different workflow languages, to understand the differences between workflow engines, and to serve as a set of benchmarks for comparing the performance of different WfMSs. These patterns mainly concern synchronisation. For example, a task can only start when all previous tasks have finished, or when at least one previous task has finished, or when precisely one previous task has finished. Similar patterns can be defined for when a task finishes: will it start all tasks downstream, at least one task, or precisely one task? We may want to impose conditions on the synchronisation links. More complicated patterns involving, for example, iteration, cancellation, and interleaved parallel execution are defined, too. By way of good practice, any WfMS should be able to support and formally validate at least each of the relevant patterns for the domain it addresses.

It is tempting to profit from the experience gained with business administration WfMSs, but in bioinformatics the prevailing trend is to implement from scratch. Nonetheless, commercial business administration WfMSs such as Microsoft's BizTalk have successfully been used for designing and running bioinformatics workflows [21].

A second strand is the use of workflows for Grid computing, i.e., massive, data-intensive and collaborative computations that are parallelised over clusters of computers. Taverna has been developed in the course of the UK myGrid-project and Kepler and Triana have originally been designed for use on grids for heavy scientific (such as astronomical, meteorological, or geological) computations. Kepler and Triana can handle massive workloads, which are several orders of magnitude larger than what is now common in bioinformatics [2]. Although originating from a Grid project, Taverna has focussed on applications in the bioinformatics domain.

A third strand of workflow use is in Laboratory Information Management Systems (LIMSs). The data model of a LIMS is determined by the nature and sequence of wet-lab processes for which it has to capture the data and metadata. A WfMS is a suitable tool for data collection, in particular now automatic registration devices make their way into the laboratory. Therefore, each piece of laboratory equipment can communicate with a computer system to hold the (meta)data and produce an automatic lab journal. Such LIMSs can then be integrated with the WfMSs used by bioinformaticians for their *in-silico* experiments. One step further, but still based on workflows, is the idea to automate the wet-lab experimentation process wholly or partially [22]. In these WfMSs, the data aspect of Grid computing and the control aspect of business applications are both prominent.

4   Workflow Topics

Returning to the themes identified in the introduction, we have encountered the following topics over the past years of practical experience with workflows and WfMSs in bioinformatics. We group them into three categories:

- *Design*
    - (a) User interface for bioinformaticians.
    - (b) Verification tools for checking properties of the workflow.
    - (c) Enactment of parts and individual tasks of a workflow.
- *Provenance*
    - (d) Handling large data volumes.
    - (e) Storing provenance.
    - (f) Accessing provenance after the workflow has been enacted.
- *Web services*
    - (g) Finding the appropriate web service for the job at hand.
    - (h) Quality of service of a web service.

- (i) Interoperability of web services.
- (j) Quality of content of a web service.

e-BioFlow pays particular attention to *Design* and to *Provenance*. In the remainder of this survey, we will discuss these topics. This list reflects our own experiences and is by no means exhaustive. Moreover, as bioinformaticians continue to design and enact workflows, other experiences will come in.

5 Design

Workflows are normally designed using a graphical user interface, in which the workflow is represented as a graph. The interface hides the representation of the technical details of the workflow. In the graphs, the tasks are the nodes of the workflow, while their relations (data flow, synchronisation) are the edges. Most design interfaces allow the user to drag and drop tasks onto the workflow pane and to connect them by means of a few mouse clicks. Still, designing a good workflow can be hard; see [23] for a more theoretical overview of design issues. A typical bioinformatician will primarily pay attention to the flow of data, but at the same time control aspects play a role [24]. Besides, the choice of resources invoked by tasks has to be addressed. The result is often information overload.

In the development of e-BioFlow, we have paid a lot of attention to the interaction with the system. We have improved the user interface, we have enabled formal verification of the workflow and, perhaps most importantly, e-BioFlow can be run as an ad-hoc WfMS, allowing the user to explore all kinds of tasks, task orderings and parameter settings. This makes e-BioFlow suited even for once-only WfMS experiments, a feature that is unique.

(a) The user interface for design

The user interface for design should take the prevention of information overload into account by not trying to squeeze all information onto a single screen. e-BioFlow has three design views, one for each aspect: control (synchronisation and iteration), data flow, and choice of resources [25]. The user can easily switch between views. Each view shows a pane that can be changed by the user. The panes are related because the same tasks are present in each of them. To help orientation, tasks are always in the same place on each of the three panes.

The three panes are related in another way as well. When we draw a data link between two tasks, this normally implies a control link, too. The data link stipulates that the task downstream needs the data output by the task upstream and therefore has to wait for the upstream task to finish. The converse is not true. A control link can be just that: a signal that a task has to wait for another task to finish even though no data are passed. As a result, every edge drawn in the data flow pane should automatically insert an edge in the control pane while an edge drawn in the control pane does not introduce an edge in the data pane. A data-oriented bioinformatician can start in the data flow pane, to switch to the control pane when the data relations are in place.

(b) Verification tools

Because a workflow is designed to run to completion when enacted, it is important to guard for deadlock and livelock (infinite loops). Another problem is tasks that will not be executed no matter how the workflow is enacted. Such tasks are called dead tasks (not to be confused with dead web services). The presence of a dead task in a workflow can indicate a workflow design error. Checking a workflow for deadlock, livelock and dead tasks can be done manually, but when the workflow gets large this becomes time-consuming, difficult and error-prone. It is far better to follow the tradition of business administration workflows and have an automatic check for such irregularities. This can be realised only when the workflow is represented in an underlying process algebra. Through the work of van der Aalst and co-workers [20], the Petri net formalism enjoys widespread popularity but there are other process algebras that will do the job. Kepler, for example, is based on the dataflow process network formalism [5,26]. e-BioFlow is based on YAWL [10] which itself is a formally correct extension of Petri Nets.

(c) Enactment of parts and individual tasks

A large problem facing designers is that in the current generation of WfMSs, the workflow has to be designed fully from start to finish before it can be enacted. A workflow engine such as Taverna does allow individual tasks to be tested, but it is not possible to incrementally add further tasks, testing underway all the time. Design will normally proceed through several design-enact-debug cycles. For a once-only workflow, the investment of designing a workflow will not pay off. Even for workflows that are to be used several times, the investment may be too large because it is impossible to test parts of the workflow. Finally, researchers very often only know what their workflow should do when they have had the opportunity to look at the data and to play with parameter settings, different algorithms, and different ways to visualise results. For them, the obligation to design a complete workflow before it can be enacted makes a WfMS the wrong tool for the job.

Such problems can be solved by means of a so-called *ad-hoc workflow management system*, also known as an adaptive WfMS [27]. In e-BioFlow, which can be run as an ad-hoc WfMS, design and enactment are interwoven. Each task and each part of the workflow can be run individually. Input data can be provided if upstream tasks have been run or if we have kept data from a previous attempt. Based on the data produced by the previous task, a decision can be made for the next task. Thus, an in-silico experiment can be run on a trial-and-error basis, which means to a bioinformatician the possibility to explore the data. This is useful for once-only experiments, but it is also a good way to design workflows that have to be run repeatedly.

In a teach-back survey [28], most of the 50 bioinformaticians with workflow experience we interviewed found the idea of an ad-hoc WfMSs appealing [29].

6   Provenance

The second cluster of problems we ran into was related to the huge volumes of data that the WfMS has to be able to handle in real-life bioinformatics cases. An OligoRAP workflow that handles a realistic amount of oligonucleotide probes, say, 20,000 probes, has to cope with approximately 3 GB of data. Business administration WfMSs, typically dealing with few data, not only pass the data as such, but also copy data between tasks. If OligoRAP were implemented that way, we would have needed a special machine to run it. However, we wanted to run OligoRAP on a commodity PC. With such amounts of data, moreover, storing and in particular accessing provenance is a challenge as well.

(d) Handling large data volumes

e-BioFlow solves the data problem by storing data in a database as soon as they are produced. When a task needs data, it fetches its data from the database by means of an SQL query. The workflow only passes pointers to the data. This is known as *pass by reference* [13]. Apart from freeing the computer system from handling massive amounts of data, pass by reference also ensures that the data are kept in a safe place in case the computer system unexpectedly breaks down. It may be argued that storage and retrieval of data makes the WfMS slower. We found this effect to be marginal or non-existent. When no provisions are made for large volumes, the system gets slow because it has to update memory and perform swaps, if the workflow can be run to end at all.

The way of working of e-BioFlow carries additional advantages. Provenance is automatically recorded. Ad-hoc design needs data at every step. The database makes ad-hoc design possible. Finally, the database can be used as cache. We will discuss these issues now.

(e) Storing provenance

The importance of provenance has been stressed by various authors [30,31,32]. In the context of WfMSs, provenance is a complete record of a single enactment of a workflow and comprises the registration of all data passed between tasks and all relevant metadata, resulting in a complete trace of the workflow enactment. This relates to the importance of verification and reproducibility for bioinformatics experimentation [33,34,35]. As we said above, e-BioFlow stores all data in a database by default. For provenance purposes, the data are decorated with metadata that provide information about the task that produced them and further details (date/time, information about the resource accessed, such as version number and URL, and similar). In this way, provenance collection is an intended side-effect of the design of e-BioFlow. The design also guarantees that provenance is complete.

Ad-hoc design is impossible without storage of results of previous steps. Moreover, these results should be immediately accessible at all times in the ad-hoc process. The database takes care of both requirements.

The database can additionally be used as cache. This idea was first proposed in the context of the Kepler system under the name of smart reruns [36]. Results of computationally demanding tasks can be stored in the cache and reused. Reuse is advantageous in case of an error downstream in the workflow or when we run a workflow repeatedly and know that certain tasks will produce output that is not changed with respect to the last time the workflow was run. e-BioFlow offers the option to treat certain data as cachable, so that they can be reused without having to re-run the task(s) that produced them.

(f) Accessing provenance

An important requirement for provenance is a data model, to extract the appropriate information from a provenance file with relative ease. The Open Provenance Model (OPM) [37] has been developed in a series of workshops with representatives of, among others, the most popular WfMSs. OPM translates the workflow and the data produced into a graph structure. When data is stored in a SQL database, the requirements of OPM can be met by installing a front-end that can translate OPM queries into SQL queries and that translates the data returned by the query into OPM format. These translations are not yet standardised. We need a so-called *OPM Profile* to lay down how tasks, edges, and actors are translated into OPM concepts. An OPM Profile has been published as [38]. To our knowledge, this is the first published OPM profile. For e-BioFlow, we designed our own profile which maps OPM onto the database schema of our provenance database and *vice versa*.

e-BioFlow is equipped with a special graphical browser for accessing provenance data after the workflow has run. It uses symbols that are de facto standards in the OPM community. The graphical browser faces challenges due the the large number of nodes and edges in the provenance graph. In OligoRAP and in similar, real-life size cases, the OPM graph has several hundred thousands of elements and relations. Such a graph can be navigated provided the workflow designer has carefully chosen the hierarchy of the workflow, so that the branching factor is low and the tree is rather deep. e-BioFlow thus uses the hierarchy of the workflow itself to facilitate access to provenance data. Biton and co-authors propose to automatically generate user views on provenance graphs [39].

7   Web Services

For many bioinformaticians, orchestrating web services has been and still is the primary reason to use workflows. Web services are invoked by means of one of several invocation methods. SOAP/WSDL, SoapLab, BioMart and BioMOBY are the most popular in bioinformatics; the latter three are even designed specifically for bioinformatics purposes [3]. To evaluate the practical use of web services in workflows, we have built a Taverna workflow that collects all Taverna workflows offered at the myExperiment website at a given time, expands all composite tasks, and groups tasks into various categories [40]. We did such a survey in December, 2008, counting the number of web service invocations per invocation method. Remarkably, the majority of all tasks in this set of workflows did not invoke a web service at all. Web service invocation apparently assumes a host of helper tasks. SOAP/WSDL was by far the most preferred method, being used in 66% of the cases. SoapLab, developed by EBI specifically for bioinformaticians, scored just 24%. BioMOBY, which as we experienced ourselves is easier to share than your toothbrush [11], and BioMart scored even less. Pure REST invocation [41,42] is very rare. Yet the original version of YAWL relies on REST [43]. The advantages of REST over SOAP/WSDL are said to include speed, scalability, security, and tool support [43, p. 149].

(g) Finding appropriate web services

Finding the appropriate web service not only involves finding a URL for a WSDL file or similar, but also requires being convinced that the web resource maintainers ensure a constant, high quality of service. The issue was earlier addressed by initiatives such as the discontinued UDDI. One of the reasons for the popularity of Taverna is that it is shipped with close to 4,000 references to web resources. BioMOBY proposes to solve the issue by means of a central registry, a BioMOBY Central. This registry can be searched using BioMOBY's service ontology. Unfortunately, it relies for its maintenance on the discipline of its users, who have widely different interests. The result is a quite flat ontology tree that contains obvious duplicates, rendering the tree unfit for searching. Recent initiatives to fill this gap are BioCatalogue (`www.biocatalogue.org`, [44]), that aims to grow into a kind of revived UDDI for bioinformatics, and Magallanes [45], that is also able to construct workflows. SADI [46], to be discussed below, proposes a solution that makes use of Semantic Web technology.

(h) Quality of service of a web service

A web service may be dead, under construction, moved to another URL and/or port, or overloaded. A web service is maintained by another party that may have other priorities and may be unable to guarantee the bandwidth necessary to satisfy hundreds of bioinformaticians worldwide who want to access the same web service. The most radical solution is to mirror all important web services in-house. For OligoRAP, this is what we did. Still, mirroring is not always good practice and it runs counter to the spirit of the Web. Mirroring is costly in terms of both money and manpower. Also, it is impossible to cover special-interest services this way. A workflow can deal with slow web-services by incorporating an iterative structure that polls the external resource to find out whether results are already available. If they are not, a wait is introduced and the polling task is iteratively called again. e-BioFlow offers predefined task templates for polling.

A related problem is that of remotely assessing what went well and what went wrong in the web service itself. Most providers do not offer extensive log files. In the absence of log files, the best one can do is to capture as much metadata as one can. This is handled by the provenance system, see below.

We have built a Taverna workflow that each month of the first half of 2009 inspected all Taverna workflows deposited at myExperiment to estimate the half-life of bioinformatics web services. Our results show that of the approximately 200 workflows that call web services, over 10% was marred by dead services. Worse, the number of broken workflows rose from 25 to 38 in just six months, an increase of over 50%.

From the perspective of the workflow designer, late binding results in workflows that are better sharable because tasks do not define resources explicitly but only roles. A role stipulates what a resource should be able to do in order to meet the requirements of the task. The resource view of the design interface of e-BioFlow supports late binding by default. Binding roles to resources is done at enactment time.

(i) Interoperability

Interoperability of web services is an important aspect in a workflow approach, but data format incompatibility is a major obstacle. In the Taverna experiment aimed at classification of tasks in myExperiment workflows we mentioned earlier [40], we tried to estimate which proportion of all tasks is devoted to data transformation. Our results indicate 30% as a lower bound, suggesting that data incompatibility still is a huge problem. Using only BioMoby services eliminates the data incompatibility problems, as we found for the OligoRAP case. The data format ontology of BioMoby however suffers from the same drawback as BioMoby's service ontology. It is evident that when users are free to define and use their own data formats, they will.

The problem is strictly speaking not technical but social. Purely technical means thus cannot solve it, but they may help. A number of projects have attempted to combat interoperability problems, among them BioMOBY, TAMBIS [47] and caBIO [48]. A newcomer is SADI (sadiframework.org, [46]), a framework based on the Semantic Web standards RDF and OWL to enable use of OWL reasoners and SPARQL. SADI assumes that web services are stateless and atomic, and that they consume and produce data in RDF format. SADI proposes to focus on data properties rather than data types. It is no longer required that the community agrees on a unifying ontology of data types; instead, it is sufficient that the community agrees on the meanings of relationships which can then be used by OWL reasoners to find compatible services. The initiative is very young with just a handful of services available. Time will tell whether SADI will be widely adopted and whether it facilitates the handling of interoperability problems.

(j) Quality of content

The quality of the content a web service offers is important because the results of a workflow can never be better than those of the worst web service. Although it is evident that the databases used by bioinformaticians are not perfect, one by and large has to guess the frequency and distribution of errors. Recently, more systematic efforts have been undertaken to assess the quality of content of databases and to improve where needed and possible [49,50,51].

8   Discussion

In the course of designing and running bioinformatics workflows, we found that existing WfMSs suitable for bioinformatics fall short of our expectations. We eventually decided to build our own WfMS, e-BioFlow. We decided to rely exclusively on open-source software, and to make e-BioFlow an open-source project as well (`ewi.utwente.nl/~biorange/ebioflow`). To profit from experience with business administration WfMSs, we did not build e-BioFlow from scratch but instead relied on the well-proven WfMS YAWL (`www.yawlfoundation.org`). The core of YAWL is largely unchanged, except that in e-BioFlow data are passed by reference while YAWL copies data between tasks. We implemented a user interface with the help of the JGraph package (`www.jgraph.com`). Finally, the provenance database is implemented in PostgreSQL (`www.postgresql.org`). Java code ties everything together. The result was satisfying. The problems we identified in particular for *Design* and *Provenance* have been solved. e-BioFlow's performance is adequate for most bioinformatics jobs. The OligoRAP use case for an oligo library for the mouse comprising 21,766 unique oligo's [13, ch. 4], for example, has been run in e-BioFlow on a commodity PC in just three hours where the original Perl version needs twice that time. Runs sometimes ran against unavailable web services. The cache function of the database saved a lot of time in those cases. When the workflow had been run to end, the provenance archive could be browsed with relative ease.

To summarise, e-BioFlow has the following features:

- The design interface allows two modes of design: an entire workflow, or adhoc design. When designing an entire workflow, information is divided over three related panes to prevent information overload.
- Ad-hoc design allows a bioinformatician to play with tasks and (partial) workflows. At all times, the bioinformatician can inspect all data produced so far. This exploratory way of working is close to the way a research bioinformatician normally works.
- Late binding: resources (web services, scripts, user interaction) are selected only at runtime. At design time, the user specifies a role. There is a database that relates roles to resources. e-BioFlow supports scripting, offering syntax highlighting for Perl, R, JavaBeans, and Sleep. It supports BioMoby services and any service that can be specified in a WSDL file.
- e-BioFlow can import workflow specifications in two languages, YAWL [10] and Scufl, the language of Taverna [7].It can export control-flow related information in the Open XML Process Definition Language, XPDL (see [52] and `www.wfmc.org/xpdl.html`).
- Data are stored in a database as soon as they are produced. In the workflow, data are passed by reference. The database can serve as cache. It also contains the complete provenance once the workflow has run to end.

– There is a provenance browser based on the de facto standard OPM that enables a user to browse a provenance archive of hundreds of thousands of nodes. In the OligoRAP case, the provenance archive contains over 3 GB of data, 2,900 composite tasks and 200,000 elements in the OPM graph. Based on our experiences, even larger archives pose no problems.

e-BioFlow was solely developed to provide a proof-of-principle that a WfMS for a commodity PC can fulfil the requirements formulated in this article. As such, we hope that these notions will find their way in the already established bioinformatics WfMSs, forming the next step in the evolution of WfMSs.

Acknowledgement

This work was part of the BioRange programme of the Netherlands Bioinformatics Centre (NBIC), which is supported by a BSIK grant through the Netherlands Genomics Initiative (NGI).

References

1. Stevens, R., Goble, C., Baker, P., Brass, A.: A classification of tasks in bioinformatics. Bioinformatics 17, 180–188 (2001)
2. Deelman, E., Gannon, D., Shields, M., Taylor, I.: Workflows and e-Science: An overview of workflow system features and capabilities. Future Generation Computer Systems 25, 528–540 (2009)
3. Neerincx, P., Leunisse, J.: Evolution of web services in bioinformatics. Briefings in Bioinformatics 6, 178–188 (2005)
4. Romano, P.: Automation of in-silico data analysis processes through workflow management systems. Briefings in Bioinformatics 9, 57–68 (2007)
5. Ludäscher, B., Altintas, I., Berkley, C., Higgins, D., Jaeger, E., Jones, M., Lee, E., Tao, J., Zhao, Y.: Scientific workflow management and the Kepler system. Concurrency and Computation: Practice and Experience 18, 1039–1065 (2006)
6. Taylor, I., Shields, M., Wang, I., Rana, O.: Triana applications within grid computing and peer to peer environments. Journal of Grid Computing 1, 199–217 (2003)
7. Oinn, T., Addis, M., Ferris, J., Marvin, D., Senger, M., Greenwood, M., Carver, T., Glover, K., Pocock, M., Wipat, A., Li, P.: Taverna: a tool for the composition and enactment of bioinformatics workflows. Bioinformatics 20, 3045–3054 (2004)
8. Wassink, I., Rauwerda, H., Neerickx, P., van der Vet, P., Breit, T., Leunissen, J., Nijholt, A.: Using R in Taverna: RShell v1.2. BMC Research Notes 2, 138 (2009)
9. Wassink, I.: Work flows in life science. PhD thesis, University of Twente, Enschede, the Netherlands (2010)
10. van der Aalst, W.M.P., ter Hofstede, A.: YAWL: Yet another workflow language. Information systems 30, 245–275 (2005)
11. BioMoby Consortium: Interoperability with Moby 1.0 – it's better than sharing your toothbrush! Briefings in Bioinformatics 9, 220–231 (2008)
12. Neerincx, P., Rauwerda, H., Nie, H., Groenen, M., Breit, T., Leunissen, J.: OligoRAP - an oligo re-annotation pipeline to improve annotation and estimate target specificity. BMC Proceedings 3, S4 (2009)
13. Neerincx, P.: Web services for transcriptomics. PhD thesis, Wageningen University and Research, Wageningen, the Netherlands (2009)

14. Kent, W.: BLAT – the BLAST-like alignment tool. Genome Research 12, 656–664 (2002)
15. Altschul, S., Gish, W., Miller, W., Myers, E., Lipman, D.: Basic local alignment search tool. Journal of Molecular Biology 215, 403–410 (1990)
16. Flicek, P., Aken, B., Ballester, B., Beal, K., Bragin, E., Brent, S., Chen, Y., Clapham, P., Coates, G., Fairley, S., Fitzgerald, S., Fernandez-Banet, J., Gordon, L., Graf, S., Haider, S., Hammond, M., Howe, K., Jenkinson, A., Johnson, N., Kahari, A., Keefe, D., Keenan, S., Kinsella, R., Kokocinski, F., Koscielny, G., Kulesha, E., Lawson, D., Longden, I., Massingham, T., McLaren, W., Megy, K., Overduin, B., Pritchard, B., Rios, D., Ruffier, M., Schuster, M., Slater, G., Smedley, D., Spudich, G., Tang, Y., Trevanion, S., Vilella, A., Vogel, J., White, S., Wilder, S., Zadissa, A., Birney, E., Cunningham, F., Dunham, I., Durbin, R., Fernandez-Suarez, X., Herrero, J., Hubbard, T.P., Parker, A., Proctor, G., Smith, J., Searle, S.J.: Ensembl's 10th year. Nucleic Acids Research 38(Database issue), D557–D562 (2010)
17. van der Aalst, W., ter Hofstede, A., Kiepuszewski, B., Barros, A.: Workflow patterns. Distributed and Parallel Databases 14, 5–51 (2003)
18. De Roure, D., Goble, C., Stevens, R.: The design and realisation of the virtual research environment for social sharing of workflows. Future Generation Computer Systems 25, 561–567 (2009)
19. van der Aalst, W., van Hee, K.: Workflow management: models, methods, and systems. MIT Press, Cambridge (2002)
20. van der Aalst, W.: The application of Petri Nets to workflow management. Journal of Circuits, Systems and Computers 8, 21–66 (1998)
21. Rygg, A., Mann, S., Roe, P., On, W.: Bio-workflows with BizTalk: using a commercial workflow engine for eScience. In: Stockinger, H., Buyya, R., Perrott, R. (eds.) e-Science 2005. Proceedings of the First International Conference on e-Science and Grid Computing, pp. 116–123. IEEE Computer Press, Los Alamitos (2005)
22. King, R., Rowland, J., Oliver, S., Young, M., Aubrey, W., Byrne, E., Liakata, M., Markham, M., Pir, P., Soldatova, L., Sparkes, A., Whelan, K., Clare, A.: The automation of science. Science 324, 85–89 (2009)
23. McPhillips, T., Bowers, S., Zinn, D., Ludäscher, B.: Scientific workflow design for mere mortals. Future Generation Computer Systems 25, 541–551 (2009)
24. Shields, M.: Control- versus data-driven workflows. In: Taylor, I., Deelman, E., Gannon, D., Shields, M. (eds.) Workflows for e-science, pp. 167–173. Springer, Berlin (2007)
25. Wassink, I., Rauwerda, H., van der Vet, P., Breit, T., Nijholt, A.: e-BioFlow: different perspectives on scientific workflows. In: Elloumi, M., Küng, J., Linial, M., Murphy, R., Schneider, K., Toma, C. (eds.) Bioinformatics Research and Development, BIRD 2008. Springer, Berlin (2008)
26. Lee, E., Parks, T.: Dataflow process networks. Proceedings of the IEEE 83, 773–801 (1995)
27. Santos, I., Göbel, M., Raposo, A., Gattass, M.: A multimedia workflow-based collaborative engineering environment for oil & gas industry. In: Proceedings VRCAI 2004 - ACM SIGGRAPH International Conference on Virtual Reality Continuum and its Applications in Industry, pp. 112–119. ACM, Singapore (2004)
28. Puerta-Melguizo, M., Chisalita, C., van der Veer, G.: Assessing users' mental models in designing complex systems. In: Borne, P. (ed.) Proceedings of the IEEE International Conference on Systems, Man and Cybernetics 2002, pp. 420–425. IEEE Computer Press, Los Alamitos (2002)

29. Wassink, I., van der Vet, P., van der Veer, G., Roos, M., van Dijk, E.: New interactions with workflow systems. In: Norros, L., Koskinen, H., Salo, L., Savioja, P. (eds.) ECCE 2009 - European Conference on Cognitive Ergonomics: Designing beyond the Product-Understanding Activity and User Experience in Ubiquitous Environments, Helsinki, Finland, VTT, pp. 349–352 (2009)

30. Greenwood, M., Goble, C., Stevens, R., Zhao, J., Addis, M., Marvin, D., Moreau, L., Oinn, T.: Provenance of e-science experiments - experience from bioinformatics. In: Cox, S. (ed.) Proceedings of UK e-Science All Hands Meeting 2003, Swindon, United Kingdom, EPSRC (2003)

31. Stevens, R., McEntire, R., Goble, C., Greenwood, M., Zhao, J., Wipat, A., Li, P.: myGrid and the drug discovery process. Drug Discovery Today: Biosilico 2, 140–148 (2004)

32. Groth, P., Miles, S., Moreau, L.: A model of process documentation to determine provenance in mash-ups. ACM Transactions on Internet Technology 9, 1–31 (2009)

33. Miles, S., Wong, S., Fang, W., Groth, P., Zauner, K.P., Moreau, L.: Provenance-based validation of e-science experiments. Web Semantics 5, 28–38 (2007)

34. Bose, R., Frew, J.: Lineage retrieval for scientific data processing: a survey. ACM Computing Surveys 37, 1–28 (2005)

35. Cohen-Boulakia, S., Davidson, S., Froideveaux, C.: A user-centric framework for accessing biological resources and tools. In: Ludäscher, B., Raschid, L. (eds.) DILS 2005. LNCS (LNBI), vol. 3615, pp. 3–18. Springer, Heidelberg (2005)

36. Altintas, I., Barney, O., Jaeger-Frank, E.: Provenance collection support in the Kepler scientific workflow system. In: Moreau, L., Foster, I. (eds.) IPAW 2006. LNCS, vol. 4145, pp. 118–132. Springer, Heidelberg (2006)

37. Moreau, L., Freire, J., Futrelle, J., McGrath, R., Myers, J., Paulson, P.: The Open Provenance Model: an overview. In: Freire, J., Koop, D., Moreau, L. (eds.) IPAW 2008. LNCS, vol. 5272, pp. 323–326. Springer, Heidelberg (2008)

38. Kwasnikowska, N., Bussche, J.: Mapping the NRC dataflow model to the Open Provenance Model. In: Freire, J., Koop, D., Moreau, L. (eds.) IPAW 2008. LNCS, vol. 5272, pp. 3–16. Springer, Heidelberg (2008)

39. Biton, O., Cohen-Boulakia, S., Davidson, S., Hara, C.S.: Querying and managing provenance through user views in scientific workflows. In: Alonso, G., Blakeley, J., Chen, A. (eds.) IEEE 24th International Conference on Data Engineering, pp. 1072–1081. IEEE Computer Press, Los Alamitos (2008)

40. Wassink, I., van der Vet, P., Wolstencroft, K., Neerincx, P., Roos, M., Rauwerda, H., Breit, T.: Analysing scientific workflows: why workflows not only connect web services. In: Zhang, L.J. (ed.) IEEE Congress on Services 2009, pp. 314–321. IEEE Computer Press, Los Alamitos (2009)

41. Fielding, R., Taylor, R.: Principled design of the modern Web architecture. In: Ghezzi, C., Jazayeri, M., Wolf, A. (eds.) Proceedings of the 22nd International Conference on Software Engineering (ICSE 2000), pp. 407–416. ACM Press, New York (2000)

42. Fielding, R.: Architectural styles and the design of network-based software architectures. PhD thesis, Information and Computer Science, University of California

43. van der Aalst, W., Aldred, L., Dumas, M., ter Hofstede, A.: Design and implementation of the YAWL system. In: Persson, A., Stirna, J. (eds.) CAiSE 2004. LNCS, vol. 3084, pp. 142–159. Springer, Heidelberg (2004)

44. Goble, C., Stevens, R., Hull, D., Wolstencroft, K., Lopez, R.: Data curation + process curation = data integration + science. Briefings in Bioinformatics 9, 506–517 (2008)

45. Rios, J., Karlsson, J., Trelles, O.: Magallanes: a web services discovery and automatic workflow composition tool. BMC Bioinformatics 10, 334 (2009)
46. Wilkinson, M., Vandervalk, B., McCarthy, L.: SADI Semantic Web Services - 'cause you can't always GET what you want? In: Ngoh, L., Teo, H. (eds.) IEEE Asia-Pacific Services Computing Conference 2009 (APSCC 2009), pp. 13–18. IEEE, Los Alamitos (2009)
47. Stevens, R., Baker, P., Bechhofer, S., Ng, G., Jacoby, A., Paton, N., Goble, C., Brass, A.: TAMBIS: transparent access to multiple bioinformatics information sources. Bioinformatics 16(2), 184–186 (2000)
48. Covitz, P., Hartel, F., Schaefer, C., De Coronado, S., Fragoso, G., Sahni, H., Gustafson, S., Buetow, K.: caCORE: A common infrastructure for cancer informatics. Bioinformatics 19(18), 2404–2412 (2003)
49. Joosten, R., Vriend, G.: PDB improvement starts with data deposition. Science 317, 195–196 (2007)
50. Ott, M., Vriend, G.: Correcting ligands, metabolites, and pathways. BMC Bioinformatics 7, 517 (2006)
51. Spronk, C., Nabuurs, S., Krieger, E., Vriend, G., Vuister, G.: Validation of protein structures derived by NMR spectroscopy. Progress in Nuclear Magnetic Resonance Spectroscopy 45, 315–337 (2004)
52. van der Aalst, W.: Business process management demystified: a tutorial on models, systems and standards for workflow management. In: Desel, J., Reisig, W., Rozenberg, G. (eds.) Lectures on Concurrency and Petri Nets. LNCS, vol. 3098, pp. 21–85. Springer, Heidelberg (2004)

MEDCollector: Multisource Epidemic Data Collector

João Zamite, Fabrício A.B. Silva, Francisco Couto, and Mário J. Silva

LaSIGE, Faculty of Science, University of Lisbon
epiwork@lasige.di.fc.ul.pt

Abstract. This paper analyzes the requirements and presents a novel approach to the development of a system for epidemiological data collection and integration based on the principles of interoperability and modularity. Accurate and timely epidemic models require the integration of large, fresh datasets. Thus, from an e-science perspective, collected data should be shared seamlessly across multiple applications. This is addressed by our approach, MEDCollector, trough workflow design enables the extraction of data from multiple Web sources. The mapping of extracted entities to ontologies will guarantee the consistency within gathered datasets, and therefore enhance epidemic modeling tools.

Keywords: Epidemic Surveillance, Data Collection, Information Integration, Workflow Design.

1 Introduction

The study of epidemic disease propagation and its control is highly dependent on the availability of reliable epidemic data. Epidemic surveillance systems play an important role in this subject, extracting exhaustive information with the purpose of understanding disease propagation and evaluating its impact in public health through epidemic forecasting tools.

International organizations, such as the World Health Organization (WHO), have epidemic surveillance systems that collect infectious disease cases. However, although official disease statistics and demographics provide the most reliable data, the use of new technologies for epidemic data collection is useful to complement data already obtained from national reporting systems.

In recent years, several projects have researched the use of the Web as a platform for epidemic data collection. The systems developed by these projects gather epidemic data from several types of sources [1], such as query data from search engines [2], internet news services[3] and directly from users [4]. Alternative sources for epidemic data are social networks, e.g. Twitter [5], which are forums where people share information that can be accessed as Web services. These alternative sources of information can be used to identify possible disease cases, or at least provide a glimpse about the propagation of a disease in a community.

S. Khuri, L. Lhotská, and N. Pisanti (Eds.): ITBAM 2010, LNCS 6266, pp. 16–30, 2010.
© Springer-Verlag Berlin Heidelberg 2010

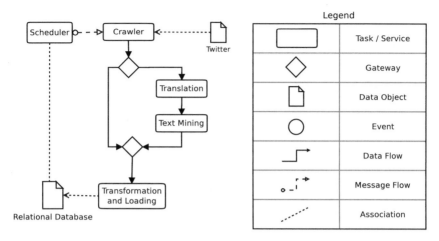

Fig. 1. Example of a workflow, to extract messages from twitter, text-mine them, and insert both the message and extracted information into the database.

The aforementioned systems use different methods for data presentation. Therefore, an integrative effort is needed to consolidate their data so it can be used in e-science data analysis.

This need is highlighted by the EPIWORK project, a multidisciplinary effort to develop an appropriate framework for epidemiological forecasting [6]. This framework is aimed at the creation of a computational platform for epidemic research and data sharing, which will encompass the design and implementation of disease incidence collection tools, the development of large-scale data-driven computational and mathematical models to assess disease spread and control.

An approach to extract and integrate data from multiple sources is the definition of workflows, which enables the composition of collection mechanisms using web services (see Fig. 1). Following this approach, this paper describes the development of MEDCollector, a system for information extraction and integration from multiple heterogeneous epidemiological data sources. MEDCollector is a component of EPIWORK's information platform, the *Epidemic Marketplace* [7]. MEDCollector enables the flexible configuration of epidemic data collection from multiple sources, using interoperable services orchestrated as workflows. Collected data can then be packed into datasets for later use by epidemic modeling tools. Through the use of Web standards for data transmission, the system enables seamless integration of web services to extend its basic functionality. This system gathers and integrates data from multiple and heterogeneous sources, providing epidemiologists a wide array of datasets obtained from the Web using its own data services, in addition to traditional data sources.

The remainder of the paper is organized as follows: Section 2 provides insight into previous related work; Section 3 is an assessment of the system requirements for an epidemic data collector; Section 4 presents our implementation; Section 5 describes a short example of the system use, showing the creation of a workflow for epidemic data collection from social networks; Section 6 presents the conclusions and perspectives for future work in MEDCollector.

2   Related Work

E-science involves the use of web, computational and information technologies to achieve scientific results [8]. It requires the development of middleware and networking technologies to perform tasks, such as data acquisition and integration, storage, management, mining and visualization. This provision of scientific environments allows global collaboration by enabling universal access to knowledge and resources. Recently, a number of initiatives, such as myGrid and its workflow environment Taverna[9] [10] in bioinformatics, and EGEE and DEISA [11] in multiple domains, have been bridging the gap between the need for computational tools and their seamless integration through the use of standards and interoperable services.

The Web presents a valuable source for collecting epidemic data, but it requires coping with a variety of formats, ranging from free text to XML documents. Disease reporting services, like the ProMED-mail newsletter [12], EuroFlu and reports from the European Center for Disease Prevention and Control (ECDC) are useful sources of epidemiological data. The ProMed-mail newsletter, maintained by the International Society for Infectious Diseases, is a notification service that sends their registered users information about new disease cases via e-mail. EuroFlu.org, a WHO website, and the ECDC's European Influenza Surveillance Network (EISN) [13] publish weekly reports on the activity of Influenza-like diseases.

Internet Monitoring Systems (IMS) can retrieve data using two distinct approaches: passive data collection and active data collection. Systems that use passive data collection mechanisms, such as Gripenet [4] and Google Flu Trends [2], provide interfaces to their users who voluntarily submit their data. On the other hand, active data collection systems, such as Healthmap [1], use crawlers that browse the Web through hyperlinks and existing web services.

The IMS Gripenet depends directly on the active participation of its voluntary users, which receive weekly newsletters about influenza activity and are requested to fill out a form about the presence, or not, of influenza symptoms during the past week. This system was based on Holland's Influenzanet [14] model and is currently implemented on seven other countries: Belgium, Italy, Brazil, Mexico, United Kingdom and Australia and Canada.

Google Flu Trends is a system that performs analysis on user queries to the Google search engine and has been shown to predict influenza activity within two weeks prior to the official sources for the North American Population. This system is currently being extended to cover other countries around the world. Both Google Flu Trends and the previously mentioned IMS collect data directly from their users.

Healthmap, takes a different approach. It is a worldwide epidemic data presentation website that represents disease cases, mostly of contagious diseases, gathered from different sources. These sources can be diverse in nature, ranging from news casting services to official epidemic reports, and have different degrees of reliability. Disease and location information is extracted via a text processing system and presented on a map via the Google Maps API.

3 Epidemic Data Collector Requirements

An epidemiological data collector should follow a set of principles and requirements enabling extensible data collection and the creation of consistent, integrated datasets, while coping with the heterogeneity associated with its sources.

- *Active data collection.* Harvesting Web data automatically using available web services and their application programming interfaces. This enables data collection from sources like Twitter, Google Flu Trends and EISN reports. Depending on the source the harvesting mechanism collects an entire message containing the name of a disease for further processing or harvest epidemiological estimates known to be published at the defined source.
- *Passive data collection.* Receiving data posts from a number of sources, including news feeds and email subscriptions (e.g. ProMED-mail). Data received by passive data collection mechanisms requires structuring before being integrated and loaded to the system.
- *Flexible Scheduling.* To cope with different periods of data update in each source the system must enable the scheduling of the activation of each data collection mechanism at their sources.
- *Local Storage.* Different data sources have variable data availability times, and data may only be available for some time period at certain sources, if any. An approach to solve the problem associated with dealing with volatile data, as well as the temporal disparity of data sources is to locally store all the data retrieved by the system in a local dedicated relational database.
- *Ontology Referencing.* Enables the use of vocabularies when referencing entities in the spatial and health domains. The use of ontologies enables the disambiguation of named entities, the mapping of entities with multiple references across data sources, and the establishment of hierarchical relationships among entities. This hierarchy becomes particularly relevant when using geographic referencing. For instance, with the support of a geospatial ontology, we could relate cities with their respective countries. This enables the aggregation of data defined for specific levels to higher levels, e.g. disease cases identified in London can be used in the United Kingdom domain.
- *Modularity and Configurability.* An epidemic data collector that retrieves data from the Web requires a degree of flexibility in order to cope with

changes or additions in its sources. By adopting a SOA architecture [15], the system has its functionality distributed through discrete units, or services Orchestrations, or workflows, enable the design of data flow sequences between the different services. Configurable workflows enable the reconfiguration and addition of new services whenever necessary by defining how services are interconnected and how information is transmitted between them [16]. By defining services with a set of configurable inputs and outputs based on Web Standards they become highly interoperable which improves the flexibility of workflow creation.

4 Implementation

The MEDCollector implements the above requirements through the dynamic design of service workflows. It is inspired in an initial prototype we developed to collect messages from Twitter containing disease and location names [17].

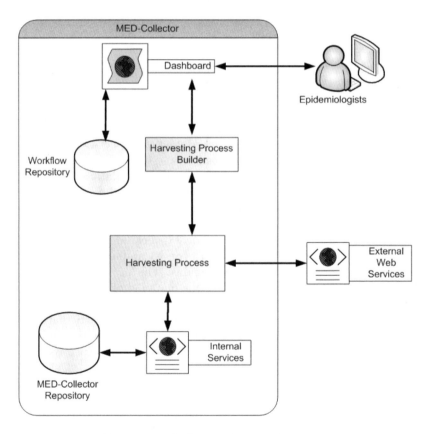

Fig. 2. MEDCollector's basic architecture

The architecture of the MEDCollector is represented in Fig. 2. Its main system components are:

- *Dashboard.* Provides user-interface capabilities to the system, enabling the user to define harvesting processes and to monitor currently deployed processes.
- *Workflow Repository.* Stores workflows designed in the Dashboard.
- *Harvesting Process Builder.* Converts designed workflows to deployed Harvesting processes.
- *Harvesting Processes.* Processes that orchestrate communications between multiple services, both internal and external, to perform data collection from external sources accordingly to workflow definition.
- *Internal Services.* Provide basic system functionalities and interact with the MEDCollector Repository.
- *MEDCollector Repository.* Stores all the data collected by the system.

The MEDCollector Repository stores both the data collected from the Web and data collection schedules. It is implemented as a MySQL relational database. For clarity in the description of this repository's implementation, we present it as storage for two types of data: a Case Data and a Scheduling Data.

4.1   MEDCollector Repository

Case Data. The collected data are organized in the repository under a classic Data Warehouse star schema [18]. The fact table, shown in Fig. 3(a), has the following dimensions describing the cases:

- *Disease*: reference to the disease name and a concept unique identified (cui) that identifies that disease in the Unified Medical Language System (UMLS) [19].
- *Location*: reference to a location monitored by the system, including a geonameid which identifies that location in the GeoNames ontology [20].
- *Source*: reference to the monitored source, its URL and, in some cases, the update interval for that source.

Scheduling Data. The schedule of data harvesting operations, represented in Fig. 3(b), has an identical organization with the harvesting events as the fact table and the same dimension tables.

The information in the repository is accessible through a series of services for inserting and selecting. The database currently includes all countries in the world and their capitals as well as a set of 89 infectious diseases.

4.2   Dashboard

The Dashboard provides the user interface to add new data sources or further ways to process information through the addition of new services or by adjustment of service parameters.

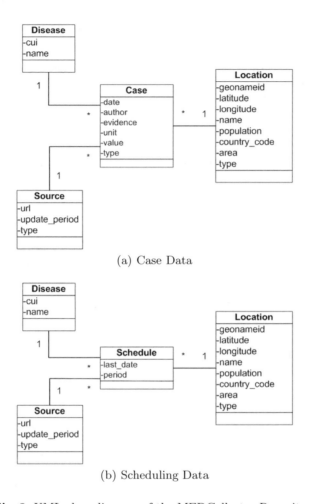

(a) Case Data

(b) Scheduling Data

Fig. 3. UML class diagram of the MEDCollector Repository

The Business Process Execution Language (BPEL) [21] is a workflow design language that uses XML to describe the interaction between services. The BPEL process, corresponding to a designed workflow, is itself a service and can be interpreted and executed by a BPEL engine.

One of the difficulties with the use of BPEL lies on the need of methods for creating process definitions by non-technical users [16], this requires the MEDCollector to have a user interface.

We considered scientific workflow systems like Taverna, but they require the direct definition of WSDLs and communication via SOAP. In addition, these systems currently do not offer on-browser interfaces, requiring users to go through local installation and configuration processes prior to using the software.

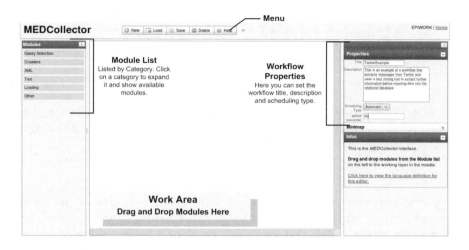

Fig. 4. Global view of the Web Interface implemented using WiringEditor and description of its components

WireIt[22] enables the definition of a "Visual Language" that specifies modules, their inputs and outputs, which represent services in MEDCollector. It is also bundled with a single-page editor that enables the definition of workflows through a wirable interface, see Fig. 4. The wirable interface consists of drag-and-drop elements which can be connected with wires between their inputs and outputs. Workflows designed in this interface are saved to the Workflow Repository.

WireIt is an open source JavaScript library for the creation of web wirable interfaces similar to Yahoo! Pipes [23] and uDesign [24]. WireIt uses Yahoo! User Interface library 2.7.0 for DOM and event manipulation and is compatible with most web browsers.

The Dashboard also enables the user to specify scheduling properties for each workflow, such as the period to wait between workflow runs.

4.3   Harvesting Processes

When the user saves a workflow from the interface, the Harvesting Process Builder receives a JSON representation of the workflow from the interface and creates the files necessary to deploy a Harvesting Process for running in the BPEL engine. Each of these processes orchestrate communications between basic services that perform the data collection accordingly to workflow definitions. A Harvesting Process consists of a process descriptor, a BPEL process and a WSDL document.

We use Apache ODE (Orchestration Director Engine) [25] to execute our Harvesting Processes. Apache ODE provides several extensions to standard BPEL engines including XPath 2.0 support, for easier variable assignments, and an HTTP binding extension that enables direct connection to RESTful Web Services. This engine also provides an interface that enables monitorization of currently deployed processes.

4.4   Services

Internal services represent the basic operations performed by the system. These can be information collection services, text mining services, transformation services, scheduler services, and others.

We have implemented the following in the current version of the MEDCollector:

1. *Query Selection Services.* These specify when each disease is actively monitored in what locations and sources. There are two types of query selection services, user defined query and a priority based query selection service. In the first the user directly specifies what query to run, and therefore which disease to monitor at what location and source. The latter uses the stored Scheduling Data, selecting the period and last search date values for each disease-location-source triple and outputting the triple with the highest positive priority value according to the formula:

$$priority = date \text{ - } last \ search \ date \text{ - } period$$

   If there are no positive values the service sends a fault message that is caught by the BPEL Process, stopping it and scheduling another run the next day. These triples can be filtered by source, location or disease, in order to create processes with specific scopes, e.g. influenza in Portugal with Twitter as a source.

   The priority is related to the amount of data collected in the past. Each week, a MEDCollector utility re-evaluates the update intervals according to the previous detected case entries:
   - Daily period: every triple with more than 1 entry the previous week.
   - Weekly period: every triple with more than 1 entry the previous two weeks and 1 or less entries the previous week.
   - Fortnightly period: every triple with more than 1 entry the previous month and 1 or less entries the previous two weeks.
   - Monthly period: every triple that does not fit the criteria mentioned above.
2. *Active Data Harvesting Services* retrieve content through APIs or provided URLs. These services structure collected cases to a XML schema compatible with other MEDCollector services. Scheduler services coordinate when these harvesting are actively querying the data sources.
3. *Passive Collection Services* receive data posted by disease reporting services and other sources such as email subscriptions.

4. *Text related services* include regular expression text mining services that search strings for patterns, text mining services and translation services that use the Google Language API [26]. Text Mining services, receive a message from harvesting and passive collection services and extract further information from them. They use a set of rules to mine previously retrieved messages for evidence that specifies number of cases, deaths or estimates.

5. *Database Loading* is done through a service that receives a XML message and accordingly performs an insert in the local relational database.

6. *Data Structuring Services* that provide functionalities such as data structure transformation and access to specific data elements to improve the flexibility of the workflows. This enables the use of external web services in the sequence flow by transforming their data into compatible data types and formats.

Furthermore, two interface modules enable the invocation of external services through REST or SOAP. These modules enable the addition of new functionalities to the system, such as gathering data from new sources or interaction with other applications.

5   Usage Example

This section illustrates the creation of workflows in MEDCollector, using again the extraction of messages from the Twitter Social Network as an example. Fig. 5 and 6 presents a step-by-step description on how to create a workflow to extract messages from Twitter, translate and mine them for epidemiological data.

To create a workflow the user starts by adding a Query Selection Service to the Interface Work Area (Fig. 5 a). To retrieve messages from Twitter the user connects the Query Selection XML output to the crawler input and specifying the source in the Query Selection input (Fig. 5 b). The Query Selection also enables filtering by disease or location so that users can specify specific entities to be searched for.

The users can also text-mine the messages extracted. Since the available text mining service is implemented only for the English language, the user uses a translation service (Fig. 5 c). Since the user does not know which language each message is in he/she leaves "input language" blank. The Translation service will identify what language the message is in prior to translating it. The user chooses the desired output language - "en" since he wants the output to be in English - then he/she connects the translation service output to the text mining service (Fig. 5 d).

The user can store both the raw messages as well as the occurrences extracted from text mining by connecting both the output of the crawler and the text mining service to a Merge Gate and then connecting it to a Loading Service (Fig. 6).

After pressing "Save" on the interface's menu, a JSON message is sent to the BPEL Process Builder, which deploys the process to be run by Apache ODE.

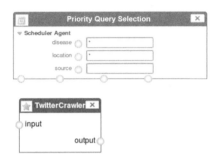

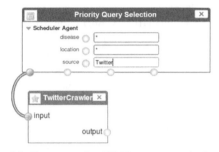

(a) Start by adding a Scheduler and an Harvesting Service to the Work Area.

(b) Connect the XML output of the Scheduler to the Harvesting Service.

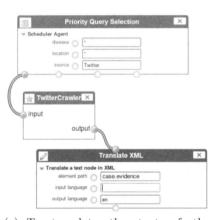

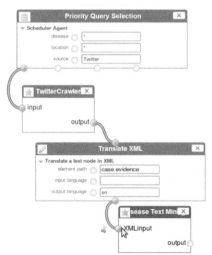

(c) To translate the text of the extracted messages use the Translation Service.

(d) After translation a text mining service can be used to extract further information.

Fig. 5. a) through d) - Step-by-Step creation of a workflow that Extracts Messages from Twitter to collect epidemiological data.

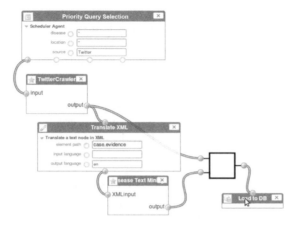

Fig. 6. Final step of the step-by-step workflow creation. To store both raw messages and text-mined cases connect both outputs to a merge game and then connect it to a loading service.

6   Conclusions and Future Directions

The MEDCollector is implemented as a component of the information platform being developed for the EPIWORK project - the Epidemic Marketplace. By enabling the collection and integration of data from multiple web sources, MEDCollector grants epidemiologists with a novel means to gather data for use in epidemic modelling tools.

The Dashboard enables users to dynamically design Web Service workflows through drag-and-drop components, without worrying about technical specifications. This enables users to directly create and modify workflows to customize data collection mechanisms according to their specific needs.

Users can set workflows to extract messages from several sources:

- *Social Network Services*, such as Twitter, where people freely share information. Text messages can be extracted from these sources.
- *Epidemiologic Surveillance Services*, such ProMED-Mail and Google Flu Trends. Each source with different data structures and formats. Users can design workflows to extract messages or disease case estimates depending on the source.
- *New Services*, such as Google News, which report RSS feeds and newsletters containing news relating to specific domains and locations. Text messages related to diseases can be extracted from these sources.

Harvesting processes collect all identified results available at the source. Should a problem occur and MEDCollector processes go offline for a period of time, when it is placed online it will retrieve missing data by continuing with its next scheduled searches.

Through the use of Web Standards for data transmission, MEDCollector enables seamless integration of externally supplied web services, granting extensibility to its basic features.

The next step is the creation a new layer for the interface that accommodates the configuration of dataset creation services. This new layer will be composed mainly of services that select information from the relational database and structure it according to the needs of the users, through XML transformation and selection. This transformation will enable the creation of aggregated and consistent datasets which can be used by other applications.

EPIWORK's information platform includes a dataset repository - the Epidemic Marketplace - where datasets can be stored for later use by epidemic modeling tools. MEDCollector will submit consistent datasets for storage in the Epidemic Marketplace at regular time periods through an upload API method being developed for this repository's mediator.

Another challenge is the development of visualization tools adequate to this data. This will enable epidemiologists to have a preliminary analysis of the data prior to its extraction from the system.

Acknowledgements

The authors want to thank the European Commission for the financial support of the EPIWORK project under the Seventh Framework Programme (Grant # 231807), the EPIWORK project partners, CMU-Portugal partnership and FCT (Portuguese research funding agency) for its LaSIGE Multi-annual support.

References

1. Brownstein, J., Freifeld, C.: HealthMap: The development of automated real-time internet surveillance for epidemic intelligence. Euro. Surveill. 12(11), E071129 (2007)
2. Ginsberg, J., Mohebbi, M., Patel, R., Brammer, L., Smolinski, M., Brilliant, L.: Detecting influenza epidemics using search engine query data. Nature 457(7232), 1012–1014 (2008)
3. Mawudeku, A., Blench, M.: Global Public Health Intelligence Network (GPHIN). In: 7th Conference of the Association for Machine Translation in the Americas, pp. 8–12 (2006)
4. Van Noort, S., Muehlen, M., Rebelo, A., Koppeschaar, C., Lima, L., Gomes, M.: Gripenet: an internet-based system to monitor influenza-like illness uniformly across Europe. Euro. Surveill. 12(7), E5 (2007)
5. Twitter (2009), http://www.twitter.com/ (accessed, December 2009)
6. EPIWORK, http://www.epiwork.eu/ (accessed, February 2009)
7. Silva, M.J., Silva, F.A., Lopes, L.F., Couto, F.M.: Building a digital library for epidemic modelling. In: Proceedings of ICDL 2010 - The International Conference on Digital Libraries, February 23-27, vol. 1. TERI Press, New Delhi (2010) (invited Paper)

8. e-IRG White Paper 2009 (2009),
   http://www.e-irg.eu/
   index.php?option=com_content&task=view&id=40&Itemid=39
9. Li, P., Castrillo, J., Velarde, G., Wassink, I., Soiland-Reyes, S., Owen, S., Withers, D., Oinn, T., Pocock, M., Goble, C., Oliver, S., Kell, D.: Performing statistical analyses on quantitative data in taverna workflows: an example using r and maxdbrowse to identify differentially-expressed genes from microarray data. BMC Bioinformatics 9(334) (August 2008)
10. Gibson, A., Gamble, M., Wolstencroft, K., Oinn, T., Goble, C.: The data playground: An intuitive workflow specification environment. In: IEEE International Conference on e-Science and Grid Computing, pp. 59–68 (2007)
11. Riedel, M., Memon, A., Memon, M., Mallmann, D., Streit, A., Wolf, F., Lippert, T., Venturi, V., Andreetto, P., Marzolla, M., Ferraro, A., Ghiselli, A., Hedman, F., Shah, Z.A., Salzemann, J., Da Costa, A., Breton, V., Kasam, V., Hofmann-Apitius, M., Snelling, D., van de Berghe, S., Li, V., Brewer, S., Dunlop, A., De Silva, N.: Improving e-Science with Interoperability of the e-Infrastructures EGEE and DEISA. In: International Convention on Information and Communication Technology, Electronics and Microelectronics (MIPRO), Opatija, Croatia, pp. 225–231 (2008)
12. Madoff, L., Yu, V.: ProMED-mail: an early warning system for emerging diseases. Clinical infectious diseases 39(2), 227–232 (2004)
13. European Influenza Surveillance Network (EISN),
    http://www.ecdc.europa.eu/en/activities/surveillance/EISN/
    (accessed, December 2009)
14. Marquet, R., Bartelds, A., van Noort, S., Koppeschaar, C., Paget, J., Schellevis, F., van der Zee, J.: Internet-based monitoring of influenza-like illness(ILI) in the general population of the Netherlands during the 2003 – 2004 influenza season. BMC Public Health 6(1), 242 (2006)
15. Durvasula, S., Guttmann, M., Kumar, A., Lamb, J., Mitchell, T., Oral, B., Pai, Y., Sedlack, T., Sharma, H., Sundaresan, S.: SOA Practitioners' Guide, Part 2, SOA Reference Architecture (2006)
16. Garlan, D.: Using service-oriented architectures for socio-cultural analysis,
    http://acme.able.cs.cmu.edu/pubs/show.php?id=290
17. Lopes, L.F., Zamite, J., Tavares, B., Couto, F., Silva, F., Silva, M.J.: Automated social network epidemic data collector. INForum - Simpósio de Informática (September 2009)
18. Utley, C.: Designing the Star Schema Database. Data Warehousing Resources (2002)
19. Bodenreider, O.: The unified medical language system (umls): integrating biomedical terminology. Nucl. Acids Res. 32(suppl_1), D267–D270 (2004),
    http://dx.doi.org/10.1093/nar/gkh061
20. GeoNames, http://www.geonames.org/ (accessed, December 2009)
21. Alves, A., Arkin, A., Askary, S., Bloch, B., Curbera, F., Goland, Y., Kartha, N., Sterling, König, D., Mehta, V., Thatte, S., van der Rijn, D., Yendluri, P., Yiu, A.: Web services business process execution language version 2.0. OASIS Committee Draft (May 2006)
22. Aboauf, E.: WireIt - a Javascript Wiring Library,
    http://javascript.neyric.com/wireit/ (accessed, January 2010)

23. Yahoo Pipes, http://pipes.yahoo.com/pipes (accessed, October 2009)
24. Sousa, J., Schmerl, B., Poladian, V., Brodsky, A.: uDesign: End-User Design Applied to Monitoring and Control Applications for Smart Spaces. In: Proceedings of the 2008 Working IFIP/IEEE Conference on Software Architecture (2008)
25. The Apache Software Foundation Foundation. Apache Orchestration Director Engine, http://ode.apache.org/ (accessed, January 2010)
26. Google AJAX Language API, http://code.google.com/apis/ajaxlanguage/ (accessed, January 2010)

Epidemic Marketplace: An Information Management System for Epidemiological Data

Luis F. Lopes, Fabrício A.B. Silva, Francisco Couto, João Zamite,
Hugo Ferreira, Carla Sousa, and Mário J. Silva

University of Lisbon, Faculty of Sciences, LASIGE
epiwork@lasige.di.fc.ul.pt
http://epiwork.di.fc.ul.pt

Abstract. The Epidemic Marketplace is part of a computational framework for organizing data for epidemic modeling and forecasting. It is a
distributed data management platform where epidemiological data can
be stored, managed and made available to the scientific community.
It includes tools for the automatic interaction with other applications
through web services, for the collection of epidemiological data from internet social networks and for discussion of related topics. This paper
defines its requirements, architecture and implementation plan based on
open-source software. This platform will assist epidemiologists and public
health scientists in finding, sharing and exchanging data.

1 Introduction

Internet technologies are becoming essential tools in Epidemiology [1]. Strong
computational competencies are necessary for the management and processing
of huge quantities of data being produced nowadays by epidemiological studies.
Data storage and management requires powerful and stable informatics platforms as well as high speed connectivity for data sharing in local networks and
in the Internet. On the other hand, epidemiological modeling requires access to
data and extreme processing capacity [2] [3].

The early detection of infectious disease outbreaks is fundamental for the efficient intervention of public health authorities and for the application of disease
control measures [4]. So, there is a constant quest for new surveillance methods,
capable of decreasing the gap between disease outbreak and its detection [5].

In the last years the internet has been increasingly regarded as a tool for the
identification of epidemiological trends and for the fast detection of epidemic
outbreaks. There are several systems that provide epidemiological insight based
on data gathered in the internet, with sources such as official alerts or news sites
[6], search engine queries [7], or even voluntary sentinels [8].

The development of new internet-based epidemiological surveillance systems,
has contributed to the continuous increase of existing epidemiological data. However, those data are heterogeneous and organized in a way that makes it hard
to share those data among scientists and health professionals.

S. Khuri, L. Lhotská, and N. Pisanti (Eds.): ITBAM 2010, LNCS 6266, pp. 31–44, 2010.

In this paper, we present the Epidemic Marketplace, a platform for data integration, management and sharing. As a repository for epidemiological data and as a discussion venue, the Epidemic Marketplace will enhance knowledge dissemination and foster data sharing and collaboration among the scientific community. Moreover, this platform is designed to integrate with epidemiological modeling and forecasting computational platforms. This will contribute to the development of a new generation of powerful tools for epidemiological forecast and disease study.

In this paper, we start by reviewing some of the related work on repositories of epidemiological resources and discuss the role of metadata annotation in these systems. We then present the Epidemic Marketplace requirements and architecture. In Section 4, we describe in more detail the Epidemic Marketplace and its modules. In Section 5, we detail the metadata model of the Epidemic Marketplace, and the role of encoding schemes and ontologies for a consistent annotation of metadata. In the following section, we describe the Epidemic Marketplace metadata model design in more detail, with a focus on its specific metadata elements. In Section 7, we discuss strategies to assist metadata content creation. Finally, in Section 8, we present the conclusions and future work.

2 Related Work

There are a large number of health and epidemic data repositories available in the internet. The United States National Library of Medicine presents a list of resources available on the web that provide access to epidemiological data and statistics [9]. One of these services is the CDC Wonder, which provides access to CDC's data in the public domain [10].

MyPubliHealth is a repository of public health resources that uses a metadata schema to organize and manage resources, making information finding easier and faster [11].

A repository of clinical trial data is made available by the National Institute of Diabetes and Digestive and Kidney Diseases (NIDDK), presenting a metadata catalogue describing the stored contents [12]. However, the metadata schema of this repository relies in few fields that are annotated mostly with free text, making metadata contained there too unstructured and semantically poor.

The HEAL (Health Education Assets Library) multimedia repository contains health-related data, such as teaching resources for health sciences education. It is designed to facilitate the sharing of high-quality, freely available multimedia resources located on the HEAL server or in other remote servers [13]. HEAL also functions as a publishing venue, for authors to submit multimedia resources for review and publication there. This repository relies on a detailed metadata schema, defined using selected elements from the IMS Meta-Data Version 1.2.1 specification [14], and several elements defined locally, specific for health sciences. This type of metadata sheme, more structured and relying less is free text, is closer to what we propose for the Epidemic Marketplace.

3   Epidemic Marketplace Architecture

The Epidemic Marketplace is envisioned as a geographic distributed network of interconnected data management nodes, sharing common canonical data models, authorization infrastructure and access interfaces. The distributed architecture should provide improved data access performance, improved availability and fault-tolerance.

Data can be either stored in one or more repositories or retrieved from external data sources using authorization credentials provided by clients. Data can also be replicated among repositories to improve access time, availability and fault tolerance. However, data replication is not mandatory; in several cases data must be stored in a single site due to, for instance, security constraints. It is worth noting, though, that any individual repository that composes the Marketplace will enable virtualized access to these data, once a user provides adequate security credentials.

According to Fig. 1, each Epidemic Marketplace node will be composed of four modules [15]: 1) a *Digital Repository*, where data will be stored, managed and made available to the community; 2) the *Mediator*, is responsible for the communication among the different modules and with foreign applications;

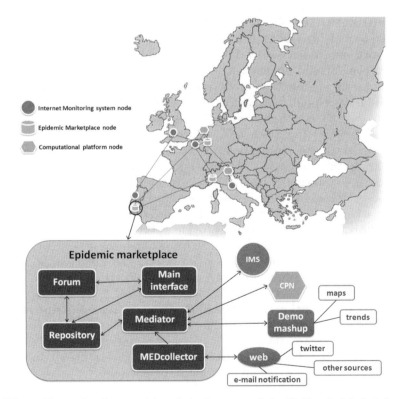

Fig. 1. Example of an envisioned deployment of the Epidemic Marketplace

3) the *MEDCollector*, which allows the harvesting of data from the web, storing it locally, through the use of workflows; 4) the *Forum*, is a venue for discussion about epidemiological topics, resources stored in the repository, such as datasets, and for the establishment of contacts among the user community.

3.1   Epidemic Marketplace Requirements

Several requirements have been identified when defining the architecture of the Epidemic Marketplace. As a data management platform it needs to:

- **Support the sharing and management of epidemiological data sets:**
  Registered users should be able to upload annotated datasets, and a dataset rating assessment mechanism should be available. The annotated data set will then compose a catalogue that will be available for users to browse, search and download according to specific permissions.
- **Support the seamless integration of multiple heterogeneous data sources:** Users should be able to have a unified view of related data sources through a common interface. Data should be available from streaming, static and dynamic sources.
- **Distributed Architecture:** The Epidemic Marketplace should implement a geographically distributed architecture deployed in several sites. The distributed architecture should provide improved data access performance, improved availability and fault-tolerance.
- **Support secure access to data:** Access to data should be controlled. The marketplace should provide single sign-on capability, distributed federated authorization and multiple access policies, customizable by users.
- **Modularity:** Not all sites where the Epidemic Marketplace will be deployed need to have all modules installed. Also, some sites may choose to implement different modules to provide new services.
- **Provide data for analysis and simulation in grid environments:**
  The Epidemic Marketplace will provide data for analysis and simulation services in a grid environment. Therefore, the Epidemic Marketplace should operate seamlessly with grid-specific services, such as grid security services, information services and resource allocation services.
- **Workflow:** The platform should provide workflow support for data processing and external service interaction. This requirement is particularly important for those services that retrieve data from the Epidemic Marketplace, process it, and store the processed data back in the marketplace, such as grid-enabled data analysis and simulation services.
- **Support the creation of a virtual community for epidemic research:**
  The platform will serve as a forum for discussion that will guide the community into uncovering the necessities of sharing data between providers and modellers. Users will become active participants, generating information and providing data for sharing and collaborating online.

Also, some non-functional requirements were identified:

- **Interoperability:** The Epidemic Marketplace must interoperate with other software. Its design must take into account that, in the future, systems developed by other researchers across the world may need to query the Epidemic Marketplace catalogue and access datasets stored there.
- **Standards-based:** To guarantee software interoperability and the seamless integration of all geographically dispersed sites of the Epidemic Marketplace, the system will be entirely built over web services, authentication and metadata standards.
- **Open-source:** Software packages to be used in the implementation and deployment of the Epidemic Marketplace should be open source, as well as the new modules developed specifically for the Epidemic Marketplace. An open-source based solution reduces development cost, improves software trustworthiness and reliability and simplifies support.

4   Implementation and Deployment

A first prototype of the Epidemic Marketplace has been deployed and is being thoroughly tested since it must be prepared to handle large amount of data and intensive user activity.

Digital Repository. The repository was built using Fedora Commons [16], with Muradora as a web frontend [17]. It also relies on other middleware, such as OpenLDAP which is be used for storing user registration an login data.

Fig. 2 depicts a snapshot of the Digital Repository frontend implemented for the Epidemic Marketplace, where users can browse availble collections.

An important architectural feature of the repository is a clear separation between data and metadata [18], since metadata may contain information not directly available in the datasets. While the data organization may be very variable, a well defined metadata schema should be used for data annotation. To complement that, the metadata schema should be based in standards. Being a widely used metadata standard in the Internet, and supported by several standard institutions, Dublin Core (DC) was adopted [19]. Furthermore, metadata must be consistent and semantically meaningful, employing encoding schemes and ontologies [20] [21].

In this work we are developing a metadata schema, which is based upon the DC standard and extended with metadata elements specific for epidemiological resources. This will enable a more meaningful annotation of the datasets contained in the repository. Moreover, ontologies such as the Unified Medical Language System (UMLS) [22], or the Open Biomedical Ontologies (OBO) [23], will be used for the creation of metadata content.

The repository is being populated with annotated datasets and descriptions of epidemiological resources. Some examples are: a dataset of cumulative cases of H1N1; datasets of Twitter messages containin references to diseases, obtained using the Epidemmic Marketplace Data Collector; a dataset with traffic information concerning the main 500 US airports.

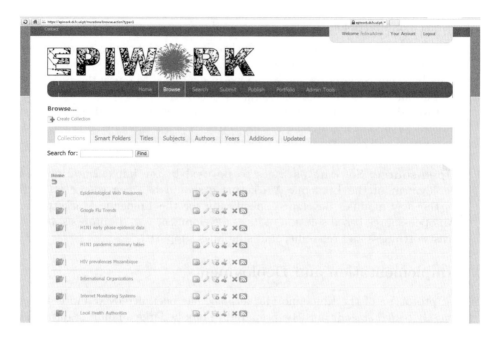

Fig. 2. A section of the repository, where collections may be browsed

Mediator. The Mediator is reponsible for the communication with foreign applications and among different Epidemic Marketplace modules. It will communicate with: 1) clients, which retrieve the data collections of the Epidemic Marketplace and produce dynamical trends graphs or maps with goreferenced data; 2) EPIWORK applications, such as Internet-based Monitoring Systems or computational platforms for epidemiological modeling, which can retrieve and store data in the Epidemic marketplace 3) other modules of the Epidemic Marketplace, for example allowing the MEDCollector [24] to automatically store datasets in the Digital Repository.

The Mediator must be able to manage the access to heterogeneous data from different sources, for different diseases, and in different formats, through either query or search interfaces. It is endowed with a RESTful interface, through which clients are able to search and query datasets and corresponding metadata. This interface obeys the principles of REST architecture [25], offering a simple, flexible and intuitive interaction.

The Mediator implements the OAI-PMH protocol [26], which enables the access to the repository metadata by external metadata harvesting applications. It will also follow the OAI-ORE standard guidelines [27], which defines rules for the description and interchange of aggregated web resources. These aggregations may combine different types of resources in digital objects.

Fig. 3 represents a diagram of the principal interactions in which the Mediator is involved. According to the diagram, the Mediator will login the users through the information contained in a LDAP directory. The mediator will search and

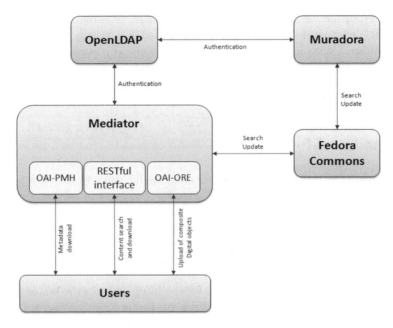

Fig. 3. Diagram of the mediator interactions

update the information contained in Fedora Commons using methods described in its API. The RESTful services will allow users to search and download of contents.

MEDCollector. Data sources such as internet based social networks and search engine query data, may present early evidence of an infection event and propagation [7]. Given the increasing popularity of social networks we can find a large amount of personal information in real time, which may be used for the early detection of epidemic events.

The objective of the MEDCollector is to take advantage of internet data sources and of the large flow of users that currently use social network services, extracting epidemiologic information from there. This module actively collecting messages from Twitter, containing references to specific diseases and locations [28]. New features are being added to this module in order to support the seamless integration of multiple heterogeneous data sources available on the internet, therefore taking not only advantage of social networks but also from a vaster array of epidemiological web data sources. It is also able to passively collect data, receiving information from other data providers, which can be done through newsfeed or e-mail subscription [24].

The data collected by this module will be stored locally in the Epidemic Marketplace. This is important, since collected data may not be available from its original source after a predefined amount of time. Data are stored in a dedicated database and can be used to create datasets.

Forum. The Epidemic Marketplace will serve as an information exchange platform, connecting modelers who search for data, for deriving their models, and those who have data and are searching for the help of modelers to interprete it. This will improve collaborations by direct trustful sharing of data within the communities. The current implementation of the forum is based on phpBB and shares authentication data with the Digital Repository, through LDAP.

5   Metadata Model

There are several metadata standards that can be used to develop metadata schemas, such as ISO/IEC 11179, a standard for storing organizational metadata in a controlled environment [29], and the Dublin Core Metadata Element Set (DC), another metadata standard used for internet resource description [30].

To keep data consistent, is necessary to use not only metadata representation standards for the design of the metadata schema, but also standards for metadata creation, making use of encoding schemes and ontologies.

The metadata model will be essential for the integration of the whole platform, for the interoperability between the different Epidemic Marketplace modules and with other applications. It will be a powerful tool for data manipulation, management and exchange.

5.1   Metadata Model Requirements

We have identified a set of requirements for the creation of a metadata model:

i) **Support well structured and meaningful metadata.** It is important to understand what kind of information is important to the target user and make sure that such information is well described by metadata.

ii) **Straightforward and easy to understand.** This is essential for the system to be accepted by the community, since the creation of metadata may be a complex and time consuming task.

iii) **Use standards to support metadata creation.** Metadata creation should rely the most possible in encoding schemes and ontologies [20] [21], avoiding whenever possible the use of unstructured free text. This makes metadata more consistent, improves information finding and machine readability.

5.2   Encoding Schemes and Ontologies

The use of encoding schemes and ontologies is essential to keep metadata simple and standardized, improving searchability and machine readability.

Encoding schemes make everyone using the same term to refer to a specific attribute. In the Epidemic Marketplace metadata model system several encoding schemes will be used, some of them proposed by Dublin Core, such as the W3C date and time format standard [31], or the RCF4646 standard that defines language codes [32].

Ontologies and databases may be used for the creation of controlled vocabularies to be used in data anotation. Existing ontologies, such as the Unified Medical Language System (UMLS) [22], or other ontologies from the OBO [23], are essential for the annotation of epidemiological and biomedical data. The International Classification of Diseases (ICD) [33], which is integrated in the UMLS [34] will be used to encode disease name. Controlled vocabularies are also useful to standardize other biomedical/epidemiological relevant concepts, providing encoding schemes for drugs [35] or medical procedures [36]. A geographic ontology, with World coverage, is also a primary need [37]. For example, to produce a standard annotation of the spatial coverage the GeoNames database [38] is being looked into as an information source.

6   Metadata Model Design

The metadata model being developed for the Epidemic Marketplace, is based on the DC standard, more specifically in the more recent DCTERMS specification defined by the Dublin Core Metadata Initiative (DCMI) Usage Board [39]. It uses several terms, from the DCTERMS namespace, and implements new ones specific for the annotation of epidemiological data. However, epidemiologic relevant data may cover different areas of knowledge, such as geographic, environmental or demographic, among others.

Table 1 describes specific metadata elements included in the Epidemic Marketplace application profile. Some of these elements may be useful only for specific type of datasets, according to the type of data contained there. For example, if the dataset contains epidemic data then probably metadata elements like

Table 1. Specific metadata terms defined in the Epidemic Marketplace metadata model. The filling of these fields in not mandatory but highly recommendable, if applicable.

Metadata element	Description
Demographic	To describe the type of demographic elements contained in the resource
Disease	To annotate the unequivocal name of a disease that is covered by the resource
Drug	Describe chemical compounds used for disease treatment
Environmental	To describe environmental data in the dataset
Host	Identifies the species of the organism that is the disease host
HostGroup	Identifies a larger taxonomic (or other) group of hosts covered
Geographic	Type of geographic data contained in the resource
Pathogen	Identifies a pathogenic species
PathoGroup	Identifies a taxonomic (or other) group of pathogens
Socio-Economic	Describe social or economic data.
Vaccine	Annotate a vaccine that is covered in the datasete
Vector	Identifies a disease vector organism covered by the dataset

```
<EM:DISEASE>MALARIA</EM:DISEASE>
<EM:ENVIRONMENT>HUMIDITY</EM:ENVIRONMENT>
<EM:HOST>HUMAN</EM:HOST>
<EM:PATHOGEN>PLASMODIUM FALCIPARUM </EM:PATHOGEN>
<EM:GEOGRAPHIC>TOPOGRAPHIC MAP</EM:GEOGRAPHIC>
<EM:VECTOR>ANOPHELES</EM:VECTOR>
<EM:DEMOGRAPHIC>ECONOMIC ACTIVITY</EM:DEMOGRAPHIC>
<EM:DEMOGRAPHIC>POPULATION SIZE</EM:DEMOGRAPHIC>
<EM:DEMOGRAPHIC>BIRTH RATE</EM:DEMOGRAPHIC>
<EM:DEMOGRAPHIC>DEATH RATE</EM:DEMOGRAPHIC>
<EM:DEMOGRAPHIC>MIGRATION</EM:DEMOGRAPHIC>
```

Fig. 4. Example annotation of data

Epidemic and Disease should be filled. If it is geographic then the Geographic element should be filled, identifying the type of geographic data in the dataset.

To test this metadata model it is important to access and annotate the most varied possible batch of datasets. This will help to reveal how well the metadata model is fully capable of describing different types of data. Since such batch of datasets is not yet available, we surveyed several epidemiological papers in order to identify types of data used there. We have derived datasets based on the data presentedused in some of those studies and then annotated these pseudodatasets to evaluate how well these concepts mapped to the metadata model. The example, presented in Fig. 4, was based on this approach using a study by Cohen and coworkers [40]. This allowed the identification of important metadata elements to be included in this model. As the Epidemic Marketplace repository is populated, a wide range of datasets will be available, allowing the testing, evaluation and improvement of this model.

7   Mechanisms to Assist Metadata Creation

Mechanisms to support the user in the process of metadata creation are essential to improve the annotation process, making it faster and easier.

First of all, users must be able to have one or more persistant metadata profiles, which they could modify, save and recover whenever needed. This feature is extremely useful when it is necessary to annotate more than one similar datasets, allowing the re-use of metadata.

Auto-filling is an essential feature to assist metadata creation. The existing implementation is able to search specific information, inserting it in the metadata form, such as the user name and organization. Other information is also inserted automatically, such as the language, title (based on the file name), date and type.

All the automatically inserted metadata can be edited by the user if deemed necessary.

Another important implemented feature are dropdown menus, so the user can select options instead of writing. Dropdown menus will be populated with controlled vocabularies, produced from sources such as thesaurus or ontologies. This will help to keep metadata simple and consistent, using specific encoding schemes.

8 Conclusion

The prototype of the Epidemic Marketplace has been developed and is now available to the Epiwork project collaborators. The system is being stress tested and some improvements are being implemented. We intend to open the platform to the general public later this year, meanwhile news and announcements can be followed at http://epiwork.di.fc.ul.pt/.

The Digital Repository is fully functional, as well as the forum. Also, there is a prototype of the Mediator, however, only part of the functions to be provided are yet implemented. Furthermore, a prototype of the MEDCollector is also available [24].

A first version of the metadata model to be used in the Epidemic Marketplace has been developed. This metadata model is based on the DC metadata standard, which was designed for simplicity and to describe resources in the internet. The DC schema was initially a vocabulary based on 15 properties. However, a recent revision has made it evolve to follow current best practice for machine-processable metadata [39]. Moreover, the DCMI has provided guidelines for the preparation of Dublin Core Application Profiles (DCAP), which can use elements from the DC-TERMS namespace and from other namespaces [41]. This allows the adaptation of DCTERMS based metadata models to very specific applications.

The Epidemic Marketplace metadata model uses elements from DCTERMS for general resource description and in addition uses specific elements for the description of epidemiological data. The inclusion of these epidemiological specific metadata elements, in the metadata schema, will allow a much better structuring of the metadata and an easier implementation of encoding schemes and ontologies. This metadata model will be common to all Epidemic Marketplace modules, where it will be used to describe, exchange and manipulate data. It will improve interoperability between different modules and with external applications that need to search, access and deposit annotated data in the Epidemic Marketplace.

An issue that needs to be overcome for the success a metadata schema is the time expended in the creation of metadata. A way to avoid this problem is having a simple and lean metadata schema. However, if the schema is too simple it might miss important concepts, so it is necessary to reach an equilibrium between simplicity and the necessity to include key information. Another way to keep the metadata creation process fast and simple is to implement automated aids, to help the user fill in the metadata.

An important factor to consider in the development of a metadata model for the description of epidemiological data is its heterogeneity, since it includes data from many different fields of study, such as behavioral, demographic or geographic data. Furthermore, the variabily of data sources and provenance, study design and collection settings add to this variability. Finally, the metadata model needs to be tested and evaluated, in order to access its efficacy and ease of use. This will allow the review and improvement of the model.

In the future the Epidemic Marketplace aims to provide a framework for the creation and development of epidemiological ontologies, openly addressing the needs of this community and fostering its active involvement. Our goal is to contribute to making ontologies widely accepted by the Epidemiological community and ensuring their sustainable evolution, by replicating the success of similar initiatives, such as the Gene Ontology in Molecular Biology [42].

Acknowledgments

The authors want to thank the European Commission for the financial support of the EPIWORK project under the Seventh Framework Programme (Grant #231807), the EPIWORK project partners, CMU-Portugal partnership and FCT (Portuguese research funding agency) for its LaSIGE Multi-annual support.

References

1. Duke-sylvester, S.M., Perencevich, E.N., Furuno, J.P., Real, L.A., Gaff, H.: Advancing epidemiological science through computational modeling: a review with novel examples. Ann. Bot. Fennici. 45, 385–401 (2008)
2. Burke, D.S., Epstein, J.M., Cummings, D.a.T., Parker, J.I., Cline, K.C., Singa, R.M., Chakravarty, S.: Individual-based computational modeling of smallpox epidemic control strategies. Academic emergency medicine: official journal of the Society for Academic Emergency Medicine 13(11), 1142–1149 (2006)
3. Bobashev, G.V., Goedecke, D.M., Yu, F., Epstein, J.M.: A hybrid epidemic model: combining the advantages of agent-based and equation-based approaches. In: Henderson, S.G., Biller, B., Hsieh, M.-H., Shortle, J., Tew, J.D., Barton, R.R. (eds.) Proceedings of the 2007 Winter Simulation Conference, pp. 1532–1537 (2007)
4. Wilson, K., Brownstein, J.S.: Early detection of disease outbreaks using the Internet. CMAJ: Canadian Medical Association journal = journal de l'Association medicale canadienne 180(8), 829–831 (2009)
5. Wagner, M.M., Tsui, F.C., Espino, J.U., Dato, V.M., Sittig, D.F., Caruana, R.A., McGinnis, L.F., Deerfield, D.W., Druzdzel, M.J., Fridsma, D.B.: The emerging science of very early detection of disease outbreaks. Journal of public health management and practice: JPHMP 7(6), 51–59 (2001)
6. Freifeld, C.C., Mandl, K.D., Reis, B.Y., Brownstein, J.S.: HealthMap: global infectious disease monitoring through automated classification and visualization of Internet media reports. Journal of the American Medical Informatics Association: JAMIA 15(2), 150–157
7. Ginsberg, J., Mohebbi, M.H., Patel, R.S., Brammer, L., Smolinski, M.S., Brilliant, L.: Detecting influenza epidemics using search engine query data. Nature 457(7232), 1012–1014 (2009)

8. van Noort, S.P., Muehlen, M., Rebelo de Andrade, H., Koppeschaar, C., Lima Lourenço, J.M., Gomes, M.G.M.: Gripenet: an internet-based system to monitor influenza-like illness uniformly across Europe. Euro surveillance: bulletin européen sur les maladies transmissibles = European communicable disease bulletin 12(7), E5–E6 (2007)
9. National Information Center on Health Services Research and Health Care Technology (NICHSR) - HSR Information Central,
   http://www.nlm.nih.gov/hsrinfo/datasites.html
10. CDC Wonder, http://wonder.cdc.gov/
11. Revere, D., Bugni, P., Fuller, S.: A Public Health Knowledge Management Repository that Includes Grey Literature. Publishing Research Quarterly 1, 65–70 (2007)
12. Cuticchia, A.J., Cooley, P., Hall, R.D., Qin, Y.: NIDDK data repository: a central collection of clinical trial data. BMC medical informatics and decision making 6(1), 19 (2006)
13. Heal, Heal Metadata Elements Description, Version 1.6 (2005), http://www.healcentral.org/services/schema/HEALmdElementsDescript_v1p6.pdf
14. IMS Global Learning Consortium. IMS Application Profile Guidelines Overview (2005), http://www.imsglobal.org/ap/apv1p0/imsap_oviewv1p0.html
15. Silva, M.J., da Silva, F.A.B., Lopes, L.F., Couto, F.M.: Building a Digital Library for Epidemic Modelling. In: Proceedings of ICDL 2010 - The International Conference on Digital Libraries, vol. 1. TERI Press, New Delhi (2010)
16. Lagoze, C., Payette, S., Shin, E., Wilper, C.: Fedora: an architecture for complex objects and their relationships. International Journal on Digital Libraries 6(2) (2006)
17. Nguyen, C., Dalziel, J.: Muradora: A Turnkey Fedora GUI Supporting Heterogeneous Metadata, Federated Identity, And Flexible Access Control. In: Third International Conference on Open Repositories 2008 (2008)
18. Stolte, E., von Praun, C., Alonso, G., Gross, T.: Scientific data repositories: designing for a moving target. In: International Conference on Management of Data (2003)
19. DCMI, The Dublin Core Metadata Initiative, http://dublincore.org/ (accessed, April 2010)
20. Goni, A., Mena, E., Illarramendi, A.: Querying Heterogeneous and Distributed Data Repositories using Ontologies. In: Proceedings of the 7th European-Japanese Conference on Information Modelling and Knowledge Bases (1997)
21. Fox, P., McGuinness, D., Middleton, D., Cinquini, L., Darnell, J., Garcia, J., West, P., Benedict, J., Solomon, S.: Semantically-enabled large-scale science data repositories. In: Cruz, I., Decker, S., Allemang, D., Preist, C., Schwabe, D., Mika, P., Uschold, M., Aroyo, L.M. (eds.) ISWC 2006. LNCS, vol. 4273, pp. 792–805. Springer, Heidelberg (2006)
22. Bodenreider, O.: The Unified Medical Language System (UMLS): integrating biomedical terminology. Nucleic acids research 32(Database issue), D267–D270 (2004)
23. Smith, B., Ashburner, M., Rosse, C., Bard, J., Bug, W., Ceusters, W., Goldberg, L.J., Eilbeck, K., Ireland, A., Mungall, C.J., Leontis, N., Rocca-Serra, P., Ruttenberg, A., Sansone, S.-A., Scheuermann, R.H., Shah, N., Whetzel, P.L., Lewis, S.: The OBO Foundry: coordinated evolution of ontologies to support biomedical data integration. Nature biotechnology 25(11), 1251–1255 (2007)
24. Zamite, J., Silva, F., Couto, F., Silva, M.J.: MEDCollector: Multisource epidemic data collector. In: Proceedings of the 1st International Conference on Information Technology in Bio- and Medical Informatics, DEXA 2010 (2010)

25. Fielding, R.T.: Architectural styles and the design of network-based software architectures. PhD Thesis, University of California, Irvine (2000)
26. OAI, The Open Archives Initiative Protocol for Metadata Harvesting (2008),
    http://www.openarchives.org/OAI/openarchivesprotocol.html
27. Tarrant, D., O'Steen, B., Brody, T., Hitchcock, S., Jefferies, N., Carr, L.: Using OAI-ORE to Transform Digital Repositories into Interoperable Storage and Services Applications. The Code4Lib Journal 6 (2009)
28. Lopes, L.F., Zamite, J.M., Tavares, B.C., Couto, F.M., Silva, F., Silva, M.J.: Automated Social Network Epidemic Data Collector. In: INForum Informatics Symposium, Lisbon (2009)
29. ISO/IEC, International Standard: Information technology - Metadata, Switzerland (2004)
30. Powell, D., Nilsson, M., Naeve, A., Johnston, P., Baker, T.: DCMI Abstract Model (2007), http://dublincore.org/documents/abstract-model/
31. Wolf, M., Wicksteed, C.: W3C Date and Time Formats (1998), http://www.w3.org/TR/NOTE-datetime
32. Phillips, A., Davis, M.: Best Current Practice - Tags for Identifying Languages (2006), http://www.ietf.org/rfc/rfc4646.txt
33. WHO, ICD-10. International Statistical Classification of Diseases and Related Health Problems. 10th Revision (2007),
    http://apps.who.int/classifications/apps/icd/icd10online/
34. Schopen, M., Nelson, S.J.: ICD-10 and the Unified Medical Language System (UMLS) Recommendations, Brisbane, Australia (2002),
    http://www.dimdi.de/static/en/klassi/koop/who/etc/etc_02_44.pdf
35. Merrill, G.H., Ryan, P.B., Painter, J.L.: Construction and Annotation of a UMLS / SNOMED-based Drug Ontology for Observational Pharmacovigilance. Methods (2008)
36. WHO. International Classification of Health Interventions (ICHI),
    http://www.who.int/classifications/ichi/en/ (accessed, April 2010)
37. Chaves, M.S., Silva, M.J., Martins, B.: A Geographic Knowledge Base for Semantic Web Applications (2005),
    http://www.lbd.dcc.ufmg.br:8080/colecoes/sbbd/2005/003.pdf
38. GeoNames Team. GeoNames, http://www.geonames.org/ (accessed, April 2010)
39. DCMI Usage Board. DCMI Metadata Terms (2008),
    http://dublincore.org/documents/2008/01/14/dcmi-terms/
40. Cohen, J.M., Ernst, K.C., Lindblade, K.A., Vulule, J.M., John, C.C., Wilson, M.L.: Topography-derived wetness indices are associated with household-level malaria risk in two communities in the western Kenyan highlands. Malaria Journal 7, 40 (2008)
41. Coyle, K., Baker, T.: Guidelines for Dublin Core Application Profiles (2009),
    http://dublincore.org/documents/2009/05/18/profile-guidelines/
42. Ashburner, M., Ball, C.A., Blake, J.A., Botstein, D., Butler, H., Cherry, J.M., Davis, A.P., Dolinski, K., Dwight, S.S., Eppig, J.T., Harris, M.A., Hill, D.P., Issel-Tarver, L., Kasarskis, A., Lewis, S., Matese, J.C., Richardson, J.E., Ringwald, M., Rubin, G.M., Sherlock, G.: Gene ontology: tool for the unification of biology. The Gene Ontology Consortium. Nature genetics 25(1), 25–29 (2000)

DCM Data Management Framework: A Data Warehousing Approach

Shehla Khalid[1], Claire Surr[2], and Daniel Neagu[1]

[1] School of Computing, Informatics and Media
[2] School of Health Studies
University of Bradford
Bradford, BD7 1DP, UK
{s.khalid3,c.a.surr1,d.neagu}@brad.ac.uk

Abstract. In health care systems the contribution of Information Technology (IT) has proven to have a dynamic role in supporting the quality of care provided to the general population. Dementia Care Mapping (DCM), an observational tool to assess the quality of care for people with dementia, still depends on spreadsheet based tools for data storage and analysis. This system does not comply with the emerging needs of DCM data to store, share, track, and compare overtime in order to monitor progress and trends in care quality. In this paper we provide an overview of the DCM system, identify the need for data management and we propose a DCM data management framework based on a data warehousing approach to facilitate the data collection, storage, sharing and analysis in an organised and consistent manner. We show the sequence of steps (designing relational and dimensional databases) required to transform DCM data into required information.

Keywords: Data Warehouse, Dementia Care Mapping, Care Quality, Dimensional Data, Relational Data, Analytical Tools.

1 Introduction

Electronic health (e-health) is an emerging innovation in health care industry. Information Technology's (IT) contribution in the health care system improves the quality, efficiency, safety, security, collaboration and informs and assists better decision making [1]. IT contribution in health care systems was initially limited to basic data storage applications and medical health records (MHR). However other examples of use of IT in health include the following applications in health care systems: computerized provider order entry (CPOE), Clinical decision support system (CDSS), Picture archiving and communications system (PACS), Radio frequency identification (RFID) [2], and Interoperability [3] in health care [4].

Information Technology and the health industry together are introducing new mechanisms for improving and monitoring the quality of patient care and quality of life. Despite of the spread of technological contributions in nearly every healthcare

S. Khuri, L. Lhotská, and N. Pisanti (Eds.): ITBAM 2010, LNCS 6266, pp. 45–56, 2010.

domain there remain areas which lack this involvement. Dementia Care Mapping (DCM) is one of them.

DCM [5], [6] was developed at the University of Bradford as a systematic observational framework and practice development process for assessing and improving dementia care quality. DCM has been used in the field since the early 1990s and has been continually developed over this time. It is now in its 8th edition and there are now over 8000 trained DCM users in over 20 countries spanning five continents. DCM has been used as both a research and practice development tool internationally [7], [8], [9], [10]. This research has shown that, if used over time, DCM can help to maintain or improve the well-being of people with dementia [11], [7] and is a useful tool for research [12], [13].

However, despite the success of DCM and the generation of a huge amount of data on dementia care quality, there are no mechanisms or framework for large scale data collection, storage, sharing and use. Currently organisations using DCM have no systematic way of saving, tracking and comparing data over time to monitor progress or trends in care quality. The lack of IT contribution in DCM reflects the incapability of variety of potential users to use the DCM data for care planning, monitoring dementia care quality, benchmarking and decision making. Currently no other solution has been proposed or developed to manage the DCM data in a structured and formatted manner so far. In this paper we propose a DCM data management framework showing a data warehousing approach to store, retrieve, analyse and mine the DCM data by different users. We also take the opportunity to provide the overview of the DCM process and the importance of DCM data management for a wide range of users in different areas.

The proposed framework consists of different stages to manage the DCM data. The DCM data will be captured and stored through a web-based interface into an international database. This will source the DCM Data Warehouse (DCMDW) for complex querying, reporting and analysis purposes. DCMDW could provide a multidimensional environment for applying different data analysis and data mining techniques. These steps will ensure the management of DCM data from capturing to storing, analysing and recognising trends over time. However we do not claim to address the comprehensive details of data warehouse development, its security and data quality in this paper, but we do introduce the relational database and dimensional database schema to clarify the entities in DCM domain. Fig.1 shows the model of our designed DCM data management framework.

The rest of the paper is organised as follows. The importance and need of DCM data management and how it will be beneficial for the wide range of users is discussed in section 2. Section 3 highlights similar work completed in health care systems. Examples of other data warehouse approaches for decision support systems are also provided and a solution for data management in various areas of health sector is described. The proposed framework with its stages is described in section 4. This paper represents the starting point of our ongoing research towards data governance for DCM. The final section, therefore, elaborates future areas for our work and concludes the paper.

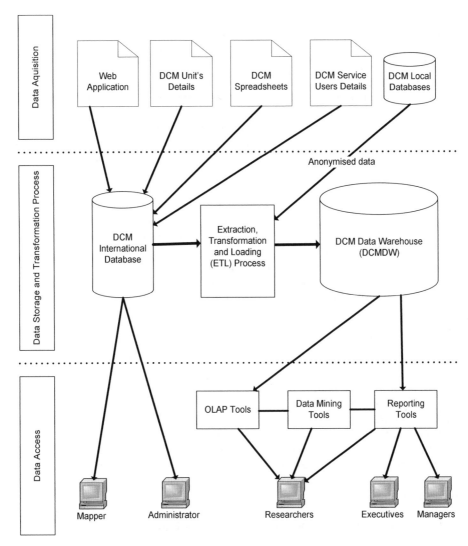

Fig. 1. A Proposed Model for DCM Data Management Framework

2   Overview of DCM Data

This section describes the DCM tool, its coding procedure and the complexity of DCM data in the context of analysis and decision making processes.

2.1 DCM Data Complexity

DCM is a complex observational tool and practice development process to evaluate and improve the quality of care of people with dementia in formal dementia care settings, such as care homes, day centres and hospital wards.

DCM observations involve continual observation of 5-8 people (participants) with dementia over a sustained period of time, usually 6 consecutive hours. Observations are carried out by a trained observer (mapper). Codes that represent the behaviours and mood and engagement levels of the participants for every five-minute period (time frame) are recorded. This is assessed by attempting to take the standpoint of the person with dementia. Two types of codes are recorded; Behaviour Category Code (BCC) and Mood and Engagement (ME). The BCC represents one of 23 different domains of a participant's behaviour. The letters from A to Z (except H, M, Z) represents the main behaviour observed within a time frame i.e. A for Articulation (when participant is being verbally or non-verbally engaged with another person or animal).ME values represent the mood and engagement of the participant associated with the BCC recorded in a time frame. The values of ME are expressed on a six point scale ranging from extreme distress (-5) to extreme positive mood and engagement (+5). So for example, a participant engaging in a positive conversation would be coded as A+3. Over a six-hour map up to 72 times frames of data may be coded for each participant. The quality of staff interactions with the people with dementia is also noted. These codes are called Personal Enhancers (PEs) and Personal Detractions (PDs). There are 17 different types of PD and PE that may be coded as and when they occur. All this information is recorded manually on a paper-based raw data sheets and then part of this data is transferred onto excel based spreadsheets for storage and basic analysis purposes. This information, in the form of reports, is then fed back to staff who develop action plans for care improvement. Observation takes places at regular intervals (3-12 monthly) to monitor progress and set new targets.

Currently, when undertaking data analysis, the mapper, for example, undertakes basic calculations such as percentage of time spent in each BCC and ME, and total number of PDs and PEs. They may also undertake further calculations such as calculating the average of all the ME values (known as the well or ill-being or WIB score), which represents the average level of well or ill-being experienced during the whole map by an individual participant or the group as a whole. The richness of the DCM data also permits other analyses to be completed for each map such as agitation and distress levels, withdrawn behaviour, passive engagement, opportunities for activity and engagement.

2.2 Limitations of Existing Data Processing Techniques

DCM data is traditionally stored in an unstructured, inconsistent and unlinked format (spreadsheets).The data recorded in one mapping session is stored in different formats i.e. BCC and ME on Spreadsheets and PD's and PE's on paper based files. Service user's basic details i.e. full name, age, gender and address are not recorded (even if recorded, for specific purposes, they cannot be related to the other recorded data about a mapping session). Lack of data management originates the integration complexities between disparate data structures. DCM data faces irregularities, incompleteness, storage, and quality issues. These data management problems currently make DCM data unsuitable for complex analysis and recognition of trends and patterns over time.

In addition, researchers and practitioners are unable to get a broad view of a large amount of historical and consistent data, which could assist with monitoring and benchmarking dementia care quality locally, nationally and internationally decision making authorities i.e. managers, executives, government bodies are restricted on their ability to utilise DCM data in decision making because of a lack of a structured, organised and efficient Decision Support System (DSS). Organisations have to go through a time consuming and costly process to bring all data together in one place to carry out very basic analysis.

This lack of data organisation and management inhibits the ability of the mapper and other potential users of DCM to utilise and analyse the DCM data to its full potential. The following queries, which can be extremely useful in care quality tracking and benchmarking cannot be answered:

1. What is the average WIB score of all male and female service users in all UK units each year over the last 5 years?
2. What is the average number of personal enhancers recorded per hour of mapping in Bradford unit from 1995 to 2000?

2.3 Importance of DCM Data Management

DCM produces a complex but rich data which needs a sustainable and consistent data management framework. This data management framework will facilitate the data storage, analysis, and efficient retrieval processes. DCM can provide the information of value to a variety of aspects of care delivery, which can help to achieve benefits on clinical, individual, group and organisational levels [14]. Our approach in introducing the data warehousing methodology to manage the DCM data will enable a variety of users (e.g. mapper, manager, researcher) to extract information relevant to them, from a historical data repository. They will be able to store and retrieve the data in an optimized manner.

Ability to process the data in this way would assist providers in monitoring and improving care quality more proficiently. Collected alongside other information about persons with dementia (e.g. diagnosis, severity of dementia, dependency, age, gender, ethnicity) and about the care setting (e.g. location, type, size, staff ratios), a single data repository of DCM data will provide a picture of the quality of dementia care internationally, nationally, regionally and locally. National and international level storage and comparison or analysis of data over time, if available, would permit national benchmarking of care quality to assist in identification of DCM care quality indices, international comparison and tracking of care quality and also highlight areas of poor and best practice. It would also provide an invaluable resource to researchers in dementia care, as it can be used in the longer term for quality of life related dementia research and for informing dementia care policy.

3 Related Work

Data warehouse technology has been effectively applied into different industries i.e. retail [15], telecommunication, finance services, and travel [16], industries. This is a challenging and complex process in health care systems because of the complexity and largely unstructured formatting of medical data. The other reasons are the volume, complexity, and security of health data [17]. But in spite of these challenges across the world attempts to develop data warehouses in different areas of health services have been made and have proved to be successful to date [18].

NHS Care Record Service (CRS) is an electronic records service in England to facilitate the link between GP's, doctors, nurses, and other health care staff and patients, to deliver better quality health care to everyone in England. Spine [19], is a national database, which is part of NHS CRS. It, stores UK patient's electronic health care records summaries, which includes the patient's demographic and medical information. There are different applications of this databases one of them is Secondary Uses Service (SUS) [20]. The SUS is a repository with anonymized patient records. This system helps researchers, analysts, practitioners and governing bodies to look at public health trends, medication and treatment efficacy, numbers of staff required by the NHS for future planning and other health care issues requiring planning or problem solving. Hospital Episode Statistics (HES) [21], is a national statistical data warehouse for NHS care provided to people living in England and those registered with NHS but are not living in England. HES repository provides the data for analysis on an individual level and organisational level by NHS authorized personnel's.

Data warehouse systems are also used in other aspects of health care and related areas. For example, [22] describe the importance and contribution of a data warehouse in bioterrorism surveillance system to recognise the patterns in medical data to identify the abnormal situations and facilitate the analytical procedures to handle these situations. In [23], the usefulness of a data warehouse approach in disease management programmes to help to maintain the health of general population is outlined. The role of a data warehouse for hospital infection control is discussed by [1]. This paper describes the importance of a clinical data warehouse for research, quality importance, organisation and accessibility of data. They also highlight the importance of a clinical data warehouse in detecting medical measures and describe how this system can help to save money and time to acquire the precision in decision making.

In [24], the contribution of a data warehouse in providing the data for analytical and decision making purposes for Comprehensive Assessment for Tracking Community Health (CATCH) is discussed. The authors assert that a data warehouse will be a most demanding future application of technology in health care sectors. A data warehouse solution for decision-based health care has also been proposed and justified by [25]. According to Stolba et al a data warehouse is a suitable solution for those medical systems which need decision support systems to enhance the quality of health care.

The mentioned work highlights the need for data warehousing in health care related issues where data is integrated from different sources in one repository and used for complex analysis and decision making purposes. Our work emphasises the need of a comprehensive solution to store and retrieve the DCM data, and we believe that data warehousing approach will solve this problem. Our proposed approach is different than most existing solutions in the way that we have distributed the load of data integration into two steps: the international database will integrate data from those sources providing data for basic analysis, for example data taken from different dementia care settings, old DCM spreadsheets and other DCM related documents. On the other hand DCMDW will accumulate the historic data from international database and other DCM organisations local databases (anonymous data) for complex analysis, reporting and decision making.

4 Proposed Stages for Data Management Framework

Different organisations have different techniques and systems to manage their data. They are based on the end-users requirements and the nature of data. Our proposed DCM data management framework constitutes different stages to collect, store and transform data into required information. The stages are depicted in Table 1.

Table 1. Four stages for DCM data management

Stages	Applications	Data Source	Users	Benefits
Stage 1	DCM Relational Database(with web interface)	Different DCM organisations, old DCM spread-sheets, other DCM related documents.	Mapper, administrator	Best for data capturing, storing, validation and integrity. Global access.
Stage 2	Extraction, Transformation, Loading (ETL) process	DCM relational databases, Other databases(with anonymised data)		Data cleansing, integration and quality check
Stage 3	DCM Data Warehouse (DCMDW)	Different data sources	Data analysis tools, data mining tools	Easy data access and retrieval from dimensional structure of data
Stage4	Analysis Applications On DCMDW	DCM data warehouse	Managers, executives, governmental authorities etc.	Decision making, bench marking, analysis and reporting

4.1 DCM International Databases

The first step towards DCM data management process is to design a web-based relational database as the primary data repository. The web application interface allows DCM data providers to enter data online and store it in a relational format. The DCM spreadsheets are transformed from zero normal form to third normal form. We have shown the recognised DCM entities and their relations with each other in Fig. 2 as a logical schema for DCM international relational databases. Different roles (users) are identified while gathering the requirements. Each role can have access to the particular data to which it is authorized to. Mapper can only see the data of a unit, he has mapped, for specific time period. The data accessed by other users i.e. researcher is pseudo-anonymous (service users are given unique identification). Mappers are able to use the data for basic calculations which will be done with pre-defined queries

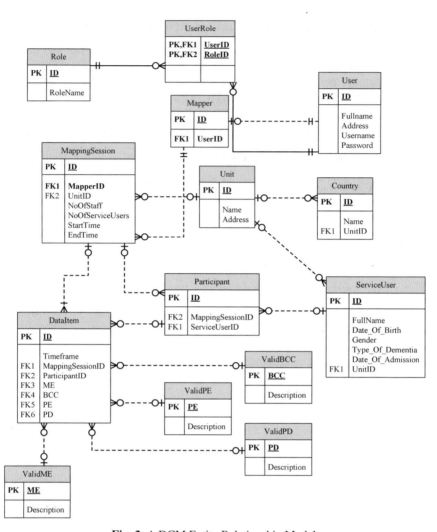

Fig. 2. A DCM Entity Relationship Model

(usually what is required from the mapping where user is able to extract the reports to feed back to the unit staff). This database will provide a platform to integrate the data, taken from different DCM data providers, at very first stage. The rule-based web interface will allow only quality data (validated DCM data) to be stored. This is the first stage where data quality is checked. There are different BCC's for example H, M, and Z which are not part of the coding system and some BCC's i.e. C (withdrawn behaviour) can only have an ME of -1 associated with it. These validations are done in database design. This procedure will ensure the correct entry of BCC's and ME's in the database. Old data (spreadsheets) will be automatically imported into the repository including the detailed data about unit and service users taken from other documents as DCM spreadsheets stores incomplete data.

4.2   Extraction, Transformation and Loading (ETL) Process

ETL process involves the data extraction, from heterogeneous sources, transformation into consistent, compatible and quality data and loading this data into data warehouse for analysis purposes [26]. DCM data from international database will be extracted and integrated with the anonymous data taken from other DCM organisation. Due to the sensitivity and security issues with DCM data, there can be disagreements regarding data provision into DCM international database by the DCM organisations from other countries. Our proposed system solves this problem by allowing these DCM organisations to provide anonymous data into DCMDW for global analysis. This data will be used by different users i.e. governmental authorities or researchers who need large amount of global data on DCM to analyse the quality of care provided in different care homes. ETL process constitutes different tools to extract the data from local DCM databases and other sources and transform this disparate data into a consistent and compatible format. This data is loaded into DCM data warehouse and used for multidimensional analysis. In this paper we do not intend to give a detailed view of ETL process and data cleansing issues.

4.3   Dimensional Database (DCMDW)

A data warehouse is a purpose built data repository to store a historical, consistent and large amount of quality data in a dimensional format for analytical and decision making purposes. The purpose of DCMDW is to provide the users with good quality data, taken from heterogeneous sources, in a consistent format which can be queried to extract the required information for analysis and reporting. The construction of the DCMDW will enable care providers and policy makers to have access to a dimensional data to make decisions to improve the quality of life and standards of care of people with dementia in formal dementia care settings. Researchers and practitioners can also have an access to a historical, consistent, non-volatile and time variant data to enhance their research and knowledge about the care quality standards.

A dimensional view of data will enable users to look at a large number of inter-dependent aspects of the data from different analytical angles for analysis and decision making activities. Star schema as a dimensional model is recognised as an effective schema for data organisation in most data warehouses [27]. The star schema consists of fact table/s and dimensional tables. A fact table consists of numeric data which contains the data at its atomic level. Dimension tables, linked to the fact table, express the details and justification of the facts for rich and detailed query function. In Fig. 3 the fact about a service user having BCC and ME on a particular date are shown with dimension tables to support this fact. The fact table has lowest level of information in it. In this fact table the lowest level information is where BCC and ME of each service user in a specific time/date in a specific unit can be determined. This atomic level of data arrangement in the data warehouse will facilitate the data mining and data analysis application on it. As most recent data mining applications support the details at the lowest grain to find the trends and patterns in the data.

The star schema in Fig.3 shows the fact table and dimension tables in DCM domain. The dimension tables provide the attribute details which are important to measure the fact in the fact table. For example unit dimension provides the attributes about the unit where mapping has taken place. This dimension can be hierarchically expanded to

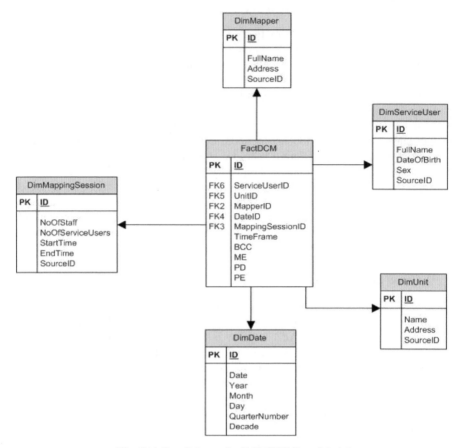

Fig. 3. A Star Schema for DCMDW Data Model

show the full address of the unit including the area and the country name. This will help to organise the units according to the areas and countries in querying process.

4.4   Applications on DCMDW

Data warehouse provides an ideal environment for multidimensional analysis [28]. Different analytical tools i.e. Online Analytical Processing (OLAP), Data Mining (DM) and Decision Support Systems (DSS) could be equipped with the data warehouse to provide different users with multidimensional analysis, patterns recognition and decision making. The OLAP tools provide a user with the facility to drill down to details to the atomic level or roll up to the aggregated data for summaries. A user is able to analyse the data from different angles. For example a DCM user will be able to find out information such as the WIB score of each service user in a particular unit in a specific time period, or in a particular year the details of all mapping session undertaken by a particular mapper etc. DCMDW will enable users at different authority levels to customise the process of information retrieval using multidimensional view of data.

5 Conclusions and Future Work

In this paper we provid the details of a novel DCM system and discuss the importance of data management to provide different users with the ability to access DCM data for various analytical purposes. We further propose a DCM data management framework comprises different stages from data capturing to dissemination. The designed relational database for DCM international database and dimensional database for DCMDW has shown DCM entities, their relationships and the dimensional view of data. DCMDW will provide a consistent and historic data repository to source different analytical tools i.e. OLAP, DM and reporting. These tools will help various users to analyse the DCM data from different perspectives and for a range of purposes to improve the quality of care in dementia care settings and quality of life in people with dementia. As this is our work in progress, we evaluated the designed databases as a small scale scenario and the results were encouraging. However further work is planned for validation, consistency checks and experimental results interpretation starting from our current contribution to the DCM data management framework.

This paper is also an introduction of our research towards DCM data governance. Currently we demonstrate the DCM data management solution by explaining the basic steps from data capturing to analysis. In the next stage we aim to study and present a detailed view of DCMDW architecture with data anonymization techniques and data cleansing process in a secure environment. In this paper we do not claim to give a comprehensive solution of data warehouse development and analysis application on it. We intend to discuss about data quality, security and anonymization, performance and scalability issues in DCM data management framework in our future work.

References

1. Wisniewski, M.F., Kieszkowski, P., Zagorski, B.M., Trick, W.E., Sommers, M., Weinstein, R.A.: Development of a Clinical Data Warehouse for Hospital Infection Control. J. Am. Med. Inform. Assoc. 10, 454–462 (2003)
2. Lahtela, A., Hassinen, M.: Requirements for Radio Frequency Identification in Healthcare. Stud. Health Technol. Inform. 150, 720–724 (2009)
3. Brailer, D.J.: Interoperability: the Key to the Future Health Care System. Health Aff. (Millwood) Suppl. Web Exclusives, W5-19–W15-21 (2005)
4. Hackbarth, G.M., Reichauer, R.D., Miller, M.E.: Medicare Payment Advisory Commission (MEDPAC). Report to the Congress: New Approaches in Medicare, 157–181 (2004)
5. Bradford Dementia Group, Evaluating dementia care: The DCM method, 7th edn. University of Bradford, Bradford (1997)
6. Bradford Dementia Group, DCM 8 User's Manual. University of Bradford, Bradford (2005)
7. Brooker, D., Foster, N., Banner, A., Payne, M., Jackson, L.: The efficacy of Dementia Care Mapping as an audit tool: report of a 3-year British NHS evaluation. Aging and Mental Health 2(1), 60–70 (1998)
8. Fossey, J., Ballard, C., Juszczak, E., James, I., Alder, N., Jacoby, R., Howard, R.: Effect of Enhanced Psychosocial Care on Antipsychotic Use in Nursing Home Residents with Dementia: Cluster Randomised Controlled Trial. BMJ 332(7544), 756–758 (2006)
9. Gigliotti, C.M., Jarrott, S.E., Yorgason, J.: Harvesting Health: Effects of Three Types of Horticultural Therapy Activities for Persons with Dementia. Dementia: The International Journal of Social Research and Practice 3(2), 161–180 (2004)

10. Sloane, P.D., Brooker, D., Cohen, L., Douglass, C., Edelman, P., Fulton, B.R., Jarrott, S., Kasayka, R., Kuhn, D., Preisser, J.S., Williams, C.S., Zimmerman, S.: Dementia Care Mapping as a Research Tool. International Journal of Geriatric Psychiatry 22, 580–589 (2007)

11. Younger, D., Martin, G.W.: Dementia care mapping: an Approach to Quality Audit of Services for People with Dementia in two Health Districts. Journal of Advanced Nursing 32(5), 1206–1212 (2000)

12. Brooker, D., Surr, C.: Dementia Care Mapping: Principles and Practice. University of Bradford, Bradford (2005)

13. Brooker, D.: Dementia Care Mapping: A Review of the Research Literature. Gerontologist 45 (Special Issue 1), 11–18 (2005)

14. British Standard Institution (BSI), PAS 800: Use of Dementia Care Mapping for Improved Person-centered Care in a Care Provider Organisations (2010)

15. Ross, D.: Retail Data Warehousing The- State-of-the-Art. In: Global Coverage of the Business Intelligence Ecosystem, US edition (2005),
    http://www.b-eye-network.com/view/769

16. The Data Warehouse Institute Awards: ARC's Fraud Prevention Solutions. TDWI Best Practices Awards (2009), http://www.arccorp.com/news/pr20090623.pdf

17. Stolba, N., Tjoa, A.M., Thomas, M., Marko, B.: Federated Data Warehouse Approach to Support the National and International Interoperability of HealthCare Information Systems. In: 15th European Conference on Information systems (ECIS), St Gallen, Switzerland (2007)

18. Protti, D.J.: How Business Intelligence is making Health Care Smarter. World View Report (10) (2005),
    http://www.connectingforhealth.nhs.uk/newsroom/worldview/protti10

19. Connecting for Health (NHS) Spine Factsheet,
    http://www.connectingforhealth.nhs.uk/resources/systserv/spine-factsheet

20. Connecting for Health (NHS) Secondary Uses Service (SUS),
    http://www.connectingforhealth.nhs.uk/systemsandservices/sus

21. Connection for Health (NHS), Hospital Episode Statistics (HES),
    http://www.connectingforhealth.nhs.uk/systemsandservices/sus/delivery/hes/index_html

22. Berndt, D.J., Fisher, J.W., Craighead, J.G., Hevner, A.R., Luther, S., Studnicki, J.: The Role of Data Warehousing in Bioterrorism Surveillance. Decision Support Systems 43, 1383–1403 (2007)

23. Ramick, C.D.: Data Warehouse in Disease Management Programmes. Journal of Health Care Information Management 15(2), 99–105 (2001)

24. Berndt, D.J., Hevner, A.R., Studnicki, J.: The Catch Data Warehouse: Support for Community Health Care Decision-making. Decision Support Systems 35, 367–384 (2003)

25. Stolba, N.: Towards a Sustainable Data Warehouse Approach for Evidence-Based Health Care, PHD Thesis (2007),
    http://publik.tuwien.ac.at/files/PubDat_141378.pdf

26. Trujillo, J., Luján-Mora, M.: A UML Based Approach for Modeling ETL Processes in Data Warehouses. In: Song, I.-Y., Liddle, S.W., Ling, T.-W., Scheuermann, P. (eds.) ER 2003. LNCS, vol. 2813, pp. 307–320. Springer, Heidelberg (2003)

27. Gray, P., Watson, H.: Decision Support in the Data Warehouse. Prentice-Hall, Englewood Cliffs (1998)

28. Ponniah, P.: Data Warehouse Fundamentals: A Comprehensive Guide for IT Professionals. John Wiley & Sons, inc., Chichester (2001)

Automatic Classification of Intrapartal Fetal Heart-Rate Recordings – Can It Compete with Experts?

Václav Chudáček[1], Jiří Spilka[1], Michal Huptych[1], George Georgoulas[5], Petr Janků[2], Michal Koucký[3], Chrysostomos Stylios[4], and Lenka Lhotská[1]

[1] Dept. of Cybernetics CTU in Prague,
[2] Dept. of Obstetrics and Gynaecology FN Brno,
[3] Dept. of Obstetrics and Gynaecology 1.LF CUNI in Prague
[4] Dept. of Communications, Informatics and Management, TEI of Epirus, Artas, Greece
[5] Dept. of Computer Applications in Finance and Management, TEI of Ionian Islands, Lefkas, Greece
chudacv@fel.cvut.cz

Abstract. Fetal heart rate (fHR) is used to evaluate the fetal well-being during the delivery. It provides information of fetal status and allows doctors to detect ongoing hypoxia. Routine clinical evaluation of intrapartal fHR is based on description of macroscopic morphological features of its baseline. In this paper we show, that by using additional features for description of the fHR recordings, we can improve the classification accuracy. Additionally since results of automatic signal evaluation are easily reproducible we can objectify the whole process, thus enabling us to focus on the underlying reasons for high expert inter-observer and intra-observer variability.

Keywords: fetal heart rate, intrapartum, classification, inter-observer variability.

1 Introduction

Correct evaluation of fetal status from the available information is crucial when difficulties occur during delivery after an otherwise normal pregnancy. Even though the baby is equipped with a defense mechanism to tackle the stress conditions during the delivery, in some cases only timely intervention can prevent the long-term consequences resulting from prolonged oxygen insufficiency - consequences such as cerebral palsy, neonatal encephalopathy or even death [1].

Instrumental evaluation of the fetal well-being during delivery is more than hundred years old. Auscultation, sensing of the fetal heart rate (fHR) using a fetal stethoscope, introduced by Pinard in 1876, was replaced in 1960's by electronic fetal monitoring (EFM) by cardiotocography (CTG - recording of fetal heart rate and force/pressure of contractions) as the most important representative.

Although introduction of the EFM was accompanied by large expectation, since it offered continuous fetal surveillance, meta-analysis of large multicentre studies [1] did not prove any significant improvements in the delivery outcomes. Some studies additionally disapproved any evidence of advantages of continuous monitoring when compared to intermittent one. Moreover, EFM became the main suspect for increased rate of cesarean sections [1].

S. Khuri, L. Lhotská, and N. Pisanti (Eds.): ITBAM 2010, LNCS 6266, pp. 57–66, 2010.
© Springer-Verlag Berlin Heidelberg 2010

In order to improve interpretation and thus lower the number of asphyxiated neo-nates CTG guidelines were introduced by International Federation of Gynecology and Obstetrics (FIGO) [2]. Even though the guidelines are available for more than twenty years poor interpretation of CTG still persists with inter-observer as well as intra-observer variations in CTG evaluation [3, 4].

First attempts of automatic CTG analysis followed FIGO guidelines that basically describe morphological changes in CTG.

Attempts to evaluate CTG using computer are as old as the guidelines. FIGO mor-phological features became fundamental features in most of clinically oriented sys-tems. Automatic extraction of morphological features was proposed by prof. Bernades and resulted in development of SisPorto [5] and later CAFE [6] by Berdinas – both automatic "expert-like" systems for CTG analysis.

In many papers, including this one, only fHR signal is used since it is the signal containing direct information about the fetal state. For fHR description different fea-tures were investigated in the past, many of them heavily influenced by the research in adult heart rate variability (HRV) analysis. Statistical description of CTG tracings was employed in works of Magenes [7] and Goncalves [8]. Another approach to fHR analysis examined frequency content by spectral analysis and paper [9] gives a short overview of works where fHR spectrum was analyzed. The fHR was also analyzed by various wavelets with different properties [10]. Other works analyzed nonlinear prop-erties of fHR such as fractal dimension of reconstructed attractor and waveform frac-tal dimension. Different estimations of fractal dimension were reviewed by [11]. The most successful nonlinear methods for HRV analysis, so far, are approximate and sample entropy. They are often used for examination of nonlinear systems and proved their applicability also in fHR analysis [12].

The paper is further structured as follows: First the data used throughout the paper are described, than follows signal pre-processing and presentation of methods for feature extraction. Afterwards selection of the useful features for the data description is presented and finally results achieved by expert as well as automatic classification are compared and discussed.

2 Data Used

The fHR signals used in this work were measured either externally using Doppler ultrasound or internally using scalp electrode. Our data set consisted of 476 delivery recordings. The data were obtained at the Obstetricians ward of General Teaching Hospital in Prague on Neoventas' STAN S21 device. Two modes of acquisition are depicted on Figure 1. In 60% (280) of all cases the measurement of fHR was done using ultrasound, in the rest electrode was attached to the scalp of the fetus. Signals were then annotated by five experts with at least five years of praxis as obstetricians; the process is described in Section 4.

Recordings obtained with the scalp electrode have usually fewer missed values and are in general less noisy.

All the recordings had to be checked for patient anamnesis and only one fold pregnan-cies delivered during $38^{th} – 42^{nd}$ week of pregnancy were chosen for the final database.

Additionally umbilical artery pH was obtained as and objective evaluation of hy-poxia. The definition of neonatal acidemia is defined in most textbooks when pH

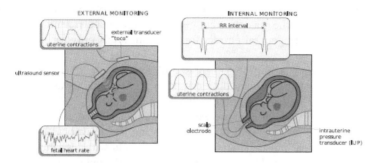

Fig. 1. Recording of the fetal heart rate and uterine activity [13]

value is below 7.05, but many recent works suggest otherwise [14]. Since pathological recordings are very hard to get and based on recommendation of cooperating obstetricians we decided to classify the fetuses as normal (i.e. without sustained hypoxia) if having pH above or equal to 7.15 and abnormal otherwise.

3   Automatic Classification Process

3.1   Signal Preprocessing

Relevance of extracted features usually highly depends on the quality of the preprocessing steps - in our work following steps were used: artifacts removal; interpolation; choice of appropriate segment; and de-trending of the signal.

The fHR signal contains a lot of artifacts caused by mother and fetal movements or displacements of the transducer. Usually between 20% and 40% of all data are affected by artifacts.

We employed the artifacts removal previously used in [5], where all abrupt changes in fHR are removed and replaced by line - see Figure 2.

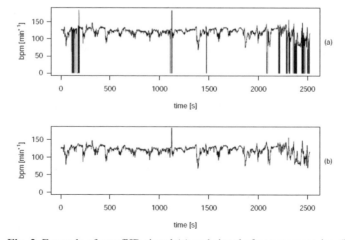

Fig. 2. Example of raw fHR signal (a) and signal after preprocessing (b)

It is important to emphasize the way the data are replaced since the results of analysis are affected by the way we treat gaps. We have used Hermit interpolation of missing data which is in general correct for fHR, but holds only for gaps of duration less then *20s*.

The fetal heart rate is non-uniformly sampled. This could affect the results of nonlinear methods, such as fractal dimension and entropy, though, since sampling is deterministically non-uniform, no problems were expected.

During the segment selection phase we tried to choose the segment as close as possible to delivery. But usually fHR directly preceding the delivery is largely contaminated with artifacts and noise. Therefore, only segments with less then 20% of erroneous signal were selected. The final segments were 20 minutes long meaning 4800 samples for signal sampled at 4 Hz.

Physiological time series are generally considered as non-stationary, i.e. statistical properties of physiological signal (mean, variance, and correlation structure) vary during time. We work with segments of short duration. Therefore, we could carefully detrend signal using third order polynomial and consider it stationary.

3.2 Feature Extraction

Since establishment of FIGO guidelines, various types of features were tested in the technical papers. Nevertheless only the classical - morphological and macroscopic features - are used in the clinical setting. In this section we thoroughly describe nonlinear features that could be used for automatic fHR classification and could bring added value to the decision process in comparison to use of classical feature set alone.

3.2.1 Classical Features

Morphological features introduced by the FIGO guidelines describe the shape and changes of the baseline such as: baseline mean (**baselineMean**); standard deviation (**baselineSD**); median of long-term (**medianLTV**) and short term variability (**STV**); and mean of interval index (**meanII**). More detailed description of the classical features is not purpose of this paper and can be found e.g. in [10].

The second category of features, that can be called classical are those used routinely in adult HRV evaluation and are standardized in [15] such as **NN50**, **RMSSD**, as well as the frequency features describing the amounts of energy in different energy bins – for example – energy in the low frequencies bin 0.05-0.15Hz (**LF**) and ratios of energies in different bins e.g. (**ratLF_HF**) [12].

3.2.2 Nonlinear Features

The nonlinear approach may reveal relevant clinical information of fHR not apparent in the time and frequency domain. Since heart-beat fluctuates on different time scales and is self-similar, fractal dimension is useful estimator of fHR dynamics. Detailed description of methods for estimation of fractal dimension entropy and complexity measures can be found in [16-19] and we will use the limited space to bring to attention the specifics of applying the methods on the fHR data.

Fractal dimension of attractor
In order to reconstruct an attractor we have estimated embedding parameters (time delay, τ, and embedding dimension, m) using mutual information approach and Cao's

method. We used only correlation dimension, $D2$, for attractor analysis since it is robust to noise. To be able to reliably estimate the fractal dimension a certain data length is necessary. There exist many theories about required data length with general agreement that the data length needed increases exponentially with data dimension. We followed data size requirements as suggested in [17]; for estimating a dimension d, a minimum data length required is $N_{min} = 10^{d/2}$.

Fractal dimension of waveform
The former approach considers signal in R^2 as a geometric object and directly uses it without any further transformation. Thus estimated dimension is always in range $(1;2)$ because the geometrical representation of signal is more complicated than line but never covers the whole 2D space. We used following methods for waveform dimension estimation: box counting (**fdBoxCountDx**), Higuchi's (**fdHiguchiDx**), and variance (**fdVarianceDx**). Note that both methods estimate Hurst exponent, H, that is related to fractal dimension $D = E + 1 - H$, where E is the Euclidian dimension which equals to one for time series. Additionally detrended fluctuation analysis (**DFA**) is used for spectral slope estimation α that is related Hurst exponent $H = 1 - \alpha$.

We used Weierstrass cosine function $w(t)$ and examined how the data length affects estimate of fractal dimension for each method. The Higuchi method provides good estimates for all data lengths while variance and box counting methods offer biased estimates of fractal dimension. The DFA method converges to the theoretical value for increasing N. The different algorithms for estimation of the fractal dimension were probed by [18]. They also concluded that Higuchi's method is the most reliable but, also, the most sensitive to noise. Since fHR certainly contains noise we will also take advantage of the variance method offering robustness to noise.

The estimated dimension is not only dependent on data length but also on the dimensionality of data. We examined bias of the estimated fractal dimension by varying the dimension D of $w(t)$ in $(1;2)$ interval. The results showed that dimension estimated by the box counting method is biased. The Higuchi's and the variance method provide unbiased estimate of the fractal dimension only for dimensions $D>1.5$. The DFA method offers biased estimation for $D<1.3$ and $D>1.7$.

Next, we estimated the two scaling regions as were described by [18]. The authors suggested two scaling regions on the log-log plot of some measurement function, e.g. number of boxes, versus size of region (e.g. size of the box). Higuchi named the time where the curve bends as critical time τ_c. To standardize estimated dimension we determined the τ_c for all methods and finally we set it to $\tau_c = 3s$.

The used data meets demands on required length. The limitation of waveform fractal analysis lies in biased estimate for low dimension - in our work we used 4800 samples long signals. Analysis performed on synthetic Weierstrass function suggests that we can reliably estimate the fractal dimension by Higuchi's method. It is necessary to point out, that Weierstrass function does not completely reflects nonlinear and stochastic properties of fetal heart rate. Hence, we have to carefully interpret results of estimated waveform fractal dimensions.

Entropy
Kolmogorov–Sinai entropy is not usable for a noisy time series of finite length; therefore, approximate entropy (**ApEn**) [19] was designed and proved its usefulness for a short and noisy time series.

However, it provides biased estimation and is dependent on data length. Sample entropy **(SampEn)** eliminated drawbacks of ApEn by reducing bias and data length dependence. Since fHR records have finite length, the entropy estimation in terms of length is of a major interest. In [19] the Pincus showed that ApEn is broadly applicable for data series of length $N > 100$. Nevertheless, this value was suggested for wide spectrum of applications and in our case, meaningful data length for ApEn is about 1000 samples. The choice of parameter m was proposed by [20]. They concluded, the best results are achieved when $m = 2$. However, this holds only in cases when a dynamical system is not purely deterministic. The tolerance r was set to $r = 0.2*$ standard deviation.

Lempel Ziv Complexity
Lempel Ziv Complexity **(LZC)** [21] examines reoccurring patterns in time series. The more reoccurring patterns - the less complex signal is. The LZC method estimates complexity of encoded signal so that dynamical changes of signal are replaced with particular character. We used binary encoding in order to avoid dependence of results on quantification criteria and normalization procedures. The required data length for LZC was examined by [22] and concluded that the minimum length is 1000 samples for binary encoded data.

3.3 Feature Selection

To determine which features to use for classification purposes feature selection algorithms were used to identify the ones containing the most of useful information. Features were ranked and since cross-validation was used only features ranked within the first ten best are presented in Table 1.

Techniques used to asses the features were computed in Weka [23]:

- **Information Gain Evaluation** (InfoGain), which evaluates attributes by measuring their information gain with respect to the class. First we discretize numeric attributes. Then based on entropy computation we define Information Gain as a criterion of impurity in a training set. Measure that reflects additional information about Y provided by X that represents the amount by which the entropy of Y decreases is called Information Gain.
- **One Rule Evaluation** uses the simple accuracy measure adopted by the One Rule classifier. It uses the minimum-error attribute for prediction, discretizing numeric attributes.
- **SVM Feature Evaluation** evaluates attributes using recursive feature elimination with a linear support vector machine. Attributes are selected one by one based on the size of their coefficients, relearning.

Based on the results of the single selectors **meta-selection** was performed to acquire one representative set of features that was used further in classification. The meta-selection was performed by simple majority voting, where only features selected by at least two selectors were picked into the final set. The results of each selection method as well as the final meta-selected set are presented in Table 1.

Table 1. Features selected by different selection methods, and the final set of features used for further classification. Features abbreviations are described in Section 3.2.1 and 3.2.2. Description of the feature selection method is in Section 3.3.

Selection method	Features selected
InfoGain	baselineSD, deltaTotal, meanLTV, medianLTV, fdBoxCountDs, ApEn, meanII, baselineMean, medianII
One Rule	baselineSD, deltaTotal, LF_HFMF, medianLTV, meanSTV, meanII, fdBoxCountDs, FdHiguchiDs, baselineMean, stdLTV
SVM	baselineSD, meanII, FdHiguchiDl, baseline_Mean, ApEn, DFA_1, FdBoxCountDs, deltaTotal, LF_HF
MetaSelection	baselineSD, deltaTotal, meanII, medianLTV, fdBoxCountDs, ApEn baselineMean,

4 Results of Expert Classification

Even though objective annotation was obtained with the data, our preliminary tests showed that sole post delivery pH measurement does not give full picture of the clinical evaluation of ongoing delivery. Therefore some tool to allow the expert obstetricians to annotate the signal was needed.

The annotator application, developed for this purpose, runs in the Java runtime environment. The application adopts the most commonly used display layout of CTG machines, therefore poses no difficulty to adjust. The centimeter grid is always preserved irrespective of display resolution - see Figure 3.

After clicking on the Java web start reference in the browser the application checks its directory in the documents folder of MyDocuments directory, unzips the data for annotation and presents them to the expert.

Expert annotation is based on three FIGO classes – normal; pathological and suspect. One of the biggest advantages of the system is its collection system, where an automatic upload is performed after every hundred annotated records. The information about annotations is then submitted to the ftp site, from which further analysis can be made.

Results of annotation depicting the sensitivity and specificity of each individual expert against the collectively built up Gold standard (computed using majority voting of three experts) is presented in Table 2.

The Table 2 also presents resulting intra-observer (IaOV) and inter-observer variability (IeOV). Finally we use kappa statistics to compare expert agreement against that which might be expected by chance – value of 0.36 corresponds to 36% above chance agreement of experts.

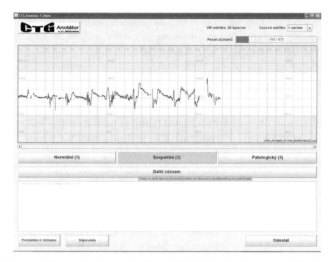

Fig. 3. Main window of the application – in the middle fHR signal on the grid where one square represents exactly one centimeter (on screen)

Table 2. Final results of expert evaluation relative to Gold standard computed as rounded average of three expert evaluations

All in [%]	**Expert1**	**Expert2**	**Expert3**
Accuracy	76	75	84
Sensitivity	75	72	79
Specificity	78	74	76
IaOV	71	56	77
IeOV		80	
Kappa statistics		36	

5   Results of Automatic Classification

When computing the results of automatic classification we have utilized 10-fold cross-validation using following classifiers: Naive Bayes, Support Vector Machine (SVM), where the polynomial kernel and penalty parameters $C = 1$ were used, and C4.5 decision tree. All methods were implemented in WEKA software [23]. Short description and further references for these methods can be found in [23].

The classification results are presented in Table 3. From all performance measures, the specificity, computed as a ratio of true positives to sum of true positive and false negative, is of major importance since a classifier with higher specificity causes lower number of false alarms that leads to lower rate of unnecessary intervention. Regarding the specificity, the SVM performed best. However, statistical tests revealed that difference between individual classifiers is statistically insignificant on $p > 0.01$ confidence level.

Table 3. Final results of automatic classification

All in [%]	NaiveBayes	SVM	C4.5 Tree
Accuracy	73	72	65
Sensitivity	84	78	74
Specificity	64	70	57
AUC	79	74	69

The same stands for the results of the automatic classification, that are well comparable to inter-observer variability and differences to expert classification were found insignificant in all three experts on confidence level $p>0.05$.

6 Discussion and Conclusion

We have evaluated 41 computed features from the classical (morphological and HRV) and non-linear domains. The best results were achieved on the meta-selected feature set based on automatic feature selection. Results achieved by automatic classification of more than 70% sensitivity and specificity are comparable with the inter-observer variability in expert evaluation.

We can conclude that automatic evaluation of the intrapartum fHR works sufficiently well. It supports our decision to use it as the first building block in the future work. Experience with the way clinicians decide on the class of the fHR record clearly suggests that additional clinical information about the patient is need to put the fHR into perspective. In the future work we will try to develop decision support system that will be built on signal processing/evaluation and clinical context.

Acknowledgments. The authors would like to thank the clinical experts who beside helping with evaluation of the signals also contributed with useful comments. Namely prof. Binder from the 2nd LF CUNI in Prague, and dr. Vít from the Bulovka Teaching Hospital.

This work was supported by the research program No. MSM 6840770012 "Transdisciplinary Research in the Field of Biomedical Engineering II" of the CTU in Prague, sponsored by the Ministry of Education, Youth and Sports of the Czech Republic.

References

1. Steer, P.J.: Has electronic fetal heart rate monitoring made a difference. Seminars in Fetal and Neonatal Medicine 13, 2–7 (2008)
2. FIGO. Guidelines for the use of fetal monitoring. International Journal of Gynecology & Obstetrics 25, 159–167 (1986)
3. Blix, E., Sviggum, O., Koss, K.S., Oian, P.: Inter-observer variation in assessment of 845 labour admission tests: comparison between midwives and obstetricians in the clinical setting and two experts. In: BJOG, Nordic School of Public Health, Gothenburg, Sweden, vol. 110(1), pp. 1–5 (2003)
4. Bernardes, J., Costa-Pereira, A., de Campos, D.A., van Geijn, H.P., Pereira-Leite, L.: Evaluation of interobserver agreement of cardiotocograms. Int. J. Gynaecol Obstet, epartamento de Ginecologia e Obstetrícia, Hospital de S. Jo?o, Faculdade de Medicina do Porto, Oporto, Portugal 57(1), 33–37 (1997)

5. Bernardes, J., Moura, C., de Sa, J.P., Leite, L.P.: The Porto system for automated cardioto-cographic signal analysis. J. Perinat. Med. 19(1-2), 61–65 (1991)
6. Guijarro-Berdinas, B., Alonso-Betanzos, A., Fontenla-Romero, O.: Intelligent analysis and pattern recognition in ctg signals using a tightly coupled hybrid system. Artif. Intell. 136, 1–27 (2002)
7. Magenes, G., Pedrinazzi, L., Signorini, M.G.: Identification of fetal sufferance Intepartum through a multiparametric analysis and a support vector machine. In: Conf. Proc. IEEE Eng. Med. Biol. Soc., Dipartimento di Informatica e Sistemistica, Pavia Univ., Italy, vol. 1, pp. 462–465 (2004)
8. Goncalves, H., Rocha, A.P., Ayres-de Campos, D., Bernardes, J.: Linear and nonlinear fetal heart rate analysis of normal and acidemic fetuses in the minutes preceding delivery. Med. Bio. Eng. Comput. 44, 847–855 (2006)
9. Laar, J., Porath, M.M., Peters, C.H.L., Oei, S.G.: Spectral analysis of fetal heart rate variability for fetal surveillance: review of the literature. Acta Obstet. Gynecol. Scand. 87(3), 300–306 (2008)
10. Georgoulas, G., Stylios, C.D., Groumpos, P.P.: Feature extraction and classification of fetal heart rate using wavelet analysis and support vector machines. International Journal on Artificial Intelligence Tools 15, 411–432 (2005)
11. Hopkins, P., Outram, N., Löfgren, N., Ifeachor, E.C., Rosén, K.G.: A comparative study of fetal heart rate variability analysis techniques. Conf. Proc. IEEE Eng. Med. Biol. Soc. 1, 1784–1787 (2006)
12. Georgoulas, G., Stylios, C.D., Groumpos, P.P.: Predicting the risk of metabolic acidosis for newborns based on fetal heart rate signal classification using support vector machines. IEEE Trans. Biomed. Eng., Laboratory for Automation and Robotics 53(5), 875–884 (2006)
13. Sundstrom, A., Rosen, D., Rosen, K.: Fetal surveillance - textbook, Gothenburg
14. Cao, L.: Practical method for determining the minimum embedding dimension of a scalar time series. Physica D 110, 43–50 (1997)
15. Task-Force. Heart rate variability. Standards of measurement, physiological interpretation, and clinical use. Task force of the european society of cardiology and the north american society of pacing and electrophysiology. Eur. Heart J. 17(3), 354–381 (1996)
16. Fraser, A.M., Swinney, H.L.: Independent coordinates for strange attractors from mutual information. Physical Review A 33(2), 1134–1140 (1986)
17. Esteller, R., Vachtsevanos, G., Echauz, J., Lilt, B.: A comparison of fractal dimension algorithms using synthetic and experimental data. In: Proceedings of the 1999 IEEE International Symposium on Circuits and Systems, ISCAS 1999, vol. 3, pp. 199–202 (1999)
18. Peng, C.K., Havlin, S., Stanley, H.E., Goldberger, A.L.: Quantification of scaling exponents and crossover phenomena in nonstationary heartbeat time series. Chaos 5, 82–87 (1995)
19. Pincus, S.: Approximate entropy (ApEn) as a complexity measure. Chaos 5(1), 110–117 (1995)
20. Pincus, S.M., Viscarello, R.R.: Approximate entropy: a regularity measure for fetal heart rate analysis. Obstet. Gynecol. 79(2), 249–255 (1992)
21. Lempel, A., Ziv, J.: On the complexity of finite sequences. IEEE Transactions on Information Theory, IT 22(1), 75–81 (1976)
22. Ferrario, M., Signorini, M.G., Cerutti, S.: Complexity analysis of 24 hours heart rate variability
23. Witten, I.H., Frank, E.: Data Mining: Practical machine learning tools and techniques, 2nd edn. Morgan Kaufmann, San Francisco (2005)

Clinical Informatics to Diagnose Cardiac Diseases Based on Data Mining

Sung Ho Ha[*] and Zhen Yu Zhang

School of Business Administration, Kyungpook National University,
1370 Sangyeok-dong, Buk-gu, 702-701 Daegu, Korea
Tel.: 82-53-950-5440, Fax: 82-53-950-6247
hsh@mail.knu.ac.kr, youchangkevin@hotmail.com

Abstract. The Emergency Department (ED) has been frustrated by the problems of overcrowding, long waiting times, and high costs over decades. With the development of computer techniques, various kinds of information systems have appeared and made people work more effectively. The Emergency Department Information System (EDIS) has been heralded as a "must" for the modern ED, which can enhance patients care, decrease the waiting time and cost, and alleviate the problem of overcrowding. This paper targets at building an engine of use in an EDIS. Based on the frameworks of patients flow in ED, real-world data were collected from the electronic medical records at the Emergency Department: more than 210000 records of 842 registered chest pain patients in total. By utilizing the data mining techniques, an engine of an expert system was proposed to help physicians with faster and more accurate decision making of diagnosis and lab test selections.

Keywords: Emergency department, Expert system, Data mining, C5.0 algorithm, Apriori algorithm.

1 Introduction

An Emergency Department (ED) in the hospital is a complex unit where the fight between life and death is only a breath away. The Emergency Department also has been frustrated by the problems of overcrowding, long waiting times, and high costs over decades [1]. Accordingly, reduction of waiting times, lowering of costs, and shortening patient care delays in the emergency department have became the hot issues in this research area.

Most hospitals today employ some sort of hospital information systems to manage their healthcare or patient data. These systems typically generate huge amount of data, which are in the form of number, text, chart, and image. This raises an important question: "How can we turn that data into useful information that would enable healthcare practitioners to make intelligent clinical decisions?" [2]. Considering the fast growth of data contents size and variety, the techniques to find useful information from collections of data have been extensively investigated in previous decades. Over

---

[*] Corresponding author.

S. Khuri, L. Lhotská, and N. Pisanti (Eds.): ITBAM 2010, LNCS 6266, pp. 67–77, 2010.

the last few years, the term 'data mining' has been increasingly used in the medical literature. The goal of predictive data mining in clinical medicine is to derive models that can use specific patient information to predict an outcome of interest and thereby support clinical decision-making. Data mining methods may be applied to the construction of decision-making models for procedures such as prognosis, diagnosis, and treatment planning, which once evaluated and verified, could then be embedded within clinical information systems [3].

The purpose of this paper is as follows: first, generate the rules using data mining techniques that can help physicians decide the selection of lab tests, which can decrease the time and costs in ED lab test processes. Second, build an expert system of EDIS that can handle the more complex problems like supporting prognoses and diagnoses, which can also help the physicians to formulate clinical decision-making faster and more accurate.

2 Theoretical Background

2.1 Data Mining in Emergency Department

In recent years, data mining has attracted a great deal of interest in Information industry, it is a young interdisciplinary field closely related to data warehousing, statistics, machine learning, neural networks and inductive logic programming. Medical data mining has been largely applied to classification and prediction for prognosis and diagnosis of patients in a small and specialized medical area [4], in order to help doctors diagnose accurately and rapidly. It was also used for training unspecialized doctors in specialized diagnostic problems [5].

So far, most researches on data in emergency departments have been based on statistical approaches like regression, and as a result, these researches have shown very low prediction accuracy, for they could not help using very limited parts of a huge amount of medical data which consists of various data types.

2.2 Chest Pain in Emergency Department

Chest pain is one of the most common causes for presentation to the emergency department. The primary cause of chest pain is cardiac diseases, and others include vascular, pulmonary, tracheobronchitis, spontaneous pneumothorax and gastrointestinal. The cardiac organ of chest pain contains three situations not common to the general practitioner. In Korea, cardiac disease is the third most common disease, and it has kept this position for more than 10 years. In 2008, 21429 people died from heart disease [6].

Accurately discerning the correct diagnosis and treatment of a patient with chest pain is one of the most difficult tasks for the emergency physician [7]. The diagnostic procedure in patients with acute chest pain should serve two major purposes:

1) To quickly identify high-risk patients quickly for the fast track.
2) To delineate patients in whom there is little or no suspicion of a life-threatening disease [8].

3   Research Methodology

3.1   Background Knowledge of ED Process

The care processes in EDs are illustrated in Fig. 1. There are six stages in total: patient arrival, triage, registration, waiting, physician assessment, and the diagnosis (discharge) [9]. Based on the processes in the ED shown in Fig. 1, the emphasis of this study focuses on the stages between the physician assessment→lab tests required (yes)→ test completed→waiting.

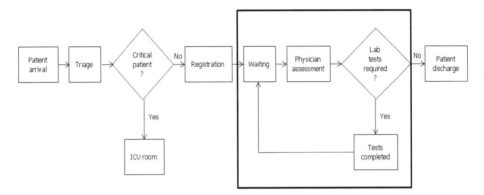

Fig. 1. Care process in emergency department

3.2   Research Methodology

The proposed methodology is displayed in Fig. 2 and consists of three stages: First, extract the information of lab test data and diagnosis data from the electronic medical data; then analyze the association relationships between the lab tests for each disease. Second, combined with the domain knowledge of an expert, the lab tests that have the relatively high frequency and include the critical lab tests mentioned in the domain knowledge of the expert are extracted from the generated association rules. Third, with the lab tests selected in second stage and other information of patient (PE data, MR data), decision models and rules to support diagnosis of chest pain are generated.

Analysis of Lab-Testing Patterns. The basic idea of the Apriori algorithm is to find frequent items in a given data set [10]. The algorithm embodies the following procedure:

1) Given the data set, the association rule mining generates all rules that have support and confidence values, which are greater than the user-specified minimum support and confidence values.

2) Candidate sets having k items are generated by joining large sets having k-1 items, and by deleting those that contain a subset whose support value is below minimum support.

3) Frequent sets of items with minimum support form the basis of deriving association rules with minimum confidence.

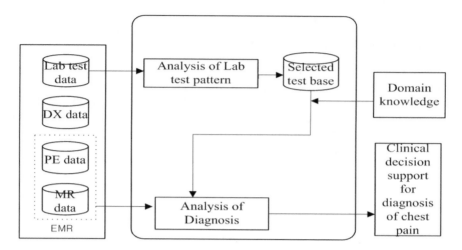

Fig. 2. Research methodology (DX: Diagnosis, PE: Patient, and MR: Medical Record)

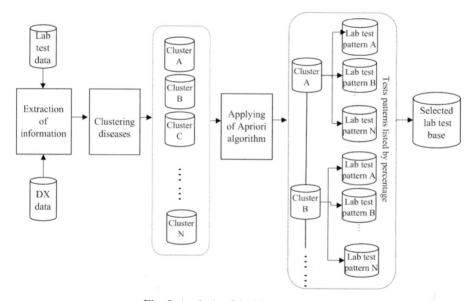

Fig. 3. Analysis of the lab test patterns

Fig. 3 illustrates the detailed processes of lab test pattern analysis. The information of lab test data and diagnosis data are extracted from the EMR in the first stage, then the chest pain diseases involved in the data can be clustered into several kinds of diseases, i.e., acute myocardial infarction angina pectoris, and so on. In the next stage, the lab test data of each disease is analyzed by the Apriori algorithm, association relationships of the lab tests can then be generated. After that, the patterns that have the relatively high frequency can be selected from the generated association rules. Combined with the domain knowledge of a medical expert, critical lab tests for each disease can be revealed, the lab tests which have the same or higher frequency with the critical lab tests are selected from the generated association rules.

Analysis of Clinical Diagnosis. The C5.0 is one of the most popular inductive learning tools originally proposed by J.R. Quinlan as the C4.5 algorithm [11]. The names of algorithms C4.5 and C5.0 are used as the names of data mining tools and software. Features and interrelations are ordered using a principle of maximization of expected information in these algorithms. Finally, these algorithms construct classification rules in form of a decision tree.

Fig. 4 illustrates the detail processes of the prediction analysis of clinical diagnosis. With the generated "Selected lab tests" in the association analysis stage, and other information like diagnosis data, patient data and medical record data, decision tree models for diagnosis of disease can be generated. Then through test and evaluation phase, the accuracy and performance of the C5.0 algorithm and the proposed method can be tested and evaluated. If the decision tree models for each diagnosis perform well enough, then the decision rules will be generated in the next stage.

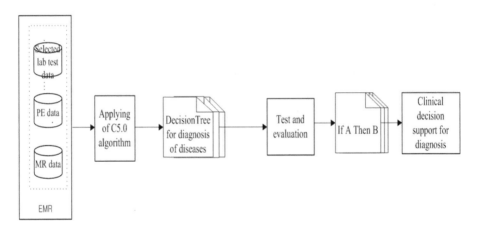

Fig. 4. Prediction analysis of clinical diagnosis

4   Data Analysis and Results

The data involved in this paper was based on the electronic medical records of chest pain patients who were treated in the Emergency Department of a hospital from July 1st, 2006 to June 30th, 2007. Because of the hospital's scale, the total number of the records reached 217108. In the preprocessing stage, the data was transformed into a form sorted in order of patient number (PNO) by EXCEL 2007, which included 842 patients in total. The values of each lab test are listed in the form of maximum values. In addition, the quantity of lab test is 410 different kinds. The attributes included in the data are listed in Table 1 below.

Table 1. Description of attributes

1. PNO (patient number)	2. Gender
3: Age	4: Date of patient arrival
5: Time of patient arrival	6: Ocode (General categories of lab tests)
7: Subcode (Segmentation of lab tests, include 410 kinds of test)	8: Oname (The medical name of lab test)
9: Result (The result of every lab test in subcode)	10: Diagnosis

All the characteristics of the patients are displayed in Table 2, males were the primary patients. From the respect of age level, the patient who was more than 60 years old accounts for 66.07% of all patients and most of them were at the age level between 71 and 80 (35.15%). While from the respect of chest pain diseases involved in this study, acute myocardial infarction (AMI) was the most typical disease, and it has a high risk to human life [13]. In the collected data for this paper, among the total 842 patients, there were 219 acute myocardial infarction patients and 259 patients with other chest pain diseases. Because 364 patients were discharged from the emergency department, they had no diagnostic information. The diseases were coded according to Korean classification of standard diseases.

Table 2. Frequency analysis of data

Category		Frequency	Percent
Gender	Male	513	60.93%
	Female	329	39.07%
Age	under 20	19	2.26%
	21-30	24	2.85%
	31-40	53	6.29%
	41-50	133	15.80%
	51-60	202	23.99%
	61-70	211	25.06%
	71-80	159	18.88%
	81-90	37	4.39%
	91-100	4	0.48%
Disease	AMI	219	26.01%
	Other	259	30.76%
	Discharge	364	43.23%

4.1 Associations of Lab Tests

As mentioned above, because of the hospital's scale, the lab tests in the form of subcode included 410 kinds of tests, in order to decrease the number of lab tests, and to decrease the time wasted with unnecessary lab test, the critical lab tests needed to be revealed from all the lab tests. According to the ocode and the subcode of the lab test, utilizing the software—Excel 2007 and Clementine 12.0, association rules of the lab test in acute myocardial infarction were generated by the Apriori algorithm. In the process of analyzing the relationship of subcodes, patient number (PNO) was set as the id, and the subcodes of the lab tests were set as both input and target data. After the association analysis, the rules (in subcode) which have the relatively high frequency needed to be revealed for the next prediction analysis.

The domain knowledge was used to find the interesting rules with the higher frequency (the value of support and confidence are both above 0.9). According to Kenneth (2006) [14] and Ren (2007) [13], acute myocardial infarction is in the range of acute coronary syndrome (ACS). Creatine Kinase (CK) and Creatine Kinase MB fraction (CK MB) are very sensitive tests for this disease, and the level of Troponin is another important factor for the diagnosis of acute coronary syndrome. For this reason, among the rules generated, the rules which contain Creatine Kinase, Creatine Kinase MB fraction and Troponin, and have the highest frequency were discovered. The results show that there are 817 association rules in total and there are 62 rules which have the support and confidence above 0.9. Through using the domain knowledge, the number of rules was reduced to 58 (Table 3). A sample of lab test association rules for AMI in subcode level are displayed in Table 4.

Table 3. Number of selected rules for AMI

	With domain knowledge	Without domain knowledge
Interesting/Total rules	58/817	62/817
Support & Confidence	S=0.9, C=0.9	S=0.9, C=0.9

Table 4. Samples of lab test patterns for AMI in subcode level

AMI			
Confidence	Support	Lift	Associations
100	99.55	1	J503942_01 → J25264001
100	99.55	1	J503942_01 → J252630_01
100	99.55	1	J503942_01 → J252620_01
100	99.55	1	J503942_01 → J252590_01
100	99.55	1	J25264001 → J252630_01
		......	

Among the 58 association rules for diagnosis of acute myocardial infarction, there are 6 lab tests that have the highest and the same frequency with test CK, CK-MB, and Troponin. All of them have the level of support and confidence above 0.9: J151600_01: Fibrinogen, J252590_01: LDH, J252620_01: Lipase, J252630_01: CK, J25264001: CK-MB, J252840_02: Actual Ca++, J252850_01: Mg, J457003_01: Pro-BNP, J503942_01: TROPONIN-I.

4.2 Prediction Analysis of Clinical Diagnosis

Of 478 patients that have the information of diagnosis, 219 among them are acute myocardial infarction patients, and the remaining 259 patients are classified as other chest pain diseases. The age of patient was randomly divided in to 8 codes: under 20

=> 1, 20 to 30 => 2 ... 90 to 100 => 9. The data was split evenly into two datasets: training dataset (283 patients' records, 60%) and testing dataset (194 records, 40%). Input variables are listed in Table 5, which includes the lab test results, patient information and the subcodes of 9 selected lab tests.

Table 5. Input and output variables for prediction of AMI patients

Output variable (Diagnosis)
Acute myocardial infarction (1),
Other chest pain diseases (0)

Input variables
Gender, Age, Symptom,

Selected lab tests: J151600_01 (Fibrinogen); J252590_01 (LDH); J252620_01 (Lipase);

J252630_01 (CK); J25264001 (CK-MB); J252840_02 (Actual Ca++); J252850_01 (Mg);

J457003_01 (Pro-BNP); J503942_01 (TROPONIN-I);

Results of lab tests

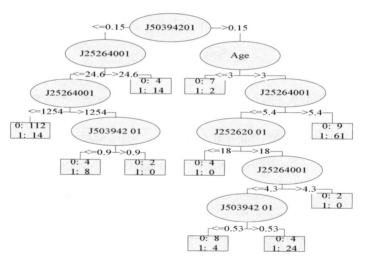

Fig. 5. Decision tree for prediction (AMI)

Fig. 5 illustrates the decision tree model for AMI prediction. There are 10 rules in the model. Each individual oval contains the lab test code. The number '0' in a leaf means the patients with other diseases and the number '1' indicates the patients with AMI. The numbers next to '0' and '1' show the number of patients. One of the rules can be read as follows:

```
If J50394201 (TROPONIN-I) > 0.15,
AGE > 3,
J25264001(CK-MB) > 5.4
Then 1 (Acute Myocardial Infarction)                    (86.9%)
```

Some explanation of the symptoms: J503942_01 (TROPONIN-I): Troponin I is a rapid qualitative test for the detection of cardiac Troponin I from whole blood or serum samples; J25264001 (CK-MB): CK-MB is CK in cardiac muscle. Various tissues and cell types express creatine kinase (CK), also known as creatine phosphokinase (CPK). CK catalyses the conversion of creatine and consumes adenosine triphosphate (ATP) to create phosphocreatine and adenosine diphosphate (ADP).

5 Validation and Comparison

5.1 Validation of Association Rules

As mentioned above, the rules whose values of support and confidence are above 0.9, were collected and sorted. In this section, we validate how the prediction performance changes as the value of support changes. Regarding another criterion – confidence, because the variation is irregular and not as significant as the change of support, therefore the explanation focuses on the alteration of support.

Fig. 6 shows the performance of the prediction model for acute myocardial infarction as the value of support altered from 0.9 to 0.2. When the value of support is above 90%, prediction accuracy is the best (88.38%), and when the value of support changed to 50% and 40%, the performance of prediction increased again, of which both are 85.21%.

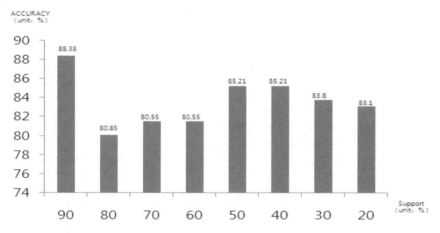

Fig. 6. Prediction accuracy as support altered (AMI)

Table 6 shows the results of a classification matrix for the prediction model. The row represents predicted values while the column represents actual values ('1' for patients with the acute myocardial infarction and '0' for patients without AMI). The left-most columns show values predicted by the models. The diagonal values show correct predictions. A classification matrix displays the frequency of correct and incorrect predictions. It compares the actual values in the test dataset with the predicted values in the trained model. In this table, the training dataset for AMI includes 254 records. There are 127 patients actually with AMI and the prediction accuracy is 107/127=0.8425. The prediction accuracy for non-AMI patients is 114/127=0.8976.

Table 6. Prediction Accuracy of C5.0 algorithm

	AMI	
	0 (Actual)	1 (Actual)
0 (Predicted)	114	13
1 (Predicted)	20	107

5.2 Comparison of Prediction Accuracy

In this section, this study evaluates the prediction accuracy by comparing the prediction accuracy with other approaches, like CART, QUEST, CHAID, and Logistic regression. Through the 40% testing data, the prediction accuracy for each algorithm is generated as with Table 7. For the testing of the models for prediction of the patient with acute myocardial infarction, testing dataset include 194 records of patients. There are 90 records of the patients with acute myocardial infarction (code 1) while other 104 records are the patients without acute myocardial infarction (code 0). From the prediction accuracy in Table 7, the validation results show that all the four data mining approaches performed with a relatively high accuracy (above 80%) and C5.0 algorithm performed the best (89.69%).

Table 7. Comparison of prediction accuracy (AMI)

	C5.0	CART	QUEST	CHAID	Logistic regression
Accuracy (%)	89.69	89.18	86.09	83.51	64.95

6   Conclusions and Further Research

The purpose of this study is to build an expert system to assist clinical decision making in the Emergency Department. This study utilized the practical data collected from the ED, used the Apriori algorithm and C5.0 algorithm, and generated the basic rule base for an expert system, which can help the physicians to make the clinical decision faster and more accurately. Through test and evaluation, the results showed that the generated decision rules perform well in diagnosis of chest pain, which can support the physician's decision-making. By comparing results with other algorithms, which include CART, CHAID, QUEST, and Logistic, the fact that the C5.0 algorithm had the best performance was proven. While comparing to the simple C5.0 algorithm, improvement of the hybrid method was also proved. As the accumulation and diversity of medical data grows, the need for an adaptive method of decision-making becomes more and more necessary. While considering the current situation of the Emergency Department Information System, more complicated and comprehensive expert systems will be necessary for the future.

References

1. Sheila, R.F., Sheila, A.T.: Shorting the Wait time: A Strategy to Reduce Waiting Times in The Emergency Department. Journal of Emergence Nursing 35, 509–514 (2009)
2. Sellappan, P., Rafiah, A.: Intelligent Heart Disease Prediction System Using Data Mining Techniques. International Journal of Computer Science and Network Security 8, 343–350 (2008)

3. Riccardo, B., Blaz, Z.: Predictive data mining in clinical medicine: Current issues and guidelines. International Journal of Medical Informatics 77, 81–97 (2008)
4. Kononenko, I.: Machine learning for medical diagnosis: history, state of the art and perspective, pp. 89–109. Elsevier, Amsterdam (2001)
5. Daniel, B., Peter, L., Roland, E.: New Insights in Clinical Impact of Molecular Genetic Data by Knowledge-driven Data Mining. In: 2nd International Conference on Systems Biology, Wisconsin, pp. 275–281 (2001)
6. Korean statistics, http://www.nso.go.kr/
7. Perey, J., Jorge, C., Joseph, G., Joseph, P., Murgo: Rapid triage of patients presenting to the emergency department with chest pain using stress echocardiography. Journal of the American Society of Echocardiography 8, 410 (1997)
8. Erhardt, L., Herlitz, J., Bossaert, L., Halinen, M., Keltai, M., Koster, R., Marcassa, C., Quinn, T., Weert, H.V.: Task force on the management of chest pain. European Heart Journal 23, 1153–1176 (2002)
9. Christine, D., Fatah, C.: Modeling and Improving Emergency Department Systems using Discrete Event Simulation. Simulation 83, 311–320 (2007)
10. Zaki, M.J.: Mining non-redundant association rules. Data Mining and Knowledge Discovery 9, 223–248 (2004)
11. Quinlan, J.R.: C4.5: programs for machine learning. Morgan Kaufmann, San Francisco (1993)
12. Mitchell, T.M.: Machine Learning and Data Mining. Communications of the ACM 42(11), 30–36 (1999)
13. Ren, H.: Clinical diagnosis of chest pain. Chinese Journal for Clinicians 36, 5–7 (2007)
14. Kenneth, H.B., Sharon, A.S.: Chest Pain: A Clinical Assessment. Radiologic Clinics of North America 44, 165–179 (2006)

The Case-Based Software System for Physician's Decision Support

Leonid Karpov and Valery Yudin

Institute for System Programming, Russian Academy of Sciences
Alexander Solzhenitsyn st. 25, 109004, Moscow, Russia
{mak,yudin}@ispras.ru

Abstract. Human body is an example of an object for which it is really impossible to build the exact behavior model. Case-Based Reasoning is a practical decision making technique used to emulate human thinking process. The article describes an approach to building intellectual systems based on Case-Based Reasoning and Data Mining techniques. A software system for physician's decision support in diagnostics and treatment selection is used as an example. This approach is based on identifying classes within the case base. The similarity measure is introduced. This measure is especially useful when the current case is incompletely described and gets to class intersection.

Keywords: decision support, diagnostics, treatment, Case-Based Reasoning, similarity measure, classifying.

1 Introduction

The most difficult objects for analyzing and decision making are those whose features cannot be formally described. This means that main factors, links and mutual interference of objects cannot be properly discovered. The lack of knowledge about the object and its environment prevents us from getting the exact behavior model of object functioning. Still the controlling of such objects is as much important and interesting as dealing with completely described objects.

Case-Based Reasoning (CBR) is a decision making technique that uses the knowledge about previously experienced situations (cases). If a case that is similar to the current one is found it can be treated as a decision. It is a frequently applied way to solve problems for humans. Among possible applications control of badly formalized objects can be seen. Human body cannot be described as control object using relatively simple model, so CBR methods are rather perspective for physician's decision support.

There exist many different software systems for decision support. The system "Doctor's Partner" is being designed and developed in the Institute for System Programming of Russian Academy of Sciences. Its aim is to support physician's decisions by using modern information technologies, and in particular Case-Based Reasoning and Data Mining techniques.

S. Khuri, L. Lhotská, and N. Pisanti (Eds.): ITBAM 2010, LNCS 6266, pp. 78–85, 2010.

2   Case-Based Problem Solving

Case-Based Reasoning is a method of looking for solution of similar problems which had already been analyzed. Instead of trying to solve a problem from scratch one can use a solution that was offered in similar situation. If current situation (case) has been slightly changed this solution may be also improved or adopted. When current case is properly analyzed it is stored to a case base, followed by the solution itself, so it may be used again later on. Case base is intended to store information about as many earlier cases as it only can, so when new cases appear, we are able to choose the situation that is most similar, and then reuse it or (if the selected situation does not match the current case properly) adopt it to match the new problem (Fig. 1) [1].

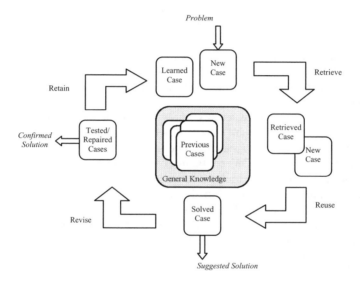

Fig. 1. The CBR Cycle

The case is a situation description. Any case consists of a problem description, which is followed by the list of actions that were issued to solve the problem. The case may be either a previously registered real case, or a typical problem solving example.

The case can be treated as an abstraction of a real event. It can either be a previously encountered and solved problem or a typical way of solving a problem. "Typically a case comprises:

- a *problem* that describes the state of the world when the case occurred,
- a solution that states the derived solution to that problem, and/or
- an outcome that describes the state of the world after the case occurred" [2].

The biggest part of existing approaches to building CBR software is focused on one aspect: choosing the most adequate case among many similar ones. All these approaches rely on estimating similarity of previously stored cases and the current case.

A metrics is established in the object features space. The point that corresponds to the current case is determined in that space. Then the metric is used to find the nearest point of previously registered cases. The particular metrics is used depending on features types. Aamodt and Plaza in [1] mark approaches to retrieve cases as syntactical similarity and semantical similarity. Semantical similarity implies that for cases choosing one will need additional knowledge about the application area (domain knowledge).

Unfortunately there exist situations when the adequate metrics cannot be chosen. These situations force us to use the similarity measure instead. The similarity measure can be introduced in different ways: all that is needed is to found a rule of cases selection.

In order to make the selection a set of cases is structured. To discover implicit knowledge about the application area different methods are used, in particular Data Mining methods. The classes of structure may be formed in different ways, either with the help of experts, or basing on learning sample, or maybe by clustering the case base. Separating the set of cases into the classes of equivalence is one of methods that may speed up the searching process: cases from the same class should be treated as more similar to each other.

The similarity measure cannot take into account all the relations of the current case and its environment, especially when the current case is located within the classes' intersection.

Pattern recognition problems usually imply that the description of objects is based on a set of features common to all objects. In other words objects and classes have the same dimensions and may be located in one features space. Sometimes real applications break this assumption. Objects themselves and classes' descriptions may have different features spaces. In medicine we can see that each disease is characterized by its own set of significant features. Finally, the case under investigation may have the set of features that differs from the set that is stored in system memory.

The current case and classes relations are clarified through the projections of classes onto the object features space. A case which is incompletely described may fall into the projection of the class to which it doesn't belong. This may happen only because of lack of the feature which may separate it from that class.

Till now they considered the situation with classes' intersection as an obstacle for case estimation. But if we can't get rid of a situation we should use it instead.

3 The Method

The method used to estimate incompletely described cases may be understood from the following:

- The case description is a feature set.
- The class description is a multidimensional parallelepiped, marginally enveloping class's cases.
- The current case is compared with classes' projections onto its features space.
- The classes to which the case falls form the differential set of the case.
- Similar cases are those cases from the class to which the case falls.
- Analogs are the most similar cases. If a case falls into the classes' projections intersection then analogs of the case are the cases from that classes that also fall into the same intersection.

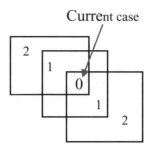

Fig. 2. Similarity degrees

(digits designate the degree of similarity between the current case and existing cases)

Depending on the complexity of the intersection we may separate the analogs and form groups (Fig. 2). Analogs from the same intersection should be treated as the most similar ones than other cases from the same class. Analogs of the highest rank are located in the intersection of all the classes from the differential set of the current case.

We can give more formal definition of the similarity measure:

Degree of similarity between the new case and the existing case is equal to the difference between the number of classes to which the current case falls and the number of classes to which the existing case falls.

The information about additional features is concentrated within analogs themselves. In Fig. 3 one-dimensional current case $x=a$ falls into the projections of classes xy and xz. To be able to be compared with analogs from xy class it lacks y feature, and for comparison with analogs from xz class it needs z feature.

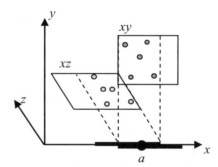

Fig. 3. Using analogs for discovering additional features of the current case

One can see the following stages of the selection cycle:

1. Choosing analogs for the current case.
2. Estimating the conformity of the formed set (is doing by a human person); if "yes" the selection is completed, if "no" – go to the next step.
3. Completing the ranked list of additional features. This list will be used to differentiate classes (features for the list are retrieving from the cases).

4. Trying to find more features (is doing by a human person). Some features can't be found out automatically. If there is the case, the cycle stops with negative result; if some more features can be offered go to the step 1.

There are no clear criteria for making a decision what cases may be used and what cases may be not. This decision should always be done by a human person. To make this decision in addition to the knowledge that is already stored in the system one should use all the knowledge about the application area.

Taking into account the approach described in [1], the method offered by authors may be introduced as *semantical similarity*.

4 Doctor's Partner System

The method described in previous chapter is practically implemented within the system named "Doctor's Partner". This system is designed for supplying physicians with the information during their attempts to diagnose the disease and to choose the treatment.

A physician communicates with the system in terms of *disease*, *treatment*, *patient*, and *sign*. The system provides physician access to the case base by transforming these terms to *classes*, *objects*, and *features* (Fig. 4).

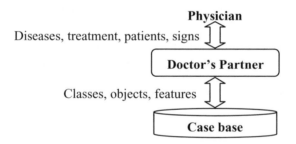

Fig. 4. Information flow in the program system

Sometimes a physician has to diagnose a case while not having all the needed signs. From one side, if the diagnose is clear even on the first stages of patient investigation, there is no need to continue with relatively expensive analyses. From the other side, it may be useful to postpone the final decision till additional examination is fulfilled or some new symptoms appear. If the set of signs leaves the possibility to make a choice among several diseases, all these diseases are gathered in the differential set of the current case.

Prior to starting the classification process we need to estimate the completeness of patient signs, we also need to choose those signs (and only them) that relate to the differential set. In order not to introduce extra signs the system is automatically choosing the needed signs. If the set is incomplete the missing signs are shown. The decision whether to estimate the situation or to continue carrying additional investigations is offered by an operator (physician).

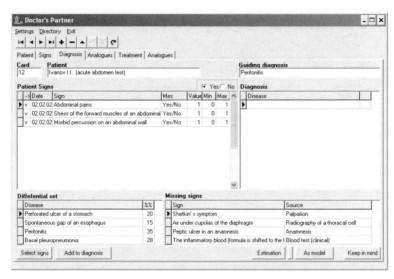

Fig. 5. Patient with symptoms of "acute abdomen"

Fig. 5 shows the system data for a patient with symptoms of "acute abdomen". The lower part of the screen represents the differential set of the current case. The list of possible diseases is also shown there. For each member of the differential set the system shows a set of the missing signs necessary for the true diagnostics of this disease.

A well-trained expert system can offer a suggestion for decision in a standard situation for which a good physician does need no prompts at all. Any physician needs help when the system provides him with ambiguous classification, when there are not enough patient signs, or when the disease goes beyond the limits of its usual symptoms manifesting itself through the signs of another disease. There may exist cases with similar, or more correctly, analogous signs. It is very useful to take these cases into account, because they may be helpful as examples. However, searching cases basing on signs, even with some tolerance, is not always appropriate. The notion of analog introduced in chapter 3 was used for the non-key selection of such patients.

Fig. 6 represents the analogs offered by the system for the symptoms mentioned above. The system has noticed that there exist patients with diagnoses of "spontaneous gap of an esophagus", "perforated ulcer of stomach", and "peritonitis". The system shows the symptoms list of an analog and marks those of them for which the patient has not been investigated yet. One patient has a diagnosis "basal pneumonia". In addition to the symptoms of "acute abdomen", he has thorax pains and rhonchus in the lungs. Evidently the physician should consider the possibility of pneumonia and check the corresponding signs.

The differential set is also used for choosing the treatment. But if it is used in making a diagnosis, one can almost always find an investigation which helps to differentiate the diseases, the choice of treatment is much more complicated because of multiplicity of variations of diseases, and different combinations of affections, which greatly limits the forms and especially the stages of treatment. It is hardly possible to train the system completely. In order to estimate the boundaries of all classes a large

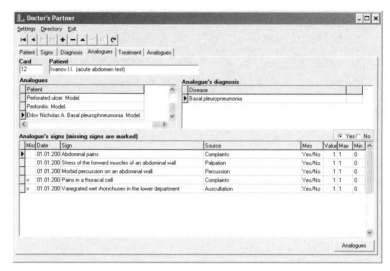

Fig. 6. Analogs in the case of symptoms of "acute abdomen"

amount of data has to be used. This leads to the situation of insufficient information when the object under investigation is to be located in intersecting classes. The use of analogs helps to solve this problem.

One can't expect a good result when an object under investigation has only one feature. The list of possible diseases, strategies of treatment, and the number of analogs will be too large. Turning back to Fig. 2, which shows the classes' intersection, it is easy to conclude that the fewer features the object has, the greater number of classes forming its differential set is.

The choice of the signs of a patient used for searching analogs depends on the qualification of the physician. Such systems operate well when the data are skillfully chosen both at the stage of learning and at the stage of investigation.

The Doctor's Partner system is implemented using the Borland C++ Builder environment. The access to the case base is carried out through the Firebird database server.

5   Conclusion

Case-based Reasoning systems shows good results in solving various problems, still they have significant drawbacks. One of these drawbacks is difficulties in case choosing, which raise from complexity of comparison of current case against previously stored cases.

This new approach offers to make a case choice on the basis of the original selection method which succeeds to retrieve the most similar case when the object under investigation is incompletely described and may be estimated ambiguously.

The results achieved may be used while dealing with incompletely described objects in the conditions of severe limits in time and resources.

The approach shown here is implemented in the software system "Doctor's Partner" intended for physician's decision support. This system may serve as a physician pocket-book, a reference book, an expert system that helps to direct one's attention to complicated situations in the conditions of ambiguous classification with incomplete set of signs, or when a disease breaks the limits of its usual symptomatology.

Acknowledgments. The authors are thankful to the Russian Fund for Basic Research that supports their work by sponsoring the projects No 09-07-00191-a and No 09-01-00351-a. The authors also thank the personnel of Moscow Regional Clinical and Research Institute (MONIKI) whose help was extremely important in designing of system prototype.

References

1. Aamodt, A., Plaza, E.: Case-based reasoning: Foundational issues, methodological variations, and system approaches. AI Communications 7(1), 39–59 (1994)
2. Watson, I., Marir, F.: Case-Based Reasoning: A Review. The Knowledge Engineering Review 9(4) (1994), http://www.ai-cbr.org/classroom/cbr-review.html

SASAgent: An Agent Based Architecture for Search, Retrieval and Composition of e-Science Models and Tools

Luiz Felipe Mendes[1], Regina Braga[1,2], and Fernanda Campos[1,2]

[1] Master Program in Computational Modeling
[2] Software Quality Research Group
Federal University of Juiz de Fora - Juiz de Fora, Minas Gerais, Brazil
{regina.braga,fernanda.campos}@ufjf.edu.br

Abstract. Scientific Computing is a multidisciplinary field that goes beyond the use of computer as machine where researchers write simple texts, presentations or store analysis and results of their experiments. Considering the increase use of computer resources applied to experiments and simulations, it is notable that the research groups are at a new level of scientific computing, well represented by e-Science domain. This work aims to propose an architecture, based on intelligent agents, to search, retrieve and compose simulation models, generated within research projects related to scientific domains. The SASAgent architecture is described and a case study is presented. Preliminary results suggest that the proposed architecture is promising to achieve requirements found in e-Science projects.

Keywords: Multi-agent systems, Semantic web services, Ontology, SOA, e-Science.

1 Introduction

Computer Science revolutionized scientific research and today is recognized as the third pillar together with theory and experimentation [1]. The use of computer resources in the development of scientific research benefits the work of scientific communities facilitating the sharing of data and computing services, and contributing to build an infrastructure of data and a distributed research community. This context, in which the computer becomes essential to the successful of scientific research from different areas, is e-Science [2], where science is performed with computer support and becomes more efficient.

Considering the e-Science scenario, it is possible to observe the extremely heterogeneous environments in which research groups, from the same domain or not, need to work, despite all available computational resources. Simulation models are generated in these heterogeneous environments. The main goal of SASAgent (Scientific Artifact Search Agent) architecture is to search, retrieve, compose and use data and tools related to computational modeling (mainly Bioinformatics), through the use of ontological annotations on them and wrapped into semantic web services, considering also the use of intelligent mechanisms that will act on those annotations.

S. Khuri, L. Lhotská, and N. Pisanti (Eds.): ITBAM 2010, LNCS 6266, pp. 86–93, 2010.

The paper is organized as follows: in section 2, we present the theoretical basis, in section 3, some proposals and related works are analyzed. The SASAgent architecture is presented in section 4, together with a case study. Finally, in section 5 conclusions and future works are presented.

2   Related Concepts

The term e-Science was introduced, in the UK, to encapsulate technologies needed to support the collaborative and multidisciplinary research that was emerging in many fields of science [2]. In essence, "an environment of e-Science should permit the co-ordinated sharing of resources in large-scale between dynamic communities of individuals, groups, laboratories and institutions, allowing the cooperative management of facilities (equipment, resources, experiments etc.) and collaborative analysis of product (data) from these facilitie's" [3]. Some characteristics of e-Science are: access to a vast collection of data, use of computer resources on a large scale, use of heterogeneous and dynamic resources of multiple organizations and dynamic workflows [4].

Simulation models are related to mathematical and computational representation of some scientific system model. Bioinformatics involves the application of information technologies to solve biological problems at molecular level, providing tools and resources needed to favor biomedical research. In this research context, biological models are related to mathematical and computational representation of some biological properties. CellML (Cell Markup Language) [15] establishes a standard format for defining and sharing biological models.

Traditionally, the Web has been seen as a distributed source of information. The emergence of Web services technology has enabled the Web to become a distributed source of services [5]. Considering the growth of the Web, there is an increasing need to automate those aspects related to Web services, such as discovery, execution, automatic selection and composition. Among the techniques needed to achieve goals of the Semantic Web, ontologies have a key role. "An ontology is a formal and explicit specification of a shared conceptualization" [6]. A language for defining ontologies is OWL (Web Ontology Language) [7]. The joint application of Semantic Web and Web service in order to generate "more intelligent" Web services, has led to Semantic Web services [8].

Agent technology is appropriate for the development of complex and distributed applications, in environments that incorporate numerous components with different expertise and interests [5]. Besides that, intelligent agents can contribute with features such as autonomy, pro-activeness and goal-oriented behavior to automate some stages of the process. Nowadays, the semantically annotated information of the semantic web can be automatically processed by agents, so that new powerful opportunities open up for developers and users.

3   Related Works

Considering semantic Web services, we can highlight two projects. FUSION [9] is a tool to register Semantic Web services. OWLS-MX [10] is a mechanism for finding Web services based on semantic rules (OWL-S) and information retrieval. FUSION is the most complete approach, as it includes semantics related to services. However, it does not consider the scientific context, as SASAgent does, including model composition and scientific workflow specification. SemWIQ [11] is an infrastructure to support e-Science. Considering the e-Science context, SASAgent has a similar proposal. However, SASAgent also includes the storage and retrieval of services, the composition of these web services, and the search for scientific artifacts, using SOA architecture.

The work of [5] is very similar to SASAgent and has as its main goal, from the use of intelligent agents and ontologies, the improvement of efficiency in the consumption of Web services and the automation of some tasks related to them. The main difference of our proposal from this one is that SASAgent performs these same tasks but also allows the composition of simulation models with these services. The work described in [5] does not have this composition functionality.

Grid researches, like Globus [17] and Unicore [18], are seeking to solve how to coordinate distributed resources among a dynamic set of individuals and organizations in order to solve a common collaborative goal. The main difference of these approaches is that SASAgent tries to discover services in specific domain, considering collaborative groups that agree in a given semantic (an ontology). Globus and Unicore are projects that turn hard the semantic agreement. Besides that, SASAgent allows a classification of the application (services) semantics in order to find service descriptions that best fit user´s intentions.

4   SASAgent: An Architecture Based on Agents for e-Science Applications

The SASAgent (Scientific Artifact Search Agent) architecture considers two distinct roles of a scientist. They can act as consumers of scientific knowledge (ConsumerScientist_Group), or can assume the role of a provider (ProviderScientist_Group). The main goal of the architecture, and therefore of research projects, is to provide, consume and compose simulation models and tools generated by scientists, in order to share and reuse knowledge that are implicit or explicit in those artifacts. The SASAgent architecture is based on three characteristics: agents with their respective roles; the knowledge base, through the use of ontologies, that provides logical inferences, and may discover new information that perhaps is implicit on the ontology; and, finally, scientific artifacts (models and tools). The knowledge base is established on the use of ontologies. We chose to use ontologies, since the use of relational databases limits the significance and capacity of expression required to the implementation of SASAgent. Thus, the knowledge will be represented by ontological terms.

Research groups generate several scientific artifacts. Our work has focus on computational tools (editors, simulators, algorithms, applications, Web Services) and models that represent the domain. These specific models are used to represent phenomena of the domain. In order to organize these specific scientific artifacts, allowing their use, sharing, management and research, we need an architecture that has scalability and can be easily integrated with other applications.

Thus, SASAgent aims the search, recovery, invocation (if it is a web service, algorithm or application) and composition of artifacts generated by scientific research groups in areas related to computational modeling, mainly Bioinformatics, through the use of intelligent agents and a semantic knowledge base. This main goal can be decomposed into a set of secondary ones: i) implementation of a multi-agent system that will serve as a mediator between the knowledge base, artifacts and scientific researchers who wish to use the architecture, ii) existence of a knowledge base that represents the knowledge needed to support the management of models through the use of ontologies, iii) independence of the domain, specifically, SASAgent should serve to any research group which wants to manage simulation models (expressed in CellML) in related domains; iv) support different roles that the "end user" (scientist) of the system can take: either as a consumer or as a provider of scientific artifacts, while allowing this user to have the ability to configure his own profile, with his main preferences.

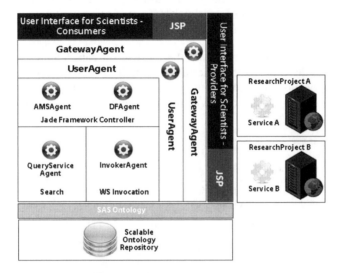

Fig. 1. SASAgent Architecture

The architecture of SASAgent is shown in Figure 1. The Agent module has seven agents that provide the necessary functionality. Four of them are outlined below:

- QueryServiceAgent (QSA): This agent is responsible for searching for scientific artifacts in the application using a SPARQL query on the related ontology. As a result, the URIs (Uniform Resource Identifier) of scientific artifacts found are returned;
- InvokerAgent (IA): When Web services are found by the QSA, this agent has the ability to invoke these services so they can be used by the user within the architecture;
- UserAgent (UA): when a new user logs on SASAgent architecture, automatically a new agent is created and his profile is loaded with information based on the ontology as, for example, the research institutions that he is interested, what are domains terms of preference, among others.
- ComposerAgent: responsible for composing new models based on discovered models by the QSA. The idea is to promote the reuse of existing components, through the composition of simpler models, producing more complex ones. The

composition produces a new CellML model, through the copy of previously defined components and the automatic connection of these components. The composition process uses a XML configuration file (Figure 2) to indicate which models will be composed and the structure of the new model. The connection of the components is made through the semantic combination of the parameters of the first component with the parameters of the second one. It is established if both parameters measure the same quantities, if both are associated to the same chemical element and, finally, if both have the same name. A SPARQL query is used to find if the output parameters are compatible to the input of the other component. This agent is also responsible for generating compositions based on the discovered services, which represent the workflow specified by the user as well as the generation of the WS-BPEL model. This composition modeling is based on syntactic and semantic compatibility of Web services discovered.

It is important to highlight that one of the most significant features of SASAgent is the use of semantic resources considering the search for scientific artifacts. For this, it uses two components: an ontology, which models the application domain, and a semantic data repository, which allows the management of ontologies and stored data.

```xml
<?xml version="1.0" encoding="UTF-8"?>
<composition>
 <global uri="http://celo.mmc.ufjf.br/noble_1962/environment.owl"/>
 <model uri="http://celo.mmc.ufjf.br/noble_1962/membrane.owl" uses="global">
  <model uri="http://celo.mmc.ufjf.br/noble_1962/leakage_current.owl" uses="global"/>
  <model uri="http://celo.mmc.ufjf.br/noble_1962/sodium_channel.owl" uses="global">
   <model uri="http://celo.mmc.ufjf.br/noble_1962/sodium_channel_h_gate.owl"/>
   <model uri="http://celo.mmc.ufjf.br/noble_1962/sodium_channel_m_gate.owl"/>
  </model>
  <model uri="http://celo.mmc.ufjf.br/noble_1962/potassium_channel.owl" uses="global">
   <model uri="http://celo.mmc.ufjf.br/noble_1962/potassium_channel_n_gate.owl"/>
  </model>
 </model>
</composition>
```

Fig. 2. Model used for testing the composition process

The ontology CelO [12] should allow inferences to be performed on the stored data to find relationships that are implicit. With this, important scientific models and tools that would not be found in a common search can be retrieved. We can consider that SASAgent architecture main difference from other similar proposals is the integration among agents and semantics. There are some works on intelligent agents, but without semantics, where intelligence is based on pure AI and also other works that try to add semantics without the use of agents. Our proposal tries to integrate these two technologies and offers a framework where research groups may share their scientific artifacts, constructing a collaborative work.

4.1 Case Study

In order to verify the applicability of SASAgent, a case study has been developed. Two different scenarios were described: i) search for Semantic Web services and

ii) search for other scientific models. In this article we present the first scenario, considering that this one is more general. We can stand out as important components of this case study, agents and the domain ontology (in this specific case study, the CelO ontology [12]) that provides the background to carry out searches applied to computational modeling domain.

The scenario was specified with focus on projects related to bioinformatics, considering our group's previous works [12]. The independence of technology and data interoperability that Web services can provide, and considering that the search for such services is not trivial, motivated the creation of this particular scenario to analyze the case study. In this context, we have chosen two services related to bioinformatics for analysis. The first one is a web service provided by the OLS framework (Ontology Lookup Service) [13] and the latter is a product of a project related to bioinformatics named PRIDE (The Proteomics Identifications database) [14]. The PRIDE project is a centralized database, which has public access to data related to proteins and peptides. This database handles multiple ontologies and the OLS project provides only one access, using this web service, to all of these ontologies. The second Web service, also related to Bioinformatics, is called PICR (Protein Identifier Cross-Reference Service) [13]. Its main objective is the ability to map protein sequences and their identifiers across multiple databases, providing the configuration of various parameters related to species involved and specific taxonomies. It uses the database UniProt Archive (UniParc) as a datawarehouse. In order to make available these Web services for SASAgent, it is necessary to store their semantic descriptions. For this, we used the SOR data repository (Scalable Ontology Repository) [15] and to check the data stored, the query language used was SPARQL.

```
1   PREFIX ufjf:<http://www.ufjf.br/escience.owl#>
2   SELECT DISTINCT ?titulo
3   WHERE
4   {
5       {
6           ?p ufjf:belongsToScientist ufjf:Maria .
7           ?p ufjf:hasScientistAssociated ?pesq .
8           ?pesq ufjf:hasPublishedScientificArtifact ?ws .
9           ?ws a ufjf:WebService .
10          ?ws ufjf:hasTitle ?titulo
11      }
12      UNION
13      {
14          ?p ufjf:belongsToScientist ufjf:Maria .
15          ?p ufjf:belongsToSubArea ?area .
16          ?area ufjf:hasPublishedScientificArtifact ?ws .
17          ?ws a ufjf:WebService .
18          ?ws ufjf:hasTitle ?titulo
19      }
20      UNION
21      {
22          ?p ufjf:belongsToScientist ufjf:Maria .
23          ?p ufjf:hasRelatedWith ?conc .
24          ?ws ufjf:hasRelatedWith ?conc .
25          ?ws a ufjf:WebService .
26          ?ws ufjf:hasTitle ?titulo
27      }
28  }
```

Fig. 3. SPARQL query

In the conducted case study, the search for these services was based on a fictitious profile of preferences belonging to a researcher named "Maria". This profile was specified considering the domain of Bioinformatics and considers ontological terms such as "Mapping", "Protein", "Cross-Reference" and "Identifiers" that are provided by CelO ontology. Figure 3 presents the SPARQL query that returns all scientific Web services, that matches Maria's profile. The query can be divided into three parts marked in sequence. In the first part selected, it returns all scientific Web services which matches Maria's profile. The second part of the query returns all models that are related to areas of interest belong to Maria's profile. Finally, the third part is responsible for returning all scientific Web services that are directly related to ontological terms selected by the researcher to compose her profile ("Mapping", "Protein", "Cross-Reference" and "Identifiers").

5 Concluding Remarks

The SASAgent architecture has as its main goal the provision of an infrastructure of a shared knowledge to researchers of computational modeling in the context of e-Science, through the use of agents, ontologies and scientific artifacts, such as Web services. In order to verify the feasibility of SASAgent, a case study was developed in the context of bioinformatics subdomain. Specifically, we can emphasize that we achieved our secondary goals, that is: i) implementation of a multi-agent system: the SASAgent was built, ii) existence of a knowledge base: use of the SOR database that store the CelO ontology, iii) independence of the domain: we can use ontologies of other related domains; iv) support different roles: the user has the ability to construct his own profile, with his main preferences. Considering these secondary goals, we can stand that our main goal was achieved with the specification and implementation of SASAgent. However, since SASAgent is a prototype, its performance has to be improved. This is one of our future works. Another one is the specification of a scientific workflow modeling tool, in order to help scientists collaborate, without worrying with the complexity of computational tools. Another work that has been developed in order to improve SASAgent is to capture provenance data of simulation tools that participate in a workflow execution. The innovation of this work, compared with similar ones is the use of an ontology base to help scientists formulate queries considering provenance data.

References

1. Atkins, D.E., Droegemeier, K.K., Feldman, S.I., Garcia-Molina, H., Klein, M.L., Messerschmitt, D.G., Messina, P., Ostriker, J.P., Wright, M.H.: Revolutionizing Science and Engineering Through Cyberinfrastructure Panel on Cyberinfrastructure (2003)
2. Hine, C.M.: New infrastructures for knowledge production: understanding E-science, 1st edn. Information Science Publishing, United Kingdom (2006)
3. NESC (2005), http://www.nesc.ac.uk (accessed, June 1, 2009)
4. Huang, L.-C., Wu, Z.-H., Pan, Y.-H.: A Grid Architecture for Scalable e-Science and Its Prototype. Journal of Software 16(4) (2005)

5. Sánchez, F.G., García, R.V., Béjar, R.M., Breis, J.T.F.: An ontology, intelligent agent-based framework for the provision of semantic web services, `http://www.sciencedirect.com` (accessed in June 1, 2009)
6. Studer, R., Benjamins, R., Fensel, D.: Knowledge engineering: Principles and methods (1998), `http://www.das.ufsc.br/~gb/pg-ia/` (accessed in June 1, 2009)
7. OWL (2004), `http://www.w3.org/TR/owl-guide/` (accessed in June 1, 2009)
8. McIlraith, S., Son, T.C., Zeng, H.: Semantic web services. IEEE Intelligent Systems 16(2), 46–53 (2001)
9. Kourtesis, D., Paraskakis, I.: Combining sawsdl, owl-dl and uddi for semantically enhanced web service discovery. In: Bechhofer, S., Hauswirth, M., Hoffmann, J., Koubarakis, M. (eds.) ESWC 2008. LNCS, vol. 5021, pp. 614–628. Springer, Heidelberg (2008)
10. Klusch, M., Fries, B.E., Sycara, K.: Automated semantic web service discovery with owls-mx. In: AAMAS 2006: Proceedings of the International joint conference on Autonomous agents and multiagent systems, NY, USA, pp. 915–922. ACM, New York (2006) ISBN 1-59593-303-4
11. Langegger, A., Wöÿ, W., Blöchl, M.: A semantic web middleware for virtual data integration on the web, pp. 493–507 (2008)
12. Matos, E.E.S., Campos, F., Braga, R., Palazzi, D.: CelOWS: an ontology based framework for the provision of semantic web services related to biological models. Journal of Biomedical Informatics (2009b), ISSN: 1532-0464, doi:10.1016/j.jbi.2009.08.008
13. Cote, R., Jones, P., Apweiler, R., Hermjakob, H.: The ontology lookup service, a lightweight cross-platform tool for controlled vocabulary queries. BMC Bioinformatics 7(1), 97 (2006)
14. Jones, P., Cote, R.: The pride proteomics identifications database: Data submission, query, and dataset comparison. In: Functional Proteomics. de Methods in Molecular Biology, vol. 484, pp. 287–303. Humana Press, Totowa (2008)
15. Lloyd, C.M., Halsted, M.D.B., Nielsen, P.: CellML: its future, present and past. Progress in Biophysics & Molecular Biology 85, 433–450 (2004)
16. Lu, J., Ma, L., Zhang, L., Brunner, J., Wang, C., Pan, Y., Yu, Y.: Sor: a practical system for ontology storage, reasoning and search. In: VLDB 2007: Proceedings of the 33rd international conference on Very large data bases, VLDB Endowment, pp. 1402–1405 (2007) ISBN 978-1-59593-649-3
17. The GLOBUS Project, `http://www.globus.org/`
18. The UNICORE Project, `http://www.unicore.eu/`

Clustering of Protein Substructures for Discovery of a Novel Class of Sequence-Structure Fragments

Ivana Rudolfova, Jaroslav Zendulka, and Matej Lexa

Brno University of Technology, Faculty of Information Technology,
Bozetechova 2, 612 66 Brno, Czech Republic
{rudolfa,zendulka,lexa}@fit.vutbr.cz
http://www.fit.vutbr.cz

Abstract. In this paper, we propose a novel method for clustering of protein substructures that we developed to study the relationships between protein sequences and their corresponding structures. We show the results of the comparison to other commonly used methods for clustering of protein structures. Finally, we outline a procedure for finding sequence profiles that tend to occur in more than one structural conformation but the number of their structural conformations is limited. This procedure is based on our method for protein substructure clustering.

Keywords: Clustering, density-based clustering, clustering of protein substructures, sequence-structure relationships in proteins.

1 Introduction

Data mining techniques may reveal interesting knowledge in various datasets and therefore, they are becoming more and more popular in bioinformatics. Nowadays, one of the key tasks in bioinformatics is the prediction of protein structure from its sequence. The analysis of the relationship between the protein sequence and its structure is still an active topic of research, since the knowledge of these relationships might help improve protein structure predictions [5,9]. In order to explore the sequence-structure relationship, cluster analysis is frequently employed [4,6,7,8].

In this paper, we propose a novel method for clustering of protein substructures. Traditionally, k-means or k-medoids techniques are used for clustering of protein structures [4,7,10]. It is not a trivial task to identify similarities between the protein substructures [4]. One possibility is to use a distance measure based on RMSD (root mean square deviation) [11]. However, the computation of RMSD markedly increases the computational time (especially for large data sets) of the clustering since it must be calculated pairwise. To overcome this shortcoming, we developed a new density-based method, where the clustering is performed over the space of torsion angles ϕ and ψ that characterize the protein substructure.

S. Khuri, L. Lhotská, and N. Pisanti (Eds.): ITBAM 2010, LNCS 6266, pp. 94–101, 2010.

We used this method in our research, where we focused on sequences that occur in more than one structural conformation, but the number of their conformations is limited. The relationship between a protein sequence and its structure has already been widely studied [2,6,7,8,10]; however, these studies searched for sequences that could be found in one given structural conformation.

In this paper, we also present the results of the comparison of our method with the traditionally used clustering methods. Further, we present the overall process that we designed to find the protein sequence profiles that tend to occur in a limited number of structural conformations.

2 DENCLUE-PS Method

DENCLUE-PS method is designed to cluster a set of protein substructures of the same length. For such set of the substructures, the method automatically determines the number of different structural conformations (the number of clusters). It is based on the ideas of the DENCLUE [3] method and on the Apriori property, generally used in association rule mining [1]. Before we describe the method, we will introduce several concepts more formally and we will formulate a lemma the method is based on.

Definition 1. A protein substructure is n-tuple of triples $s = (\langle \phi_1, \psi_1, \omega_1 \rangle, \ldots, \langle \phi_n, \psi_n, \omega_n \rangle)$ where n is the length of the substructure and $\langle \phi_i, \psi_i, \omega_i \rangle$ is the triple of the values of the torsion angles for the $i - th$ position in the substructure.

Each protein substructure of length n can be conceived as a point in an $3n$-dimensional data space. Such data space will be referred to as a substructures data space. According to the DENCLUE method we employ the density function (based on influence function) that we define as follows:

Definition 2. Let $S = \{s_1, s_2, \ldots, s_k\}$ be a set of protein substructures in a substructures data space. The density function at point x of the substructures data space is defined as:

$$f^S(x) = \sum_{i=1}^{k} f^{s_i}(x) \tag{1}$$

where $f^{s_i}(x)$ is an arbitrary influence function of the substructure s_i on the point x.

The set of protein substructures in a substructures data space that are to be clustered will be referred to as an input set. On the basis of the definition 2, we define the dense region, maximal dense region, and the cluster of substructures as follows:

Definition 3. The region R in the substructures data space is dense, if $f^S(x) \geq \xi, \forall x \in R$ where x is an arbitrary point in region R and ξ is the threshold of the density function.

Definition 4. The dense region R in the substructures data space is maximal if $\forall y \notin R$ holds:

1. $f^S(y) < \xi$ or
2. $\neg \exists x \in R$ such that $d(x, y) < \epsilon$, where $d(x, y)$ is the distance between two points x and y, and ϵ is the threshold of the distance between two dense regions.

Definition 5. Let R be a maximal dense region in the substructures data space. Cluster of substructures is the set of the substructures $C = \{s_i | s_i \in R, i = 1...k\}$, where k is the number of the substructures in the input set.

In the next paragraphs we will refer a data space of torsion angles ϕ, ψ and ω to as a $\phi\psi\omega$-space. Now we introduce a projection of a substructures $i - th$ position to the $\phi\psi\omega$-space and a projection of n-dimensional substructures data space to $\phi\psi\omega$-space:

Definition 6. The projection of a substructure s into the $\phi\psi\omega$-space for the $i - th$ position is an unary operation that chooses the triple of values $\langle \phi_i, \psi_i, \omega_i \rangle$: $\prod_i(s) = \langle \phi_i, \psi_i, \omega_i \rangle$.

Definition 7. The projection of a set of substructures $S = \{s_1, s_2, \ldots, s_k\}$ into the $\phi\psi\omega$-space for the $i - th$ position is an unary operation that chooses the triple of values $\langle \phi_i, \psi_i, \omega_i \rangle$ for each substructure of S: $\prod_i(S) = \{\prod_i(s_a) | a = 1 \ldots k\}$, where the result is a multiset.

In our DENCLUE-PS method we also exploit the Apriori property. The Apriori property, adapted for density-based clustering methods states the following:

Lemma 1 (Apriori property). If a d-dimensional region in the data space is dense, then so are its projections in $(d - 1)$-dimensional space. [1]

Based on this property we can formulate a lemma that represents the core of our DENCLUE-PS method:

Lemma 2 (cluster construction). Two protein substructures $s_1 = (\langle \phi_1, \psi_1, \omega_1 \rangle_1, \ldots, \langle \phi_n, \psi_n, \omega_n \rangle_1)$ and $s_2 = (\langle \phi_1, \psi_1, \omega_1 \rangle_2, \ldots, \langle \phi_n, \psi_n, \omega_n \rangle_2)$ are assigned to the same cluster if the projections $\prod_i(s_1)$ and $\prod_i(s_2)$ inhere in the same dense region in the $\phi\psi\omega$-space, $\forall i = 1 \ldots n$.

Proof. The proof follows directly from Lemma 1.

The DENCLUE-PS method performs the clustering on the individual projections into $\phi\psi\omega$-space and afterwards, it combines the results on the basis of the Lemma 2. To describe this process, we define the partition of the set of protein substructures and the minimal partition of the set of substructures as follows:

Definition 8. The set $P = \{P^1, \ldots, P^m | P^i \neq \emptyset \ \forall i = 1 \ldots m\}$ is a partition of the set of protein substructures S if the following conditions hold:

1. $P^1 \cup \ldots \cup P^m = S$,
2. the intersection of any two distinct elements of P is empty, i.e. if $P^i \cap P^j \neq \emptyset$ then $P^i = P^j$ $\forall P^i, P^j \in P$.

Definition 9. Let $M = \{M_1, M_2, \ldots, M_n\}$ be the set of partitions of the set of substructures $S = \{s_1, s_2, \ldots, s_k\}$. The partition R of the set S is the minimal partition defined by the set of the partitions M if the following conditions hold:

1. R is the partition of the set S,
2. $s_a \in R^i \wedge s_b \in R^i \mid a \neq b \iff s_a \in M_t^j \wedge s_b \in M_t^j \; \forall t = 1 \ldots n$, where $R^i \in R$, $M_t^j \in M_t$ and $s_a, s_b \in S$.

The minimal partition of the set S is such partition, that consists of the minimal possible number of the sets and, at the same time, any set of minimal partition cannot contain any two elements that are found in two different sets of any of the defining partitions.

Generally, our method consists of two steps. In the first step, we employ the Apriory property and we perform the clustering on the projections into the $\phi\psi\omega$-space for each position in the substructures. By this step, we determine the clusters of the preferred combinations of the torsion angles for each position. In the second step, we combine the results of the clustering for individual projections. Therefore, we search for a minimal partition of the input set of the substructures that is defined by the partitions given by clustering of the individual projections.

The algorithm is applicable on an arbitrary set of protein substructures of a given length and it returns the number of clusters (preferred structural conformation) if at least the given percentage share of the input substructures are included in the final clusters. Otherwise, the algorithm ends with the result that there are no strong structural preferences in the given set of substructures. The algorithm is summarized in Figure 1.

Input: set of protein substructures of a given length described by the torsion angles.
Parameters:
    minobj - minimal number of the substructures that can form a cluster
    minsupp - minimal percentage share of the input set of substructures that has
        to be included in the final clusters
Output: number of clusters - structural conformations
Algorithm:
    1. Set up the influence of each input substructure for each grid.
    2. Compute an overall density function for each grid and identify the maximal dense regions. Quantify the number of such regions (clusters) for each grid.
    3. Find a minimal partition of the input set of the substructures defined by the partitions given by the individual grids. (Combination of the results for the individual projections.)
    4. Split the clusters according to the values of the torsion angle ω for each position in the substructure.
    5. Discard the clusters that contain less than minobj substructures.
    6. Check the number of structures included in the clusters. If this number is less than minsupp of the input substructures, the number of structural conformations for the given set of structures is considered as unlimited.

Fig. 1. A summarization of the DENCLUE-PS method

3   Experimental Results

In order to evaluate DENCLUE-PS method, we compared it to the k-medoids method that utilizes the distance measure based on RMSD. We chose this method, because the partitioning methods are the most frequently used methods for clustering of protein fragments. We compared the results and the computational complexity of both methods. All experiments described in this section were carried out on Intel Pentium 4 / 2.8GHz, 2GB RAM.

For the comparison, we used the real data from PDB. We selected the set of sequence-structure fragments that we found to occur in two different structural conformations. We prepared an input set of 150 substructures. We compared the results and the processing time of clustering of the sets of 10, 50, 100 and 150 substructures. The input sets of 50, 100 and 150 substructures contain some outlier substructures each.

To estimate the RMSD between each pair of the input set, we used a python program match.py taken from [12]. This program finds an optimal superposition of the given structures and calculates the RMSD for this optimal superposition.

To cluster the substructures with DENCLUE-PS method, we have to compute the values of the torsion angles ϕ, ψ and ω for each amino acid. The RMSD determination and the torsion angle values calculation present the step of data preparation for the particular clustering. Figure 2 compares the computational complexity of these data preparation operations.

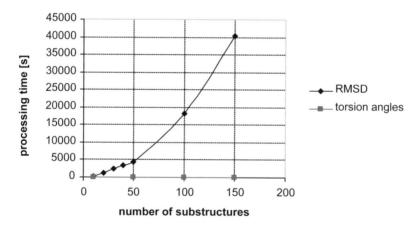

Fig. 2. The computational complexity of the RMSD determination and the torsion angle values calculation. The processing time of the torsion angle values calculation was between 2,88 seconds for 10 substructures, and 22,57 seconds for 150 substructures.

In the comparison of the DENCLUE-PS method, as a clustering method, we used k-medoids method implemented in Open source Clustering library developed at the University of Tokyo [13]. The processing time of k-medoids clustering fairly depends on the initial clustering. To reduce the impact of the initial

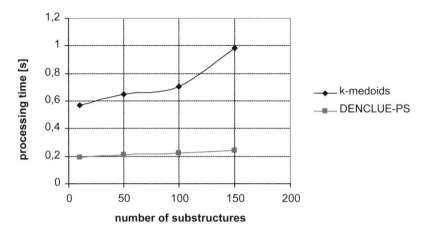

Fig. 3. The computational complexity of the k-medoids clustering and the DENCLUE-PS clustering

clustering on the processing time, we computed the average processing time for 100 runs of the algorithm. The results are shown in Figure 3.

From the Figures 2 and 3, it is clear that the computational complexity of DENCLUE-PS method is better than that of k-medoids clustering based on RMSD distance measure. The RMSD determination rapidly decreases the efficiency and the scalability of the methods based on RMSD distance measure. The computational complexity of the clustering itself does not differ much; however the observed processing time of our density-based method was any time slightly better than that of k-medoids method.

We also compared the results of both clustering methods. We set the number of clusters for k-medoids to the value of 2. With this setting, both methods divided the input set of 10 substructures into the same clusters. For the rest of the input sets, the results slightly differed since the DENCLUE-PS method detected outlier substructures in the input set, while the k-medoids assigned these substructures to one of the clusters. However, the partition of the other substructures was the same for the both methods. The outliers could be assigned to some cluster; however, it will decrease the solidity of the clusters.

The main advantage of our method is its very good scalability. On the other hand, our method handles the torsion angle for each position separately. This approach denotes two substructures as dissimilar even if their torsion angles significantly differ for only one position. The RMSD is calculated for the whole substructures and, therefore, it might accept larger variability on some positions.

4 Application

We developed the DENCLUE-PS method for clustering of protein substructures in order to find such sequences that occur in nature in more than one structural conformation, but the number of its conformations is limited. The goal of our research is to find and characterize the sequence motifs of the sequences that tend to occur in nature in limited number of the same structural conformations. To achieve this goal, we decided to perform the following steps:

1. To select the sequence fragments that occur predominately in the given number of structural conformations.
2. In this list, to find the sequences with the same preferred structures (seeds).
3. To develop an algorithm for an automatic refinement of the sequence profiles of the individual seeds.

We designed and implemented two algorithms that automatically perform the second and the third step. Both algorithms are based on the DENCLUE-PS method.

5   Conclusions

In this paper, we present the DENCLUE-PS method which is a density-based method for clustering of protein substructures. The DENCLUE-PS method is highly scalable, its processing time is almost independent on the number of input substructures and it grows linearly with their length. Experiments showed that the DENCLUE-PS method is significantly faster than commonly used techniques - partitioning clustering techniques based on RMSD distance measure. Qualitative results of the DENCLUE-PS method are comparable with other commonly used methods. The other advantage of the DENCLUE-PS method is that it does not require specifying the number of clusters; instead, the method detects the number of native clusters.

Our research is focused on studying protein sequences that occur in more than one structure conformation, but the number of its conformations is limited. DENCLUE-PS method is a tool that can help us.

Up to this time, we have found a few sequence profiles that predominately occur in two given structural conformations. More computations are needed to find all relevant sequence-structure fragments. Next, it is desirable to characterize the identified sequence-structure fragments according to their length and preferred structural conformations and to build up a database of these fragments. For the future, we also plan to encompass our knowledge into protein structure prediction techniques.

Acknowledgments. This work was partially supported by the BUT FIT grant FIT-S-10-2 and the research plan MSM0021630528.

References

1. Han, J., Kamber, M.: Data Mining: Concepts and Techniques. Academic Press, London (2001) ISBN: 1-55860-489-8
2. Han, K.F., Bystroff, C., Baker, D.: Three-dimensional structures and contexts associated with recurrent amino acid sequence patterns. Protein Science 6, 1587–1590 (1997)

3. Hinneburg, A., Kaim, D.A.: An Efficient Approach to Clustering in Large Multimedia Data-bases with Noise. In: Proceedings of the ACM SIGKDD 1998 (1998)
4. Park, S.H., Park, C.Y., Kim, D.H., Park, S.H., Sim, J.S.: Protein Structure Abstraction and Automatic Clustering Using Secondary Structure Element Sequences. In: Gervasi, O., Gavrilova, M.L., Kumar, V., Laganá, A., Lee, H.P., Mun, Y., Taniar, D., Tan, C.J.K. (eds.) ICCSA 2005. LNCS, vol. 3481, pp. 1284–1292. Springer, Heidelberg (2005)
5. Rohl, C.A., Strauss, C.E., Misura, K.M., Baker, D.: Protein structure prediction using Rosetta. Methods Enzymol. 383, 66–93 (2004)
6. Sander, O., Sommer, I., Lengauer, T.: Local protein structure prediction using discriminative models. BMC Bioinformatics 7, 14 (2006)
7. Tang, T., Xu, J., Li, M.: Discovering Sequence-Structure Motifs from Protein Segments and Two Applications. In: Pacific Symposium on Biocomputing, vol. 10, pp. 370–381 (2005)
8. Tendulkar, A.V., Joshi, A.A., Sohoni, M.A., Wangikar, P.P.: Clustering of Protein Structural Fragments Reveals Modular Building Block Approach of Nature. Journal of Molecular Biology 338, 611–629 (2004)
9. Zaki, M.J., Bystroff, C.: Protein Structure Prediction, 2nd edn. Humana Press (2008) ISBN: 978-1-58829-752-5
10. Zhong, W., Altun, G., Harrison, R., Tai, P.C., Pan, Y.: Improved K-means Clustering Algorithm for Exploring Local Protein Sequence Motifs Representing Common Structural Property. IEEE Transactions on Nanobioscience 4, 255–265 (2005)
11. Zhou, X., Wong, S.T.C.: Computational systems bioinformatics: methods and biomedical applications. World Scientific Publishing (2008) ISBN: 978-981-270-704-8
12. Trapped in the USA: match.py - calculating the RMSD of PDB structures, http://boscoh.com/protein/matchpy/
13. Open source Clustering software, http://bonsai.ims.u-tokyo.ac.jp/~mdehoon/software/cluster/software.htm

A Comorbidity Network Approach to Predict Disease Risk

Francesco Folino, Clara Pizzuti, and Maria Ventura

Institute for High Performance Computing and Networking (ICAR)
Italian National Research Council (CNR)
Via P. Bucci 41C
87036 Rende (CS), Italy
{f.folino,pizzuti}@icar.cnr.it

Abstract. A prediction model that exploits the past medical patient history to determine the risk of individuals to develop future diseases is proposed. The model is generated by using the set of frequent diseases that contemporarily appear in the same patient. The illnesses a patient could likely be affected in the future are obtained by considering the items induced by high confidence rules generated by the frequent diseases. Furthermore, a phenotypic comorbidity network is built and its structural properties are studied in order to better understand the connections between illnesses. Experimental results show that the proposed approach is a promising way for assessing disease risk.

1 Introduction

Health care is one of the most important research activity because of its implications in every day life of individuals. An emerging perspective in the last few years aims at identifying individuals most at risk for developing diseases plaguing present age. In fact, prevention or intervention at the disease's earliest onsets allow advantages for both the patient, in terms of life quality, and the medicare system, in terms of costs. However, recognizing the origin of an illness is not an easy task because it can be generated by multiple causes. Hospitals and physicians collect thousands of patient clinical histories containing important information regarding illness correlations and development. This phenotypic information can be exploited to build a model that predicts disease risk by studying the comorbidity relationships between diseases whenever they contemporarily appear in the same individual. Advanced risk assessment tools are currently at disposal, mainly based on statistical techniques. Another approach for addressing the problem, which is gaining increasing interest, is the use of methodologies coming from the fields of knowledge discovery [5] and network analysis [6]. Some recent proposals in these contexts are those of [2,3,4].

In this paper we apply network and association analysis on a data set of patient medical records. Our aim is twofold: *(i)* study the relationships of comorbidity appearing in the data set, and *(ii)* generate a predictive model that uses the

S. Khuri, L. Lhotská, and N. Pisanti (Eds.): ITBAM 2010, LNCS 6266, pp. 102–109, 2010.

past patient medical history to determine the risk of individuals to develop future diseases. Analogously to [3] and [4], we construct a phenotypic comorbidity network and analyze its structural properties to better understand the connections between diseases. Then, differently from these approaches, we propose the utilization of association analysis [5] to generate a disease risk predictive model. The model is built by using the set of frequent diseases that contemporarily appear in the same patient. The diseases the patient could likely be affected in the future are obtained by considering the items induced by high confidence rules generated by recurring disease patterns. The medical record of a patient is then compared with the patterns discovered by the model, and a set of illnesses is predicted. Experimental results show that approach is a promising method to predict individual risk disease by taking into account only the illnesses a patient had in the past.

The paper is organized as follows. The next section describes the data set used. Section 3 builds two phenotypic disease networks and analyzes its structural properties. In section 4 the predictive model is described. Finally, section 5 reports the evaluation of the proposed predictive approach on the patient data records.

2 Data Description

The data set consists of medical records of 1462 patients of a small town in the south of Italy. Each record contains a unique patient identifiers, date of birth, the gender, and the list of disease codes with the date of the visit in which that disease has been diagnosed. The age distribution for the study population is reported in Figure 1(a). The disease codes are those defined by the International Classification of Diseases, Ninth Revision, Clinical Modification (ICD-9-CM). Every health condition is associated with a unique category and given a code, up to five digits long. The first three digits constitute the principal diagnosis, while the other two identify secondary diagnoses.

The data is completely anonymized, thus there is no way to identify the patients. In our database the number of diagnoses are 8768 spanning from 1990 to 2009. From an analysis of the patient records, we found that the raw data

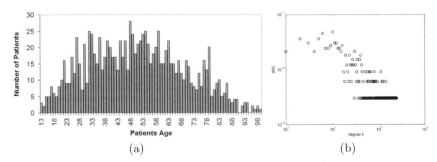

Fig. 1. Age distribution for the study population (a), degree distribution of the disease network computed using 3-digit codes (b)

contained some uninteresting information. These patients have been discarded because not useful for the phenotypic network construction. After this prepro-cessing phase, the database reduced to 1105 patients and the number of diseases was 972. However, the number of diseases was still too high. As described above, the first three digits of a code denote the general diagnosis. Even if some details can be missed, these three digits are sufficiently informative to study the dis-ease correlations. In order to obtain a more manageable network, the five digits ICD-9-CM codes have been collapsed to these first three digits, so the number of diseases was reduced to 330.

3   Phenotypic Disease Network

The patient medical records contain important enlightenment regarding the co-occurrences of diseases affecting the same individual. A comorbidity relationship between two illnesses exists whenever they appear simultaneously in a patient more than chance alone [3]. Our first goal was to make discernible the correla-tions among the diseases contained in our data set by building a network whose nodes are the diseases and a link between two nodes occurs when a comorbidity relation appears, i. e. when the couple of diseases affects at least one patient. The edges were labelled with the number of patients showing both the illnesses. An important property to study about networks is the degree distribution [1]. Fig-ure 1(b) reports the degree distribution of our disease network. The figure points out that the network is a scale-free network, i.e. the degree distribution follows a power-law $p_k \approx k^{-\alpha}$, where $\alpha \approx 0.59$. Furthermore the clustering coefficient is 0.69 and the diameter is 4.

The number of edges computed between the nodes was 5736, a too high value to be visualized in a comprehensible manner. Since many edges had weight 1, we adopted the same statistical approaches proposed by Hidalgo et al. [3] to measure the strength of comorbidity relationships, and thus to discard those edges deemed less meaningful. The measures employed to quantify the strength between two sicknesses are the *Relative Risk (RR)* and the *ϕ-correlation*. The *RR* of observing a pair of diseases i and j appearing in the same patient is given by $RR_{ij} = \frac{CC_{ij}(N-CC_{ij})}{P_i P_j}$, where CC_{ij} is the number of patients affected by both diseases, N is the total number patients in the data sets, and P_i, P_j are the numbers of patients affected by diseases i and j, respectively. The *ϕ-correlation* is defined as $\phi_{ij} = \frac{CC_{ij}(N-CC_{ij})-P_i P_j}{\sqrt{(P_i P_j (N-P_i)(N-P_j))}}$.

The distribution of RR values for our data set is shown in Figure 2(a), and that of *ϕ-correlation* in Figure 2(b). As pointed out in [3], the Relative Risk overestimates relations involving rare diseases and underestimates relationships between very common sicknesses. On the other hand, *ϕ-correlation* underesti-mates comorbidity between rare and frequent diseases, and accurately discrim-inates associations between illnesses of similar appearances. Thus, we built a network by selecting only the statistically significant edges having $RR > 20$, and

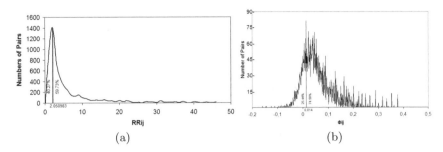

(a)   (b)

Fig. 2. Distribution of the Relative Risk between all disease pairs (a), and distribution of the ϕ-correlation between all disease pairs (b)

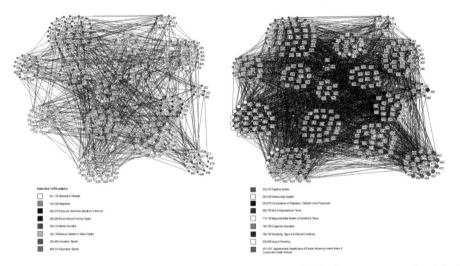

Fig. 3. Disease network with Relative Risk above 20 (left). Disease network with ϕ-correlation above 0.06 (right). Different colors denote the ICD-9-CM categories appearing in the dataset. Codes labeling bigger points are those that do not appear in the RR network.

another network by discarding all the edges having $\phi \leq 0.06$. The two networks are depicted in Figure 3. The network on the left contains 618 edges, the other one has 2515 connections. The figure confirms the observation that the Relative Risk underestimates very common diseases. In fact, for example, illnesses like hypertension (code 401), diabetes mellitus (code 250), osteoarthrosis (code 715), or general sysmptons (780), do not appear in Figure 3 (left) because a high percentage of the population is affected by these problems. They are instead depicted in the figure on the right, together with all the others excluded. To better distinguish them, their size is bigger than those already present in the figure on the left.

4   Disease Risk Prediction

A general predictive model to assess disease risk can be realized by studying the patterns of co-occurrences across the medical patient records. Each patient can be associated with the list of diseases he has been affected during his life. Groups of illnesses occurring frequently in many patient records can be exploited to capture comorbidity relations and generate predictions about the diseases a patient can incur, given the past history of his health conditions. To this end, a valuable help can come from *association analysis*. Association analysis [5] is an important data mining methodology for discovering interesting hidden relationships in large data sets. It relies on the concept of *frequent itemset* to extract strong correlations among the items constituting the data set to study.

Let DS be the set of medical patient records, $D = \{d_1, \ldots, d_n\}$ the set of illnesses appearing in DS, and $T = \{t_1, \ldots, t_m\}$ a set of m patient transactions, where each t_i is a subset of D, i.e. a set of diseases. Groups of diseases occurring frequently together in many transactions are referred to as *frequent itemsets*. The concept of frequency is formalized through the concept of *support*. Given a set $I = \{I_1, \ldots, I_k\}$ of frequent itemsets on T, the support of an itemset $I_i \in I$, $\sigma(I_i)$, is defined as $\sigma(I_i) = \frac{|\{t \in T | t_i \subseteq t\}|}{|T|}$, where $|\,.\,|$ denotes the number of elements in a set. The support, thus, determines how often a group of diseases appears together. It is a very important measure since very low support discriminates those groups of items occurring only by chance. Thus a frequent itemset, in order to be considered interesting, must have a support greater than a fixed threshold value, *minsup*. An association rule is an implication expression of the form $X \Rightarrow Y$, where X and Y are disjoint itemsets. The importance of an association rule is measured by its *support* and *confidence*. The support of a rule is computed as the support of $X \cup Y$ and tells how often a rule is applicable. The confidence is defined as $\frac{\sigma(X \cup Y)}{\sigma(X)}$, and determines how frequently items in Y appear in transactions that contain X.

Frequent itemsets having a support value above a minimum threshold are used to extract high confidence rules, and can be exploited to build a risk prediction model by matching the medical record of a patient against the patterns discovered by the model. In this scenario, the support determines how often a group of diseases appears together, while a rule like $X \Rightarrow \{d\}$, where $X \subseteq D$ is a subset of diseases and d is a single disease, having a high confidence allows to reliably infer that d will appear together with the items contained in X. The idea we pursue in this paper thus consists in using frequent itemsets of diseases for predicting a set of diseases a patient could likely be affected in the future, given the patient clinical history.

We use a sliding window of fixed size w over the medical records for capturing the patient's history depth used for the prediction. A sliding window of size w means that only the last (in time order) w diseases appearing in the record influence the prediction of possible forthcoming illnesses. Given a fixed window size w, we consider only the frequent itemsets of size $w + 1$ that contain the w items appearing in the current medical patient record t_i. The prediction of the next disease is based on the confidence of the corresponding association rule whose consequent is exactly the disease to be predicted. Thus, if the rule has a confidence value greater than a fixed threshold, the disease on the right of the arrow is added to the set of predicted illnesses.

In order to explain the way our prediction approach works, let the transactions reported in the top table of Figure 4 be a set of some patient's medical records. By fixing the minimum support threshold σ to 0.8 (i.e., an itemset is frequent if it is present at least 4 times in the transaction set), the algorithm finds the patterns in the bottom table.

t_1	{401, 722, 723, 715}
t_2	{401, 722, 715, 462, 723}
t_3	{401, 722, 715, 462}
t_4	{722, 715, 401, 462}
t_5	{723, 401, 722, 715, 462}

Length 1	Length 2	Length 3	Length 4
{401} (5)	{401, 722} (4)	{401, 722, 462} (4)	{401, 722, 462, 715} (4)
{722} (5)	{401, 462} (4)	{401, 722, 715} (5)	
{462} (4)	{401, 715} (5)	{401, 462, 715} (4)	
{715} (5)	{722, 462} (4)	{722, 462, 715} (4)	
	{722, 715} (5)		
	{462, 715} (4)		

Fig. 4. Example of transactions involving some common diseases (a). Frequent itemsets mined by the algorithm(b).

Now, let $t = \{722, 715, 401, 733\}$ be a new medical record. If the window size w is set to 2, this means that only the two first diseases are used to generate the predictions, i.e., $\{722, 715\}$. By matching $\{722, 715\}$ against the 3-frequent itemsets, the items with code 401 and 462 are proposed as likely, next diseases. The scores of predicted illness 401 and 462 are 1 and 0.8. As previously described, these scores correspond to the confidences of the association rules $\{722, 715\} \Rightarrow \{401\}$ and $\{722, 715\} \Rightarrow \{462\}$, respectively.

5   Experimental Results

In this section we first define the measures used to test the effectiveness of our approach. Next, we present the results and evaluate them on the base of the introduced metrics. As discussed in Section 2, the dataset we used for the experiments consists of 1105 transactions involving 330 distinct diseases. In order to perform a fair evaluation we applied the well-known *k-fold cross validation* method [5], with $k = 10$.

We tested our approach in the following way. Each transaction t in the evaluation set is divided in two groups of diseases. The first group of diseases, called $head_t$, are used for generating predictions, while the remaining, referred as $tail_t$, are used to evaluate the predictions generated. The length of $head_t$ is tightly related to the maximum window size allowable for the experiments. In our case, since the mining phase of frequent patterns produced itemsets of size at most 5, the length of $head_t$ has been fixed to 4. Thus, given a window size $w \leq |t|$, we

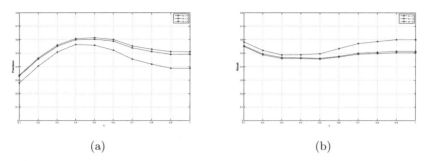

(a)   (b)

Fig. 5. Impact of w on precision and recall measures when $\sigma = 0.01$

select the first w diseases for generating the predictions and the remaining $|t| - w$ for testing their prediction. Fixed $head_t$ and a confidence threshold τ, we produce the prediction set $P(head_t, \tau)$ containing all the predictions whose score is greater than τ. Then the set $P(head_t, \tau)$ is compared with $tail_t$. The comparison of these sets is done by using two different metrics, namely *precision* and *recall*. Precision and recall are two widely used statistical measures in the data mining field. In particular, precision is seen as a measure of exactness, whereas recall is a measure of completeness. In order to obtain an overall evaluation score for each measure (fixed a confidence threshold τ) we computed the mean over all transactions in the test set. In the experiment presented we measured both precision and recall by varying τ from 0.1 to 1. Moreover, in order to evaluate the impact of window size w on the quality of predictions, we ranged w from 2 to 4.

Figure 5 shows the impact of w on precision and recall of the predictions. We obtained these results by fixing the overall support for the mining of frequent patterns to 0.01. As expected, the results in Figure 5(a) clearly reveal that the precision increases as a larger portions of patient's medical history, i.e. an increasing number of diseases, are used to compute predictions. Conversely, the recall is negatively biased by larger window sizes, but this effect slightly fades for higher values of τ (see Figure 5(b)).

Figure 6 displays the behavior of precision and recall metrics when the support threshold varies. We used $w = 2$ since it is the maximum allowable window size when the support reaches the value 0.1. Increasing the support threshold has two main positive effects: *(i)* improving the precision of predictions, and *(ii)* ensuring the scalability of the association rule mining algorithm, since a lower number of frequent itemsets are computed. However, as a side effect, a higher support results in a potential loss of some important, yet infrequent, diseases in the prediction set. In the medical context, this kind of illnesses could be particularly important and more informative for producing a correct diagnosis. Figure 6(a) clearly points out better performances of precision when the support threshold increases. Indeed, it is easy to notice that, for $w = 2$ and $\tau = 0.4$, we obtain a precision of 0.5635 if $\sigma = 0.01$, whereas the precision reaches the value 0.7608 and 0.8593 for $\sigma = 0.05$ and $\sigma = 0.1$, respectively. An inverse trend can be noted in Figure 6(b) for the recall which, even for $w = 2$ and $\tau = 4$,

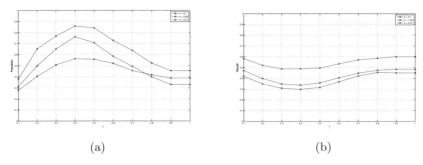

(a)   (b)

Fig. 6. Impact of σ on precision and recall measures when $w = 2$

progressively decreases from the value 0.4903, when $\sigma = 0.01$, to 0.2985, when $\sigma = 0.1$, respectively.

6   Conclusions

We constructed a phenotypic comorbidity network and studied its structural properties to better understand the connections between diseases. Then we presented a methodology based on associative rules to generate a predictive model that uses the past medical history of patients to determine the risk of individuals to develop future diseases. Experimental results showed that the technique can be a viable approach to disease prediction. Future works aims to compare our method with other proposals in literature, in particular with a collaborative filtering technique based on the k-nearest-neighbor, like that employed by [4].

Acknowledgements. This work has been partially supported by the project *Infrastruttura tecnologica del fascicolo sanitario elettronico*, funded by Technological Innovation Department, Pres. Cons. Min.

References

1. Albert, R., Barabási, A.-L.: Staistical mechanics of complex networks. Reviews of modern physics 74, 47–97 (2002)
2. Davis, D.A., Chawla, N.V., Christakis, N.A., Barabási, A.-L.: Time to CARE: a collaborative engine for practical disease prediction. Data Mining and Knowledge Discovery Journal 20, 388–415 (2010)
3. Hidalgo, C.A., Blumm, N., Barabási, A.-L., Christakis, N.A.: A dynamic network approach for the study of human phenotypes. PLoS Computational Biology 5(4) (2009)
4. Steinhaeuser, K., Chawla, N.V.: A network-based approach to understanding and predicting diseases. In: Social Computing and Behavioral Modeling. Springer, Heidelberg (2009)
5. Tan, P.-N., Steinbach, M., Kumar, V.: Introduction to Data Mining. Pearson International Edition, London (2006)
6. Wasserman, S., Faust, K.: Social Network Analysis. Methods and Applications. Cambridge University Press, Cambridge (1994)

Mining and Post-processing of Association Rules in the Atherosclerosis Risk Domain

Petr Berka[1,2] and Jan Rauch[1,2]

[1] Dept. of Information and Knowledge Engineering, University of Economics, Prague,
Czech Republic
[2] Centre of Biomedical Informatics,
Institute of Computer Science of the Academy of Sciences,
Prague, Czech Republic

Abstract. The paper presents a novel approach to post-processing of
association rules based on the idea of meta-learning. A subsequent association rule mining step is applied to the results of "standard" association rule mining. We thus obtain "rules about rules" that help to better
understand the association rules generated in the first step.

A case study of applying this approach to data about atherosclerosis
risk is described in the paper.

1 Introduction

Atherosclerosis is a slow, complex disease that typically starts in childhood
and often progresses when people grow older. Atherosclerosis involves the slow
buildup of deposits of fatty substances, cholesterol, body cellular waste products, calcium, and fibrin (a clotting material in the blood) in the inside lining
of an artery. The buildup (referred as a plaque) with the formation of the blood
clot (thrombus) on the surface of the plaque can partially or totally block the
flow of blood through the artery. Atherosclerosis-related diseases are a leading
cause of death and impairment in the developed countries. So understanding
(based either on experts' knowledge or on results of data mining) the causes of
atherosclerosis and it's risk factors is important for health care professionals.

The paper is organized as follows: Section 2 describes the data collected within
a longitudial study of atherosclerosis primary prevention that was carried out
in several hospitals in Prague. Section 3 reviews the area of association rule
mining and presents our novel approach to mining association meta-rules from
the original set of association rules. Section 4 describes a case study of applying
this approach to the atherosclerosis risk data.

2 The STULONG Study

In the early seventies of the twentieth century, a project of extensive epidemiological study of atherosclerosis primary prevention was developed under the
name "National Preventive Multifactor Study of Hard Attacks and Strokes"
in the former Czechoslovakia. The study included data of more than 1400 men

S. Khuri, L. Lhotská, and N. Pisanti (Eds.): ITBAM 2010, LNCS 6266, pp. 110–117, 2010.

born between 1926-1937 and living in Prague 2. The men were divided according to presence of risk factors (hypertension, hypercholesteromia, smoking, obesity, positive family history), overall health conditions and ECG result into following three groups: normal (a group of men showing no RF defined above), risk (group of men with at least one RF defined above) and pathological (group of men with a manifested cardio-vascular disease). Long-term observation of patients was based on following the men from normal group and risk group (randomly divided into intervened risk group - RGI and control risk group - RGC).

STULONG is the data set concerning this longitudinal study of the risk factors of the atherosclerosis. Four data tables have been created when transforming the collected data into electronic form[1]. The table ENTRY contains values of 224 attributes obtained from entry examinations. The table CONTROL contains results of observation of 66 attributes recorded during follow-up control examinations oriented on risk factors and clinical demonstration of atherosclerosis. Additional information about health status of 403 men was collected by the postal questionnaire, resulting values of 62 attributes are stored in the table LETTER. There are 5 attributes concerning death of 389 patients who died during the study, values of these attributes are stored in the table DEATH. For details see `http://euromise.vse.cz/stulong-en/index.php`.

The STULONG data were analyzed using both statistical and machine learning (data mining) methods. Refer to [3] for description of various analyses performed within the ECML/PKDD Discovery Challenge workshops. One of the mostly used methods in this contest were association rules.

3   Association Rules Mining and Post-processing

An association rule is commonly understood to be an expression of the form

$$X \Longrightarrow Y,$$

where X and Y are sets of items. This expresses that transactions containing items of set X tend to contain items of set Y. The term association rules was coined by R. Agrawal in the early 90th in relation to so called market basket analysis [1]. In this analysis, transaction data recorded by point-of-sale (POS) systems in supermarkets are analyzed in order to understand the purchase behavior of groups of customers (e.g. {eggs, bacon} $\Longrightarrow$ {cheese}). The idea of association rules has been later generalized to any data in the tabular, attribute-value form. So data describing properties (values of attributes) of some examples

---

[1] The study was realized at the 2nd Department of Medicine, 1st Faculty of Medicine of Charles University and Charles University Hospital, U nemocnice 2, Prague 2 (head. Prof. M. Aschermann, MD, SDr, FESC), under the supervision of Prof. F. Boudík, MD, ScD, with collaboration of M. Tomečková, MD, PhD and Ass. Prof. J. Bultas, MD, PhD. The data were transferred to the electronic form by the European Centre of Medical Informatics, Statistics and Epidemiology of Charles University and Academy of Sciences (head. Prof. RNDr. J. Zvárová, DrSc).

can be analyzed in order to find associations between conjunctions of attribute-value pairs (categories). Let us denote these conjunctions as *Ant* and *Suc* and the association rule as $Ant \implies Suc$.

The two basic characteristics of an association rule are *support* and *confidence*. Let (for the analyzed data) a be the number of examples (rows in the data table) that fulfill both *Ant* and *Suc*, b the number of examples that fulfill *Ant* but do not fulfill *Suc*, c the number of examples that fulfill *Suc* but do not fulfill *Ant*, and d the number of examples that fulfill neither *Ant* nor *Suc*. Then, the support of an association rule is defined as

$$sup = \frac{a}{a+b+c+d},$$

and confidence of an association rule is defined as

$$conf = \frac{a}{a+b}.$$

When looking for association rules, we are usually interested in rules with support and confidence that exceed some given thresholds.

3.1 Association Rules Mining

There is a number of algorithms, that perform the association rule mining task. These algorithms repeatedly generate syntactically correct rules (i.e. rules, in which two different values of an attribute cannot occur) and then test if the rules meet given thresholds *minconf* and *minsup*. The best-known algorithm *apriori* proceeds in two steps. All frequent itemsets are found in the first step. A frequent itemset is a set of items that is included in at least *minsup* transactions. Then, association rules with a confidence of at least *minconf* are generated from frequent itemsets in the second step [1].

3.2 Association Rules Post-processing

The result of association rule mining task is usually a huge list of rules (thousands, tens of thousands) that have to be visually interpreted and evaluated by the domain expert. So some kind of post-processing of the results would be very helpful for the user. And indeed, various approaches have been used to post-process the huge list of found associations: filtering, selection, visualization, grouping and clustering (see e.g.[5], [6]). In this section, we present our alternative approach based on the idea of meta-learning.

We propose to apply association rule mining algorithm to the set of "original" association rules obtained as a result of particular data mining task. This idea thus follows the stacking (meta-learning) concept used in data mining to combine classifiers [2], but has not been presented yet for descriptive tasks. The input to the proposed meta-learning step will be association rules encoded as data, the output will be a set of association meta-rules uncovering relations between various characteristics of the original set of rules.

We will distinguish two types of association meta-rules: *qualitative* and *quantitative*. Qualitative rules will represent the meta-knowledge in the form "if original association rules contain a conjunction of categories *Ant*, then they also contain the conjunction of categories *Suc*", i.e qualitative rules have the form

$$Ant \implies Suc.$$

Quantitative rules will represent the meta-knowledge in the form "if original association rules contain a conjunction of categories *Ant*, then they have quantitative characteristics *Q*", i.e

$$Ant \implies Q.$$

or, "if original association rules have quantitative characteristics *Q*, then they contain a conjunction of categories *Suc*", i.e

$$Q \implies Suc.$$

where Q can be e.g "confidence $\in [0.9, 1]$". We can also search for conjunctions of categories, that frequently occur in the list of original association rules (let call them *frequent cedents*).

To find association meta-rules, standard association rule mining algorithms can be used. The only thing to do is to represent the original association rules as input data. In our experiments, we encoded the association rules using the attributes from the original data set and extended this representation by the information about support and confidence. So e.g. the first rule from the list shown in Table 1 will be encoded using the values `PIVO=v1`, `VINO=v11`, `LIH=v12`, `KAVA=v1`, `abssup=132`, `conf=0.89`. Attributes not occurring in a rule will take the missing value code. The values of absolute support and confidence must then be discretized to fit into the apriori algorithm; we used equifrequent discretization into 5 intervals for support and equidistant discretization into 4 intervals for confidence. The corresponding part of the data table is shown in Table 2. Let us stress that the chosen representation does not reflect the distinctions between *Ant* and *Suc* of the original rules.

Table 1. Association rules

```
1. VINO=v11 LIH=v12 KAVA=v1 148 ==> PIVO=v1 132 conf:(0.89)
2. ZOD=v3 AKTPZ=v2 VINO=v11 LIH=v12 143 ==> PIVO=v1 127 conf:(0.89)
3. ZOD=v3 AKTPZ=v2 PIVO=v1 LIH=v12 144 ==> VINO=v11 127 conf:(0.88)
 . . .
```

Of course, the main question is: does such post-processing make sense from the user's point of view? We believe that it makes, if we answer positively at least one of the following questions:

– Do the meta-rules give better insight into the list of "original" rules?
– Is the list of meta-rules easier to evaluate?

We performed several experiments to find answers to these questions.

Table 2. Encoded association rules

ZOD	AKPTZ	PIVO	VINO	LIH	KAVA	abssup	conf
?	?	v1	v11	v12	v1	(-inf-136.5]	(0.8425-inf)
v3	v2	v1	v11	v12	?	(-inf-136.5]	(0.8425-inf)
v3	v2	v1	v11	v12	?	(-inf-136.5]	(0.8425-inf)
			...				

4 STULONG Data Mining and Post-processing

A number of analyses of the STLULONG data has been performed (see). We
will show in this paper some results related to the analytic questions related to
the entry examination (what are the relations between social factors, or physical activity, or alcohol consumption and the risk factors). All the experiments
reported in this paper were performed using the *apriori* algorithm implemented
in the *Weka* data mining system [7].

Let us start with a closer look at the analysis that tries to find relations
(associations) between social characteristics, smoking, drinking of alcohol, coffee
or tea. First rules resulting from this analysis are shown in Table 1, the total
number of rules is 385. This corresponds to the parameter *minsup* set to 0.1
and the parameter *minconf* set to 0.7. After encoding these rules (example see
in Table 2) we can run the *apriori* algorithm again to find different types of
meta-rules defined in Section 3.2.

At first we will look for *qualitative* meta-rules. Table 3 shows the listing of
all qualitative meta-rules for the parameters $minsup = 0.1$ and $minconf = 0.7$;
we intentionally used the same setting of parameters as for the analysis of the
original data to compare the number of found rules and meta-rules.

Table 3. Qualitative meta-rules

```
1. VINO=v0 45 ==> LIH=v0 39 conf:(0.87)
2. LIH=v0 55 ==> VINO=v0 39 conf:(0.71)
3. KAVA=v1 27 ==> PIVO=v1 19 conf:(0.7)
```

Due to the way how the rules have been encoded for meta-learning, the meta-
rules have the same syntax as the original rules. But their meaning is completely
different. Recall that the rules are obtained from the original data but the meta-
rules are obtained from rules. So the first rule from Table 1 says that in the
group of 148 persons who drink wine (VINO=v11), liquors (LIH=v12) and coffee
(KAVA=v1), 132 of them also drink beer (PIVO=v1). But the last rule from
Table 3 (that also refers to categories KAVA=v1 and PIVO=v1) says that the
resulting list of association rules contains 27 rules that refer to drinking coffee,
19 of them also refer drinking beer. We thus have found a subset of original rules
with the same categories.

Table 4. Quantitative meta-rules

```
1. abssup=(155.5-180] conf=(-inf-0.7475] 30 ==> AKTPZ=v2 22 conf:(0.73)
2. conf=(0.795-0.8425] 51 ==> VINO=v11 37 conf:(0.73)
3. abssup=(237.5-inf) conf=(-inf-0.7475] 38 ==> AKTPZ=v2 27  conf:(0.71)
4. conf=(0.795-0.8425] 51 ==> LIH=v12 36 conf:(0.71)
```

The next step in our running example will be the mining for *quantitative* meta-rules. The input data (encoded rules) remain the same as in the previous step. We again used the parameters $minsup = 0.1$ and $minconf = 0.7$ and we obtained 4 meta-rules shown in Table 4. The third meta-rule says, that 71% of all rules with high support and low confidence refer to people with moderate physical activity after a job (AKTPZ=v2). We thus obtained some quantitative characteristics of subsets of the original rules.

To be able to use the Weka system also for the last type of analysis, for looking for frequent cedents, we added a dummy category "true=t" to the data that encoded the original association rules. We are thus able to identify frequent cedents from the rules

$$true = t \Longrightarrow Suc,$$

that have sufficiently high confidence. Table 5 shows the 27 respective rules for $minsup = 0.1$ thus showing the conjunctions of categories that occur in at least

Table 5. Frequent cedents

```
 1. true=t 385 ==> AKTPOZAM=v2 228 conf:(0.59)
 2. true=t 385 ==> PIVO=v1 201 conf:(0.52)
 3. true=t 385 ==> VINO=v11 142 conf:(0.37)
 4. true=t 385 ==> LIHOV=v12 130 conf:(0.34)
 5. true=t 385 ==> AKTPOZAM=v2 PIVO=v1 93 conf:(0.24)
 6. true=t 385 ==> VINO=v11 LIHOV=v12 85 conf:(0.22)
 7. true=t 385 ==> DOPRAVA=v3 83 conf:(0.22)
 8. true=t 385 ==> AKTPOZAM=v2 VINO=v11 83 conf:(0.22)
 9. true=t 385 ==> PIVO=v1 VINO=v11 81 conf:(0.21)
10. true=t 385 ==> PIVO=v1 LIHOV=v12 79 conf:(0.21)
11. true=t 385 ==> CAJ=v5 76 conf:(0.2)
12. true=t 385 ==> AKTPOZAM=v2 LIHOV=v12 70 conf:(0.18)
13. true=t 385 ==> TELAKTZA=v1 65 conf:(0.17)
14. true=t 385 ==> ZODPOV=v3 60 conf:(0.16)
15. true=t 385 ==> LIHOV=v0 55 conf:(0.14)
16. true=t 385 ==> PIVO=v1 VINO=v11 LIHOV=v12 50 conf:(0.13)
17. true=t 385 ==> AKTPOZAM=v2 DOPRAVA=v3 48 conf:(0.12)
18. true=t 385 ==> KAVA=v2 46 conf:(0.12)
19. true=t 385 ==> VINO=v0 45 conf:(0.12)
20. true=t 385 ==> PIVO=v1 CAJ=v5 45 conf:(0.12)
21. true=t 385 ==> DOPRAVA=v3 PIVO=v1 44 conf:(0.11)
22. true=t 385 ==> AKTPOZAM=v2 PIVO=v1 VINO=v11 42 conf:(0.11)
23. true=t 385 ==> AKTPOZAM=v2 VINO=v11 LIHOV=v12 41 conf:(0.11)
```

Table 6. Summary of results

task	no. attributes	assoc rules	qualitative rules	quantiative rules	frequent cedents
T1	18	12389	36	28	142
T1 red.	12	385	3	4	27
T2	14	5186	23	35	162
T3	17	2369	16	24	59
T4	13	3391	6	6	110

10 percents of the original association rules. The results e.g. show, that more than one half of the original rules refer to moderate physical activity after a job or to drinking beer.

Table 6 summarizes the results of our analysis (both mining association rules and meta-rules) for different analytical questions asked for the STULONG data. Task "T1" refers to the analysis of relation between social characteristics, smoking, drinking of alcohol, coffee or tea. Task "T1 red.", refers to our running example where the task was the same as for "Task1" but the set of social characteristics was reduced. Task "T2" refers to the analysis of relation between smoking, drinking of alcohol, coffee or tea and risk factors. Task "T3" refers to the analysis of relation between smoking, drinking of alcohol, coffee or tea and physical examinations (blood pressure, BMI, skinfold). Task "T4" refers to the analysis of relation between smoking, drinking of alcohol, coffee or tea and biochemical examinations (cholesterol, triglycerides, urine). The numbers in the table show the number of attributes from the original data used for analysis, the number of found association rules, the number of qualitative meta-rules, the number of quantitative meta-rules, and the number of frequent cedents. In all experiments, the setting for *minsup* and *minconf* remain the same as described in the running example above.

The results support our working hypothesis, that the number of meta-rules will be significantly smaller than the number of original rules. Thus the interpretation of meta-rules by domain expert will be significantly less time consuming and difficult compared to the interpretation of the original association rules.

5   Conclusions

The paper presents a novel idea of using meta-learning approach to post-process the results of association rule mining. We used the described method in the atherosclerosis risk domain, where an interesting data set has been collected within a longitudial study of atherosclerosis primary prevention. This data has been extensively analyzed using association rule mining algorithms. We believe, that the proposed meta-rules can help the experts to better understand the results of the "standard" data mining step (and our results show this is true). Moreover, the number of meta-rules is (in all our experiments) significantly smaller than the number of "standard" rules and thus the meta-rules are easier to inspect.

Our further work in this area will be oriented on the question how to mine meta-rules if the association rules have more complex structure and on the question of other types of meta-rules. An additional topic of our research is related to using domain knowledge via application of logic of association rules [4].

Acknowledgement

The work is supported by the grant MSMT 1M06014 (from the Ministry of Education of the Czech Republic) and the grant GACR 201/08/0802 (from the Grant Agency of the Czech Republic).

References

1. Agrawal, R., Imielinski, T., Swami, A.: Mining Association Rules Between Sets of Items in Large Databases. In: SIGMOD Conference, pp. 207–216 (1993)
2. Bauer, E., Kohavi, R.: An Empirical Comparison of Voting Classification Algorithms: Bagging, Boosting, and Variants. Machine Learning 36(1/2), 105–139 (1999)
3. Berka, P., Rauch, J., Tomečková, M.: Lessons Learned from the ECML/PKDD Discovery Challenge on the Atherosclerosis Risk Factors Data. Computing and Informatics 26(3), 329–344 (2007)
4. Rauch, J.: Considerations on Logical Calculi for Dealing with Knowledge in Data Mining. In: Ras, Z.W., Dardzinska, A. (eds.) Advances in Data Management, pp. 177–202. Springer, Heidelberg (2009)
5. Sigal, S.: Exploring interestingness through clustering. In: Proc. of the IEEE Int. Conf. on Data Mining (ICDM 2002), Maebashi City (2002)
6. Toivonen, H., Klementinen, M., Roikainen, P., Hatonen, K., Mannila, H.: Pruning and grouping discovered association rules. In: Workshop notes of the ECML 1995 Workshop on statistics, machine learning and knowledge discovery in databases, Heraklion, pp. 47–52 (1995)
7. Weka - Data Mining with Open Source Machine Learning Software, http://www.cs.waikato.ac.nz/ml/weka/

Optimized Column-Oriented Model: A Storage and Search Efficient Representation of Medical Data

Razan Paul and Abu Sayed Md. Latiful Hoque

Department of Computer Science and Engineering,
Bangladesh University of Engineering and Technology, Dhaka 1000, Bangladesh
razanpaul@yahoo.com, asmlatifulhoque@cse.buet.ac.bd

Abstract. Medical data have a number of unique characteristics like data sparseness, high dimensionality and rapidly changing set of attributes. Entity Attribute Value (EAV) is the widely used solution to handle the above challenges of medical data, but EAV is neither storage efficient nor search efficient. In this paper, we have proposed a storage & search efficient data model: Optimized Column-Oriented Model (OCOM) for physical representation of high dimensional and sparse data as an alternative of widely used EAV. We have implemented both EAV and OCOM models in a medical data warehousing environment and performed different relational and warehouse queries on both the models. The experimental results show that OCOM is dramatically search efficient and occupy less storage space compared to EAV.

Keywords: OCOM, Sparse Data, Open Schema, EAV, Data Model.

1 Introduction

A number of exciting research challenges as described in [1] is posed by health care data that make them different from the data in other industries. Data sparseness arises because doctors perform only a few different clinical lab tests among thousands of test attributes for a patient over his lifetime. It requires frequent schema change because healthcare data need to accommodate new laboratory tests, diseases being invented every day. For the above reasons, relational data representation requires too many columns and hence the data is high dimensional.

Integrating Large-scale medical data is important for knowledge discovery. Once this knowledge is discovered, the results of such analysis can be used to define new guidelines and to improve patient care. We require an open schema data model to support dynamic schema change, sparse data, and high dimensional data. In open schema data models, logical model of data is stored as data rather than as schema, so changes to the logical model can be made without changing the schema. EAV is the widely used open schema data model to handle these challenges of data representation. However, EAV suffers from higher storage requirement and not search efficient. In this paper, we have proposed a storage and search efficient open schema data model: OCOM.

S. Khuri, L. Lhotská, and N. Pisanti (Eds.): ITBAM 2010, LNCS 6266, pp. 118–127, 2010.

Section 2 describes the related work. The overview of COM and EAV, the details organizational structure and analysis of OCOM are given in section 3. A data transformation is required to adopt the existing data suitable for data warehouse representation. The transformation is elaborated in section 4. Analytical details of performance of the proposed models are given in section 5. Section 6 offers the result and discussion. Section 7 is the conclusion.

2   Related Work

EAV [2] gives us extreme flexibility in data representation but it is not search efficient as it keeps attribute name as data in attribute column and has no tracking of how data are stored. The EAV model for phenotype data management has been given in [3]. Use of EAV for medical observation data is also found in [4], [5], [6]. The Entity-Relationship Model is proposed in [7]. Storage and querying of high dimensional sparsely populated data is proposed in [8], But this model does not keep the data in search efficient way. Agarwal et al. in [9] propose several methods for the efficient computation of multidimensional aggregates. In [10], authors proposed data cube as a relational aggregation operator generalizing group-by, crosstab, and subtotals.

3   Open Schema Data Models

3.1   Column Oriented Model (OCM)

A column-oriented model [11], [12] stores data separately for each column, so a new column can be added without changing existing data. This model has several advantages: high performance in aggregate operation on a small number of columns over many rows and we can perform various operations on a particular column values without touching other column values. OCM can represent high dimensional data but cannot handle sparse data. This model suffers from higher storage requirement to represent sparse data.

3.2   Entity-Attribute-Value Model (EAV)

EAV is   an open schema data model, which is suitable for High Dimensional and sparse data like medical data. In EAV, every fact is conceptually stored in a table, with three sets of columns: entity, an attribute, and a value for that attribute. In this design, one row actually stores a single fact. It eliminates sparse data to reduce database size and allows changing set of attributes. Moreover, EAV can represent high dimensional data, which cannot be modeled by relational model because existing RDBMS only support a limited number of columns. EAV gives us extreme flexibility but it is not search efficient as it keeps attribute name as data in attribute column and has no tracking of how data are stored.

3.3   Optimized Column-Oriented Model (OCOM)

To remove the search inefficiency problem of EAV whilst preserving its efficiency of representing High Dimensional and sparse data, we have developed a search efficient

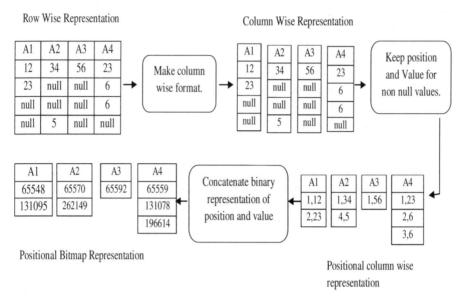

Fig. 1. Optimized Column-Oriented Model

open schema data model OCOM. This model keeps data in a search efficient way. This approach is a read-optimized representation whereas the EAV approach is write-optimized. Most of the data warehouse systems write once and read many times, so the proposed approach can serve the practical requirement of data warehouse. Figure 1 shows the transformation of sparse relational data representation to an equivalent OCOM representation. In this model, data is represented in a column wise format. The minimum amount of information that needs to be stored is the position of all non-null elements with their values in a column. Then both the position and the value are converted into a compact single integer PV by concatenating their binary representation. In OCOM, every single fact is conceptually stored with a single field: the PV.

This model maps position and value of non-null elements to p-bit and q-bit integer respectively and concatenate them to form a single compact n-bit integer PV. For medical domain, position represents patient ID and value represents various attribute of patients. This model stores every fact in sorted order of PV and the first p-bit of PV is entity. Hence, facts in this model are stored in sorted order of entity and we can perform binary search on it based on entity.

We have considered both the position and value is 16 bit. 16 bit is good enough to represent medical information, as cardinality of medical data is not high. However, it is not good enough for position, as the number of patients can be large. To handle this problem, we have developed a multilevel index structure for each attribute as shown in Figure 2. Each segment pointer table contains pointer of up to 2^{16} segments of positional data. Each segment can hold up to 2^{16} positional bitmaps. In this way, we can store facts of 2^{32} =4294967296 patients. To store value of an attribute of a

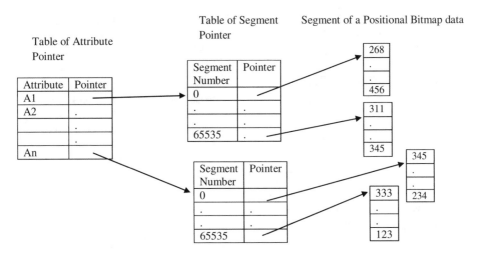

Fig. 2. Multi level index structure for OCOM

particular patient ID, this model select segment pointer table of that attribute, and find segment number = patient ID/65536. Then it finds the segment and stores the positional bitmap in that segment in sorted order of PV.

4   Data Transformation Using Domain Dictionary and Rule Base

For knowledge discovery, the medical data have to be transformed into a suitable transaction format to discover knowledge. We have addressed the problem of mapping complex medical data to items using domain dictionary and rule base. The medical data of diagnoses, laboratory results, allergies, vital signs, and etc are types of categorical, continuous numerical data, Boolean, interval, percentage, fraction and ratio. Medical domain expert have the knowledge of how to map ranges of numerical data for each attribute to a series of items. For example, there are certain conventions to consider a person is young, adult, or elder with respect to age. A set of rules is created for each continuous numerical attribute using the knowledge of medical domain experts. A rule engine is used to map continuous numerical data to items using these developed rules.

Data, for which medical domain expert knowledge is not applicable, we have used domain dictionary approach to transform these data to numerical forms. As cardinality of attributes except continuous numeric data are not high in medical domain, these attribute values are mapped integer values using medical domain dictionaries. Here the mapping process is divided in two phases. Phase 1: a rule base is constructed based on the knowledge of medical domain experts and dictionaries are constructed for attributes where domain expert knowledge is not applicable, Phase 2: attribute values are mapped to integer values using the corresponding rule base and the dictionaries.

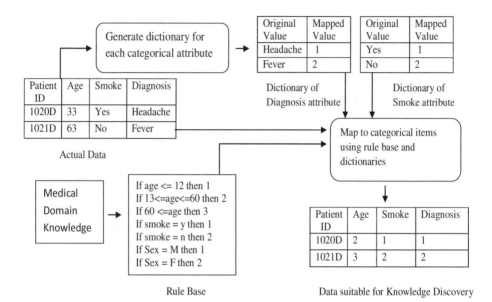

Fig. 3. Data Transformation of Medical Data

5   Storage Analysis of EAV and OCOM

Let b be the total number of blocks of observation table and k is the total number of attributes of observation table.

5.1   Analysis of Storage Capacity of EAV

Let n = total number of facts, q = Average length of attribute names, g = Average length of values. In EAV, 32 bits (4 bytes) is required to represent entity. Size of each fact in EAV is $(4 + q + g)$ bytes. Hence, the total size to hold all facts is $S = n \times (4 + q + g)$ bytes.

5.2   Space Complexity of Medical Domain Dictionaries and Rule Base

Let C_i = cardinality of ith categorical medical attribute, L_i = average length of ith attribute value, u = number of categorical attributes. Integer codes of categorical attribute values, shown in data transformation, are not stored explicitly and the index of attribute is the code. Domain Dictionary Storage of ith attribute is $C_i \times L_i$ bytes. Total domain dictionaries storage (SD) is $\sum_{i=1}^{u} \left(C_i \times L_i \right)$ bytes. If the size of rule base storage is R, the dictionary and rule base storage (SDR) is $\sum_{i=1}^{u} \left(C_i \times L_i \right) + R$ bytes.

5.3 Analysis of Storage Capacity of OCOM

In OCOM, 16 bits is required to represent entity and 16 bits is required to represent value individually. Size of each fact in OCOM is 32 bits = 4 bytes. Let, n = total number of facts, m = total number of facts in a block, w = word size (bytes). Total number of blocks is $\lceil n/m \rceil$. If word size is less than or equal to size of each fact, the number of words per fact is $\lceil 32/w \rceil$. The number of words per block is $\lceil (m \times \lceil 32/w \rceil) \rceil$, the size of each block is $w \left(\lceil (m \times \lceil 32/w \rceil) \rceil \right)$ and hence the total size to hold all facts is $S = \lceil n/m \rceil \times w \times \left(\lceil (m \times \lceil 32/w \rceil) \rceil \right)$. If word size is greater than size of each fact, the number of facts per word is $\lceil w/32 \rceil$, the number of words per block is $\lceil (m / \lceil w/32 \rceil) \rceil$, the size of each block is $w \left(\lceil (m / \lceil w/32 \rceil) \rceil \right)$ and hence the size to hold all facts is $\lceil n/m \rceil \times w \times \left(\lceil (m / \lceil w/32 \rceil) \rceil \right)$. In OCOM, total size to hold all facts = storage for facts + storage for domain dictionaries and rule base

$$= \lceil n/m \rceil \times w \times \left(\lceil (m \times \lceil 32/w \rceil) \rceil \right) + \sum_{i=1}^{u} \left(C_i \times L_i \right) + R \text{ (If w <= size of fact) or}$$

$$= \lceil n/m \rceil \times w \times \left(\lceil (m / \lceil w/32 \rceil) \rceil \right) + \sum_{i=1}^{u} \left(C_i \times L_i \right) + R \quad \text{(If w > size of fact).}$$

6   Results and Discussion

The experiments were done using PC with core 2 duo processor with a clock rate of 1.8 GHz and 3GB of main memory. The operating system was Microsoft Vista and implementation language was c#. We have designed a data generator that generates all categories of random data: ratio, interval, decimal, integer, percentage etc. This data set is generated with 5000 attributes and (5-10) attributes per transaction on average. We have used highly skewed attributes in all performance evaluations to measure the performance improvement of our proposed open schema data models in worst case. For all performance measurement except storage performance, we have used 1 million transactions.

6.1   Storage Performance

Figure 4 shows the   storage space required by EAV and OCOM. The EAV occupies significantly higher amount of storage than OCOM. This is due to the data redundancy of EAV models.

6.2   Time Comparison of Projection Operations

Figure 5 shows the performance of Projection operations on various combinations of attributes. Almost same time is needed with different number of attributes in EAV, as it has to scan all the blocks whatever the number of attributes. In OCOM, it can be observed that the time requirement is proportional to the number of

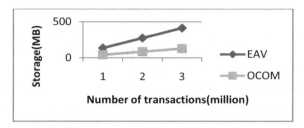

Fig. 4. Storage Performance

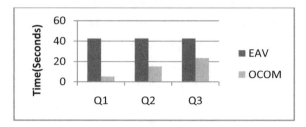

Fig. 5. Time Comparison of Projection Operations

attributes projected. This is because that the query needs to scan more number of blocks as the number of attributes increases.

6.3   Time Comparison of Multiple Predicates Select Queries

Figure 6 shows the performance of multiple predicates select queries on various combinations of attributes in three different open schema data models. In OCOM, It can be observed that the number of attributes in select queries leads to the time taken. It is because as number of attributes in select queries increases, it has to scan more number of attribute partitions. Almost same time is taken with different number of attributes in EAV as it has to scans all the blocks twice whatever the number of attributes in predicate. This experiment shows that EAV requires much higher time compared to other models. It is because that EAV has no tracking of how data are stored, so it has to scans all the blocks once to select entities and has to scan all the blocks again to retrieve the attribute values for the selected entities.

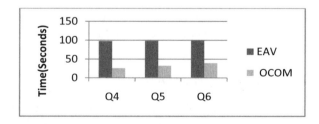

Fig. 6. Time Comparison of Select Queries

6.4   Time Comparison of Aggregate Operations

Aggregate operations compute a single value by taking a collection of values as input. Figure 7 shows the performance of various Aggregate operations on a single attribute. Time is not varied significantly from one aggregate operation to another as different aggregate operations need same number of data block access for most of the cases. Figure 7 shows EAV has taken much higher time than OCOM as it has to scan all the blocks to compute each operation. OCOM has taken almost same time to find count, min, max, average on a single attribute. This is because for all operations, it needs to scan the blocks of the attribute for which particular operation is executing.

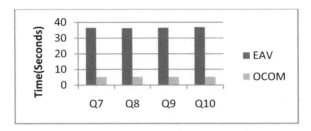

Fig. 7. Time comparison of Aggregate Operations

6.5   Time Comparison of Statistical Operations

Figure 8 shows the performance of various statistical operations on a single attribute. Time is varied significantly from one statistical operation to another as different statistical operations need different sorts of processing. This experiment shows EAV has taken much higher time compared to OCOM. It is because it has no tracking of how data are stored, so it has to scans all the blocks to compute each operation. For median, mode and standard deviation, OCOM has to scan the blocks of attribute for which particular operation is running one, two and two times respectively.

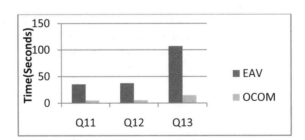

Fig. 8. Time comparison of Statistical Operations

6.6   Time Comparison of CUBE Operations

The CUBE operation is the n-dimensional generalization of group-by operator. The cube operator unifies several common and popular concepts: aggregates, group by, roll-ups and drill-downs and, cross tabs. Here No pre-computation is done for

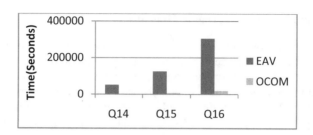

Fig. 9. Time comparison of CUBE operations

Q1: Select A_i from observation;
Q2: Select A_i, A_j, A_k from observation.
Q3: Select A_i, A_j, A_k, A_l, A_m from observation.
Q4: Select * from observation where A_i='XXX'.
Q5: Select * from observation where A_i='XXX' AND A_j='YYY'.
Q6: Select * from observation where A_i='XXX' AND A_j='YYY' AND A_k='ZZZ'.
Q7: Select AVG (A_i) from observation.
Q8: Select Max (A_i) from observation.
Q9: Select Min (A_i) from observation.
Q10: Select   Count (A_i) from observation.
Q11: Select Median (A_i) from observation.
Q12: Select Mode (A_i) from observation.
Q13: Select   Standard Deviation (A_i) from observation.
Q14: Select A_i, A_j, Max (A_m) from observation CUBE-BY (A_i, A_j)
Q15: Select A_i, A_j, A_K, Max (A_m) from observation CUBE-BY (A_i, A_j, A_k)
Q16: Select A_i, A_j, A_K, A_m, Max (A_n) from observation CUBE-BY (A_i, A_j, A_k, A_m)

aggregates at various levels and on various combinations of attributes. Figure 9 shows the performance of CUBE Operations on various combinations of attributes. It can be observed that the number of attributes in cube operations leads to the time taken as CUBE operation computes group-bys corresponding to all possible combinations of CUBE attributes. The experiment results show that EAV has taken much higher time compared to OCOM as it is not partitioned attribute wise and it has no entity index, so every search becomes full scan of all blocks. OCOM does not need to read unused attributes but does read unused values during the binary search.

7   Conclusion

EAV is a widely used solution to model data which are sparse, high dimensional and need frequently schema change, but EAV is not a search efficient data model for knowledge discovery. In this paper, we have proposed a storage and search efficient open schema data models OCOM to model high dimensional and sparse data as an alternative of EAV. We have implemented both EAV and OCOM models in a data warehousing environment and performed different relational and warehouse queries on both the models. We have achieved a query performance faster in the range of 15 to 70 compared to existing EAV model. These efficiencies arise due to binary data representation in OCOM and partition of data attribute wise where as string representation is used in EAV model. The experiment results show our proposed open schema data model is dramatically efficient in knowledge discovery operation and occupy less storage compared to widely used EAV model.

References

1. Torben, P.B., Christian, J.S.: Research Issues in Clinical Data Warehousing. In: Proceedings of the 10th International Conference on Scientific and Statistical Database Management, Capri, pp. 43–52 (1998)
2. Stead, W.W., Hammond, E.W., Straube, J.M.: A chartless record—Is it adequate? Journal of Medical Systems 7(2), 103–109 (1983)
3. Li, J., Li, M., Deng, H., Duffy, P., Deng, H.: PhD: a web database application for phenotype data management. Oxford Bioinformatics 21(16), 3443–3444 (2005)
4. Anhøj, J.: Generic design of Web-based clinical databases. Journal of Medical Internet Research 5(4), 27 (2003)
5. Brandt, C., Deshpande, A., Lu, C.: TrialDB: A Web-based Clinical Study Data Management System. In: Proceedings of the American Medical Informatics Association Annual Symposium, Washington, p. 794 (2003)
6. Nadkarni, P.M., Brandt, C., Frawley, S., et al.: Managing Attribute—Value Clinical Trials Data Using the ACT/DB Client—Server Database System. The Journal of the American Medical Informatics Association 5(2), 139–151 (1998)
7. Chen, P.P.: The entity-relationship model—toward a unified view of data. ACM Transactions on Database Systems 1(1), 9–36 (1976)
8. Hoque, A.S.M.L.: Storage and Querying of High Dimensional Sparsely Populated Data in Compressed Representation. In: Shafazand, H., Tjoa, A.M. (eds.) EurAsia-ICT 2002. LNCS, vol. 2510, pp. 418–425. Springer, Heidelberg (2002)
9. Agarwal, S., Agrawal, R., Deshpande, P., et al.: On the Computation of Multidimensional Aggregates. In: Proceedings of the 22th International Conference on Very Large Data Bases, pp. 506–521 (1996)
10. Jim, G., Surajit, C., Adam, B.: Data Cube: A Relational Aggregation Operator Generalizing Group-By, Cross-Tab and Sub-Totals. Data Mining and Knowledge Discovery 1(1), 29–53 (1997)
11. Copeland, G.P.: A decomposition storage model. In: International Conference on Management of Data, Austin, Texas, United States (1985)
12. Stonebraker, M., Abadi, D.J., Batkin, A., et al.: C-Store: A column-oriented DBMS. In: Proceedings of the 31st VLDB Conference, Trondheim, Norway (2005)

A Semantic Query Interface for the OGO Platform

José Antonio Miñarro-Giménez, Mikel Egaña Aranguren,
Francisco García-Sánchez, and Jesualdo Tomás Fernández-Breis

Facultad de Informática, Universidad de Murcia,
CP 30100 Murcia, Spain
jose.minyarro@um.es, mikel.egana.aranguren@gmail.com,
frgarcia@um.es, jfernand@um.es

Abstract. In the last years, a number of semantic biomedical systems
have been developed to store biomedical knowledge in an accessible manner. However, their practical usage is limited, since they require expertise
in semantic languages by the user, or, in the other hand, their query interfaces do not fully exploit the semantics of the knowledge represented.
Such drawbacks were present in the OGO system, a resource that semantically integrates knowledge about orthologs and human genetic diseases,
developed by our research group. In this paper, we present an extension
of the OGO system for improving the process of designing advanced
semantic queries. The query module requires the users to know and to
manage only the OGO ontology, which represents the domain knowledge,
simplifying the process of query building.

Keywords: Ontology, Semantic Web, Semantic Querying, Biomedical
Informatics.

1 Introduction

An ontology is a formalisation of a knowledge domain, a set of concepts and
their relationships, on which machines can perform automated reasoning. In the
last years, there has been an increasing interest in the development and application of ontologies in biomedical domains, in order to computationally represent
and efficiently manage biomedical knowledge. As a representative example, the
OBO Foundry community attempts to develop a set of orthogonal biomedical
ontologies to support biomedical research[1].

The Knowledge Representation (KR) technology used for building biomedical
ontologies is closely related to the Semantic Web. The Semantic Web is a next
generation web in which automated processing of information will deliver more
concise results to the user, and allow machines to perform time consuming tasks
[1]. For the Semantic Web to work, information must be codified with precise
semantics, thus in a computationally accessible manner, *via* ontologies.

---

[1] http://www.obofoundry.org/

S. Khuri, L. Lhotská, and N. Pisanti (Eds.): ITBAM 2010, LNCS 6266, pp. 128–142, 2010.

Semantic Web technologies have been increasingly used for data integration in life sciences and provide a useful framework for translational medicine (see, for instance, [3]). Different Semantic Web technologies such as RDF[2], OWL[3] and SPARQL[4] have been used for developing such semantic biological solutions. OWL, the Web Ontology Language, a W3C[5] official recommendation, is one of the most widely used ontology languages. OWL is designed to act as a standard for producing web interoperable ontologies in the Semantic Web, and it provides an optimal balance between decidability and expressive power.

The Orthology Gene Ontological (OGO) system, developed by our research group, also exploits semantic technologies to integrate life sciences information [6]. The OGO system connects data about orthologous genes and human genetic diseases, facilitating the labour of life scientists. The OGO Knowledge Base (KB) is based on a domain ontology that guides the semantic integration of the information collected from the repositories about orthology and human genetic diseases. The original implementation of the OGO system provided a keyword-based query interface and the semantic query was automatically generated. However, this query interface did not allow users to make complex queries exploiting the semantics of the domain.

Most biomedical semantic systems provide query interfaces based on powerful semantic query languages such as OWL DL or SPARQL, since such languages allow the exploitation of the semantics of the represented domain at query time, by incorporating all the restrictions modelled in the ontology in the queries. These languages are not specially difficult for users with a computing background or with some expertise in relational query languages such as SQL. However, they are currently not usable by the average biomedical researcher, who should be the final user of these semantic systems. Therefore, mechanisms for making query construction simpler for such users are required.

It has already been noted that "*the casual user is typically overwhelmed by the formal logics of the Semantic Web*" [2]. This is due to the fact that ontology users have to be familiar with [14]: (1) the ontology syntax (*e.g.* RDF, OWL), (2) some formal query language (*e.g.* SPARQL), and (3) the structure and vocabulary of the target ontology. In recent years, Controlled Natural Languages (CNL) [10] have received much attention due to their ability to reduce ambiguity in natural language. CNLs are characterised by two properties [11]: (1) their grammar is more restrictive than that of the general language, and (2) their vocabulary only contains a fraction of the words that are permissible in the general language. These restrictions aim at reducing or even eliminating both ambiguity and complexity. In recent years, the use of CNLs in the context of the Semantic Web has received much attention. Several platforms have been developed to work as either natural language ontology editors or natural language query systems. Two important examples in the first category are CNL Editor [8] (formerly OntoPath [5]) and

---

[2] http://www.w3.org/RDF

[3] http://www.w3.org/TR/owl-features

[4] http://www.w3.org/TR/rdf-sparql-query

[5] http://www.w3c.org

GINO [2]. Moreover, our research group has recently developed OWLPath [13]. Such systems rely on the existence of a grammar that guides the querying process and also constrains the expressivity of the queries, therefore not providing rich results for complex domains. As a result, we decided to extend the functionality of the OGO query interface by using the ontology to guide the users in the design of the queries, providing an interface that has the same expressivity of a semantic query language. Such extension is described in this paper.

2   The OGO System

OGO is a system based on Semantic Web technologies that integrates and stores up to date information about orthology and human genetic diseases, continuously updating it. The orthology information (clusters of ortholog genes) is collected and integrated from KOG[6], Inparanoid[7], OrthoMCL[8] and Homologene[9], reducing the heterogeneity and redundancy of such information. The data about genetic diseases is collected from OMIM[10]. The current version of the OGO system[11] contains more than 90,000 ortholog clusters, more than a million of genes, *circa* a million of proteins, approximately 16,000 human genetic disorders and more than 17,000 references to PubMed articles.

The KB is based on the OGO ontology, which imports[12] other bio-ontologies in order to organise, in classes, the information provided by individuals (orthologs, genetic diseases, *etc.*). The imported semantics can be exploited at query time. The imported bio-ontologies are listed as follows:

- Gene Ontology (GO) [7], linking ortholog genes to their molecular function, cellular component or biological process.
- Evidence Codes Ontology[13] (ECO), providing a hierarchy for classifying GOA (Gene Ontology Annotation) evidence codes [4].
- NCBI taxonomy (NCBI) [9], providing a hierarchy for the taxonomic classification of organisms.
- Relationship Ontology (RO) [12], providing a common set of relationships for bio-ontologies, to facilitate integration of the OGO system with other "RO friendly" bio-ontologies and resources.

The OGO ontology[14] (Figure 1) contains the links between orthologous genes but also provides information about other gene-related concepts like organisms, proteins and GO terms. The information about genetic diseases was integrated

---

[6] http://www.ncbi.nlm.nih.gov/COG/grace/shokog.cgi
[7] http://inparanoid.sbc.su.se/cgi-bin/index.cgi
[8] http://www.orthomcl.org/cgi-bin/OrthoMclWeb.cgi
[9] http://www.ncbi.nlm.nih.gov/sites/entrez?DB=homologene
[10] http://www.ncbi.nlm.nih.gov/sites/entrez?db=OMIM\&itool=toolbar
[11] http://miuras.inf.um.es/~ogo
[12] http://www.w3.org/TR/2009/REC-owl2-syntax-20091027
[13] http://www.berkeleybop.org/ontologies/owl/ECO
[14] http://miuras.inf.um.es/ontologies/OGO.owl

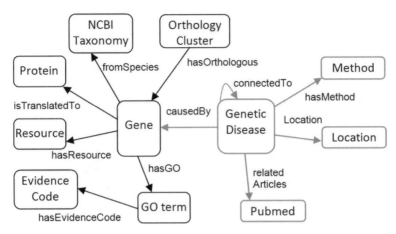

Fig. 1. The OGO ontology

with orthology information using the relationship *causedBy*. Cardinality constraints and disjoint axioms were also defined in the ontology, for example each gene can only belong to one species and also each genetic disease instance has to be caused by at least one gene.

The information was integrated using the OGO methodology [6], which requires the definition of mapping rules between the resources and the OGO ontology. These mapping rules indicate the correspondences between data fields in the source files and the concepts, properties and relations in the ontology. The rules must be defined manually as they depend on the structure of each file belonging to different repositories. The Jena Semantic Web framework[15] was used for manipulating the ontology, building the repository, executing the integration process and implementing the persistence of the model. Jena is an open source Java framework for building Semantic Web applications which provides a programmatic environment for RDF, OWL and SPARQL. The SPARQL functionality is provided by the ARQ module. Since the persistency of the KB is supported by a relational database, the ARQ module translates SPARQL queries into SQL ones in order to retrieve the information from the KB.

2.1 Keyword-Based Query Interface

The first query application interface, developed for querying the OGO repository, was based on keywords to be matched against genes or genetic diseases. Figure 2 shows this interface, which offers two different querying perspectives: orthology and genetic diseases.

The first perspective allows for querying using the ID or names of a gene. The results are its orthologous genes, and those can be filtered by species or the resource from which the orthologous gene was retrieved, using the check boxes. Once the keyword has been input by the user, a SPARQL query pattern (Table 1) is

---

[15] http://jena.sourceforge.net/

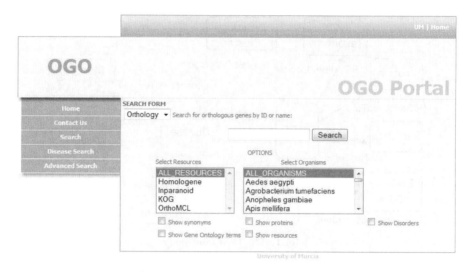

Fig. 2. Keyword-based query interface

automatically applied to create the query. The $<KEYWORD>$ corresponds to the gene name or ID, the $<ORGANISMn>$ corresponds to the URI of any of the organism in the NCBI taxonomy and the $<RESOURCEn>$ corresponds to the URI of any of the orthology repositories.

The genetic diseases perspective allows to query the repository by disease name or OMIM identifier. The orthology information can be reached through this perspective by clicking on the gene name that appears in its results. Table 2 shows the SPARQL query pattern applied to the user input, where $<KEYWORD>$ corresponds to the genetic disease name or OMIM identifier.

Table 1. Basic orthologs query pattern

```
@prefix ogo: <http://miuras.inf.um.es/ontologies/OGO.owl>.
SELECT
 ?Gene0
WHERE {
 ?Gene1 ogo:Name ?literal .
 FILTER (regex(?literal, <KEYWORD>)) .
 ?OrthologyCluster ogo:hasOrthologous ?Gene1 .
 ?OrthologyCluster ogo:hasOrthologous ?Gene0 .
 {
  ?Gene1 ogo:fromSpecies <ORGANISM1> .
  UNION
  ?Gene1 ogo:fromSpecies <ORGANISM2> .
  UNION
  ...
 }.
 {
  ?Gene1 ogo:hasResource <RESOURCE1> .
  UNION
  ?Gene1 ogo:hasResource <RESOURCE2> .
  UNION
  ...
 }.
}
```

Table 2. Genetic disease query pattern

```
@prefix ogo: <http://miuras.inf.um.es/ontologies/OGO.owl>.
SELECT
  ?Disease
WHERE {
  ?Disease ogo:Name ?literal .
  FILTER (regex(?literal, <KEYWORD>)) .
}
```

As it can be appreciated by looking at the previous query patterns, the expressivity of the queries is very limited. This was due to the fact that our initial work focused on obtaining the integrated repository and providing an user-friendly query interface for any user. Once these users have realized that the system provides semantically rich information, more powerful methods are required because queries such as "finding all genes orthologous to the gene which is translated to a particular protein" or "finding all the genes belonging to a particular species that are related to the gene that causes a certain disease" cannot be defined with these query interfaces, even though the ontological repository would answer such queries.

2.2 The Semantic Query Interface

In this section, we describe the semantic query interface that we have developed for the OGO system. The interface was developed to assist biomedical users to formulate complex semantic queries. Its architecture is depicted in Figure 3, comprising (1) the communication interface, (2) the Jena module for accessing the semantic RDF/OWL repository, (3) the query ontology, and (4) the guided search subsystem.

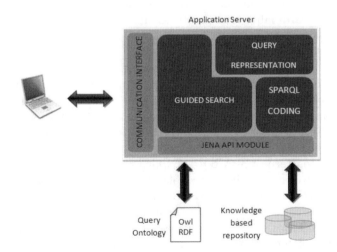

Fig. 3. The architecture of the semantic flexible query system

The web user interface was implemented using Ajax, Javascript, Servlets and JSP. The communication interface module facilitates the communication between users and the server application, *via* Web. The Jena API module allows the combination of the KB with the ontology used for guiding the definition of the semantic query. The query ontology is the same ontology that was used for defining the KB. However, the query ontology can also be customised for improving the user experience. These changes permit to define user-friendly names in the ontology elements to help users identify such elements in the query interface. It is also possible to hide concepts and relationships of the ontology that might not be interesting for querying purposes.

The modules that implement the ontology guided search method are described as follows:

- *Query representation module:* It stores the query defined by the users through the web interface. This module is responsible for ensuring the consistency of the query since it verifies that the values and conditions introduced are valid for the ontology. Thus, this module has to cooperate with the guided search module, which limits the options offered during the definition of the query, and with the SPARQL coding one, which generates the final SPARQL queries (see below).
- *Guided search module:* This module guides users throughout the different stages of the definition of the query and it is also responsible for gathering, formatting and showing the query results to the users. It assists users in the design of the query by managing the available knowledge from the query ontology. Thus, only allowed queries are defined and executed in the repository. Currently, the queries that can be defined form a subset of the potential SPARQL expressivity. The grammar describing the types of SPARQL queries that can be defined is depicted in Table 3. However, some axioms defined in the ontology, such as cardinality or disjointness, and properties such as *label* or *comment*, are not allowed to be retrieved. These elements of the ontology are excluded to simplify the query interface and thus provide users with only the elements of the ontology containing information about the domain.
- *SPARQL coding module:* This module transforms the user-defined query into an optimised SPARQL query. The process is divided in two phases. Firs, the user-defined query is translated into a SPARQL-based query, and then, the SPARQL query is optimised in order to reduce the response time. The way that users define the query condition clauses is very similar to the basic graph pattern of SPARQL, in which the subject, predicate and object of the RDF triple may be a variable. Therefore, the translation is mainly focused on identifying the proper URI of the ontology elements and satisfying the grammar rules of the query language. In terms of optimisation, we sort the different types of condition clauses to make the SPARQL queries run faster. The sorting takes into account the details of our KB (it contains few concepts and relationships compared to the number of individuals). Thus, conditions which contain less variables are planned to be executed first during the sorting phase.

Table 3. Query Grammar

Query::="SELECT" **ListVar** (**WhereClause**)?
ListVar::=**Var** (**Var**)*
WhereClause::="WHERE {" **ConditionClause** (**ConditionClause**)* "}"
ConditionClause::=[**VarCondition** | **LiteralCondition**] "."
VarCondition::=[**Var** | **Individual**] **Property** [**Var** | **Individual**]
LiteralCondition::=[**Var** | **Individual**] **Property** [**Var** | **Individual**] "."
    "FILTER (regex (" **Var** "," **Literal** "))"
Var → This term represents a variable in the query which can be matched to any concept or individual in the ontology.
Individual → This term represents a concept or individual identified by an URI in the ontology.
Property → This term represents a relationship or property identified by an URI in the ontology.
Literal → This term represents any data value defined by the user.

Fig. 4. The web interface for the design of the queries

The ontology guided search user interface is shown in Figure 4. The "Search for" text area contains the variables that are returned by the server application. By clicking on "Select Concept", the ontological tree is shown to the user, who selects the concept to add into the query. An example of the ontology tree is shown in the Figure 5. Later, each selected concept is associated with a unique variable in the query. Therefore, it is possible to select the same concept several times. These selected concepts can be removed from the "Search for" area by clicking on "Delete concept". This is only possible if the concept does not participate in any condition clause defined in the query. Figure 4 also contains the "Execute Query" and "Clear Query" buttons. The "Execute Query" button is activated once the user has added a concept in the query and allows its execution.

Once the concepts have been selected, the users have to define the conditions the data must meet to be included in the list of results. The conditions defined for the current query are shown in the "Query Requirements" area, and they can be added by clicking on "Add new requirement". When this occurs, the list of all allowed conditions for each variable node are shown. The left part of Figure 6 shows the allowed conditions for a query about the variable that represents the *Gene* concept of the ontology. The concept *Gene[0]* has some data type properties associated, such as *Name* and *Identifier*, for which the only allowed values are strings. The *Gene[0]* has also relationships that link a gene to other

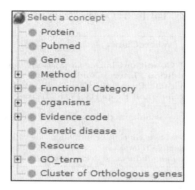

Fig. 5. Example of an ontology tree

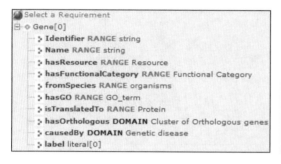

Fig. 6. Defining a requirement

ontology concepts, such as *hasResource* which associates a gene to the repository from which it was collected; the *hasFunctionalCategory* relationship relates
a gene to a Functional Category in the ontology; the *fromSpecies* relationship
identifies the organism that belongs to the gene; the *hasGO* relationship associates genes with Gene Ontology terms; and the *isTranslatedTo* relationship
associates instances of genes with instances of proteins. Finally, the *Gene[0]* par-
ticipates in some relationships but in its range, such as *hasOrthologous* which
relates a *Cluster of Orthologous genes* to its gene instances; and the *causedBy*
relationship which associates a *Genetic disease* and the genes which are involved
in. Once a property is selected, new options are offered to the user to specify
the value condition. This is shown in the right part of Figure 6. In case the
property has associated a simple data type such as a string, the user can input
the value, such as in *Name* or *Identifier* properties of the Figure 6. In case a
relationship relates the selected concept to another one and this has subclasses
or instances, the user is given the possibility of choosing one by clicking on
"Edit Object", such as in *fromSpecies* or *isTranslatedTo* relationships in Figure
6. Even more, when defining the domain of a relationship, a subclass or individual may also be selected by clicking on "Edit Subject". If the condition adds new

variable concepts in the "Query Requirement" area, then new conditions for these variables will be generated when clicking on the "Add new requirement" button. The variables which only appear in conditions but not in the "Search for" area do not appear in the results table.

Once the query is executed, the results are displayed in a table on which columns are the ontology concepts shown in the "Search for" area, and rows are the clickable and browseable results. Examples of such output are shown in Figures 7 and 8, on Section 3.

3   Query Examples

This section describes how advanced semantic queries can be designed and executed in the OGO system using the new query interface. In previous sections, we mentioned two queries that could not be formulated with the previous interface: (1) Finding all genes orthologous to a gene which is translated to the protein "NP_008816.3" protein; and (2) finding all the genes belonging to a particular species that are related to the gene that causes a certain disease.

The first query illustrates how to obtain orthology information without using gene names. The second query shows how translational bioinformatics can be done with the semantic integration of the repository. It also shows how semantic query languages can be used for retrieving the suitable instances by filtering the repository results with relationships or properties of ontology concepts. Each example can be defined in a single query and therefore researchers can obtain the suitable results in one step avoiding querying several repositories and manually integrating the information.

3.1   Finding All Genes Orthologous to a Gene Which Is Translated to the Protein "NP_008816.3"

Table 4 shows the representation of the query after the selection of the concepts and properties in the user interface. In this query, we want to retrieve all the instances of *Gene* that belong to the same cluster of orthologous genes. Such cluster must contain a gene that is translated into the protein "NP_008816.3". This query is translated into the following conditions: (1) A gene, which is represented by the variable *Gene[1]*, is translated to the *Protein[2]*; (2) the variable *Protein[2]* has the property *Name* with the "NP_008816.3" string value; (3) the

Table 4. Query one: Find all genes orthologous to the gene which is translated into "NP_008816.3" Protein

Search for:
   Gene[0]
Query requirements:
   Gene[1]→is translated to→Protein[2]
   Protein[2]→Name→"NP_008816.3"
   Cluster of orthologous genes[3]→Has Orthologous→Gene[1]
 	
   Cluster of orthologous genes[3]→Has Orthologous→Gene[0]

variable *Gene[1]* belongs to a cluster of orthologous genes, which is identified
by the variable *Cluster of orthologous genes[2]*; and finally, another variable of a
gene concept, that is called *Gene[0]*, belongs to the same cluster variable, *Cluster
of orthologous genes[2]*. The [i] suffixes indicate that they refer to different instances among requirements. For instance, the two Gene instances *Gene[0]* and
Gene[1] refer to different instances but *Cluster of orthologous genes[2]* refers to
the same instance.

Therefore, the user defines the query without knowing the full URIs and the
amount of manual typing is minimised, thus reducing the possibility of making
mistakes. The corresponding automatically generated SPARQL query is shown
in Table 5. For the query generation, the "Search for" and "Query requirements"
areas are changed into SELECT and WHERE SPARQL clauses. Each concept and
property graphically selected are identified in the ontology by means of its URI and
are constrained by the corresponding condition clauses in the WHERE area.

Table 5. Query one in SPARQL

```
@prefix ogo: <http://miuras.inf.um.es/ontologies/OGO.owl>.
SELECT
  ?Gene_0
WHERE {
  ?Protein_2 ogo:Name ?literal_4 .
  FILTER (regex(?literal_4, "NP_008816.3")) .
  ?Gene_1 ogo:isTranslatedTo ?Protein_2 .
  ?Cluster_of_Orthologous_genes_3 ogo:hasOrthologous ?Gene_1 .
  ?Cluster_of_Orthologous_genes_3 ogo:hasOrthologous ?Gene_0 .
}
```

The left-side of Figure 7 shows part of the results obtained for this query. It
contains the identifiers of all gene instances that belong to the same cluster of
orthologous genes and this cluster has a gene that is translated into the protein
"*NP_008816.3*". The interface allows us to navigate through the results and
view their properties. An example of this navigation is shown on the right-side
of Figure 7: the information about the human gene "*atbf1*", which is translated
into the protein "*NP_008816.3*", is shown.

3.2 Finding All the Orthologous Genes of the Gene That Causes Prostate Cancer and belong to *Rattus Norvegicus*

The representation of this query in the interface is shown in Table 6. To define
this query, we first added the variables *Genetic disease[0]*, which corresponds
to the Genetic disease concept, and *Gene[1]*, which corresponds to the Gene
concept. We then linked *Genetic disease[0]* to *Gene[2]* through the *caused by*
relationship, and we defined the value "prostate cancer, susceptibility to" for
its property *Name*. Finally, the orthologous genes were obtained by means of
the definition of the requirements for *Cluster of orthologous genes[3]*, *Gene[1]*

Fig. 7. Query one: Results

Table 6. Query Two: Find all genes orthologous to the genes that cause the Prostate cancer disease and belongs to the *Rattus norvegicus* organism

> **Search for:**
>   Genetic disease[0]
>   Gene[1]
> **Query requirements:**
>   Gene[1]→from species→Rattus norvegicus
>   Genetic disease[0]→caused by→ Gene[2]
>   Genetic disease[0]→Name→"prostate cancer, susceptibility to"
>   Cluster of orthologous genes[3]→Has Orthologous→Gene[2]
>
>   Cluster of orthologous genes[3]→Has Orthologous→Gene[1]

Table 7. Query 2 in SPARQL

```
@prefix ncbi: <http://um.es/ncbi.owl>.
@prefix ogo: <http://miuras.inf.um.es/ontologies/OGO.owl>.
SELECT
 ?Genetic_disease_0
 ?Gene_1
WHERE {
 ?Gene_1 ogo:fromSpecies ncbi:NCBI_10116 .
 ?Genetic_disease_0 ogo:Name ?literal_4 .
 FILTER (regex(?literal_4,"Prostate cancer, susceptibility to")) .
 ?Genetic_disease_0 ogo:causedBy ?Gene_2 .
 ?Cluster_of_Orthologous_genes_3 ogo:hasOrthologous ?Gene_2 .
 ?Cluster_of_Orthologous_genes_3 ogo:hasOrthologous ?Gene_1 .
}
```

and *Gene[2]*, as in the first example. Table 7 shows the SPARQL query that is automatically generated for this particular query. Some results are shown in Figure 8. The left column contains the identification of the *Genetic diseases*, and the right column shows the names of the genes that belong to *Rattus norvegicus* and are orthologous to the genes that cause the genetic disease.

Genetic disease[0]	Gene[1]
104155, prostate cancer, susceptibility to, zinc finger homeobox 3	pex12, 116718
	rgd1560268, zfhx3.predicted, 307829
	rgd1563022, zfhx4.predicted, 310250
600020, neurofibrosarcoma, prostate cancer, susceptibility to, max-interacting protein 1	clec5a, 679787
	ensrnog00000026306, loc684510
	loc689617, 689617
	loc689629, 689629
	max, mgc124611, 60661
	mxi.wr, mxi1, 25701
	tgap1, 294892

Fig. 8. Query Two: Results

4 Conclusions

Providing usable and flexible mechanisms for querying biomedical semantic repositories is fundamental for the success of the application of the Semantic Web in life sciences. To date, many efforts have been invested on the semantic representation and integration of biomedical data, so very interesting semantic repositories have been generated. However, most of the currently available systems have problems for facilitating the definition of expressive, semantic queries. This is due to the fact that they require knowing complex languages such as SPARQL or limit the expressivity of the queries, as it happens with most CNLs.

We have experienced ourselves this problem in the development of the OGO project, which has generated a large integrated KB of biomedical knowledge relating orthology information with human genetic diseases. However, the query and exploitation mechanisms of such knowledge and data were limited in the initial version of the OGO system. To overcome this flaw, we have presented in this paper a system that guides users in the design of powerful semantic queries. Our main goal was to facilitate the exploitation of our semantic repositories by biomedical researchers.

In this work, we present our initial results, moving the complexity of using the OGO system from mastering semantic languages such as SPARQL to working with a domain ontology. Although the researchers need to know the ontology and its structure, they do not have to define the query manually. In fact, using a SPARQL-based query interface does not only require expertise in SPARQL but also expertise in the underlying ontology. Our system reduces the need to know precisely the concepts and how they are related since these are displayed to the user during the query definition. In addition, the need to be an expert on SPARQL is eliminated because the interface guides the definition of the query by enabling/disabling options. This query design assistance is performed by using the OGO ontology. Consequently, the learning curve for executing advanced queries on the semantic repository is reduced. Even more, the interface avoids the misuse of the relations and properties between concepts in the ontology and typos in queries. Therefore, the interface guides the researchers for defining the query properly.

An interesting property of this query module is the fact that it is a generic solution. Although it has been developed for and applied to the OGO system, it is possible to use it for any semantic system that uses SPARQL-based queries. This is possible because we would only need to change the ontology that guides the process and to connect the system to the new semantic repository. We are applying it to our repository of clinical archetypes. We would like to allow users to define semantic queries without noticing that they are using an ontology, by reducing the number of clicks and selections for adding a particular ontological entity or requirement into the query. We are also exploring the possibility of using a reduced version of the OGO ontology for guiding the process due to the overload produced by handling large amounts of data managed and transferred during the design of the query. The ontology can also be simplified to constraint the queries to a particular set of concepts and properties. Furthermore, the definition of labels in the ontology concepts, relations and properties would make it possible to show alternative names of these entities, so friendlier names would be shown to the users and multilingual interfaces could be easily developed.

Acknowledgements

This work has been funded by the Spanish Ministry for Science and Education through grant TSI2007-66575-C02-02 and the Comunidad Autónoma de la Región de Murcia through grant BIO-TEC 06/01-0005. JA Miñarro is supported by the Fundación Séneca and the Servicio de Empleo y Formación through the grant 07836/BPS/07.

References

1. Berners-Lee, T., Hendler, J., Lassila, O.: The Semantic Web. Scientific American 284(5), 34–43 (2001)
2. Bernstein, A., Kaufmann, E.: GINO - A Guided Input Natural Language Ontology Editor. In: Cruz, I., Decker, S., Allemang, D., Preist, C., Schwabe, D., Mika, P., Uschold, M., Aroyo, L.M. (eds.) ISWC 2006. LNCS, vol. 4273, pp. 144–157. Springer, Heidelberg (2006)
3. Bodenreider, O., Sahoo, S.S.: Semantic Web for Translational Biomedicine: Two Pilot Experiments. In: Proceedings of the AMIA Summit on Translational Bioinformatics, vol. 148 (2008)
4. Camon, E., Magrane, M., Barrell, D., Lee, V., Dimmer, E., Maslen, J., Binns, D., Harte, N., Lopez, R., Apweiler, R.: The Gene Ontology Annotation (GOA) Database: sharing knowledge in Uniprot with Gene Ontology. Nucleic Acids Res. 32, D262–D266 (2004)
5. Jiménez-Ruiz, E., Berlanga, R., Nebot, V., Sanz, I.: OntoPath: A Language for Retrieving Ontology Fragments. In: Meersman, R., Tari, Z. (eds.) OTM 2007, Part I. LNCS, vol. 4803, pp. 897–914. Springer, Heidelberg (2007)

6. Miñarro Giménez, J., Madrid, M., Fernández-Breis, J.: OGO: an ontological approach for integrating knowledge about orthology. BMC Bioinformatics 10, S10–S13 (2009)
7. GO, C.: Gene Ontology: tool for the unification of biology. Nature Genetics 23, 25–29 (2000)
8. Namgoong, H., Kim, H.G.: Ontology-based Controlled Natural Language Editor Using CFG with Lexical Dependency. In: Aberer, K., Choi, K.-S., Noy, N., Allemang, D., Lee, K.-I., Nixon, L.J.B., Golbeck, J., Mika, P., Maynard, D., Mizoguchi, R., Schreiber, G., Cudré-Mauroux, P. (eds.) ASWC 2007 and ISWC 2007. LNCS, vol. 4825, pp. 351–364. Springer, Heidelberg (2007)
9. Sayers, E., Barrett, T., Benson, D., Bolton, E., Bryant, S., Canese, K., Chetvernin, V., Church, D., Dicuccio, M., Federhen, S., Feolo, M., Helmberg, W., Geer, L., Kapustin, Y., Landsman, D., Lipman, D., Lu, Z., Madden, T., Madej, T., Maglott, D., Marchler-Bauer, A., Miller, V., Mizrachi, I., Ostell, J., Panchenko, A., Pruitt, K., Schuler, G., Sequeira, E., Sherry, S., Shumway, M., Sirotkin, K., Slotta, D., Souvorov, A., Starchenko, G., Tatusova, T., Wagner, L., Wang, Y., Wilbur, J., Yaschenko, E., Ye, J.: Database resources of the National Center for Biotechnology Information. Nucleic acids research (2009)
10. Schwitter, R.: A controlled natural language layer for the semantic web. In: Zhang, S., Jarvis, R.A. (eds.) AI 2005. LNCS (LNAI), vol. 3809, pp. 425–434. Springer, Heidelberg (2005)
11. Smart, P.: Controlled natural languages and the semantic web. Tech. rep., School of Electronics and Computer Science, University of Southampton, Technical Report ITA/P12/SemWebCNL (2008)
12. Smith, B., Ceusters, W., Klagges, B., Kohler, J., Kumar, A., Lomax, J., Mungall, C., Neuhaus, F., Rector, A., Rosse, C.: Relations in Biomedical Ontologies. Genome Biology 6, R:46 (2005)
13. Valencia-García, R., García-Sánchez, F., Castellanos-Nieves, D., Fernández-Breis, J.: OWLPath: An OWL Ontology-Guided Query Editor. IEEE Transactions on Systems, Man, and Cybernetics - Part A: Systems and Humans (2010), doi:10.1109/TSMCA.2010.2048029
14. Wang, C., Xiong, M., Zhou, Q., Yu, Y.: PANTO: A Portable Natural Language Interface to Ontologies. In: Franconi, E., Kifer, M., May, W. (eds.) ESWC 2007. LNCS, vol. 4519, pp. 473–487. Springer, Heidelberg (2007)

BioMedical Information Retrieval: The BioTracer Approach

Heri Ramampiaro*

Department of Computer and Information Science
Norwegian University of Science and Technology (NTNU)
N-7491, Trondheim, Norway
heri@idi.ntnu.no

Abstract. With the large amount of biomedical information available today, providing a good search tool is vital. Such a tool should not only be able to retrieve the sought information, but also to filter out irrelevant documents, while giving the relevant ones the highest ranking. Focusing on biomedical information, the main goal of this work has been to investigate how to improve the ability for a system to find and rank relevant documents. To achieve this, we apply a series of information retrieval techniques to search in biomedical information and combine them in an optimal manner. These techniques include extending and using well-established information retrieval (IR) similarity models like the Vector Space Model (VSM) and BM25 and their underlying scoring schemes, and allowing users to affect the ranking according to their view of relevance. The techniques have been implemented and tested in a proof-of-concept prototype called BioTracer, extending a Java-based open source search engine library. The results from our experiments using the TREC 2004 Genomic Track collection seem promising. Our investigation have also revealed that involving the user in the search will indeed have positive effects on the ranking of search results, and that the approaches used in BioTracer can be used to meet the user's information needs.

Keywords: Biomedical information retrieval, evaluation.

1 Introduction

The continuous increase in the amount of available biomedical information has resulted in a higher demands for and on biomedical information retrieval (IR) systems. While their use has helped researchers in the field to stay updated on recent literature, many of the existing search systems tend to be either too restrictive – i.e., low recall, or too broad – i.e., low precision, in terms of the returned results. For this reason, we believe there is still a need to improve existing search systems, especially with respect to retrieval performance, such as maximising the values of both precision and recall.

---

* This work was partially done while the author was on sabbatical at the Dept. of Computer Science, University of California, Irvine.

S. Khuri, L. Lhotská, and N. Pisanti (Eds.): ITBAM 2010, LNCS 6266, pp. 143–157, 2010.

1.1 Challenges

From the information retrieval point of view, the challenges in retrieving biomedical information, such as MEDLINE[1] abstracts, are many. First, as in most scientific domains, there is a wide use of domain-specific terminology [14]. Therefore, it might be hard to offer a unified method for indexing and retrieving biomedical information. Second, the mixture of (natural) English terms and biomedical-specific terms can pose problems due to high term ambiguity. A single word can have different meanings [4]. This may in turn result in challenges for traditional IR methods, such as thesaurus-based extension of queries, as well as identifying relevant documents. For this reason, there is a strong need for word sense disambiguation, which is not easy, and is in itself an area of active research [4]. To illustrate, the term "*SOS*" normally refers to "urgent appeal for help", but it could also mean the gene symbol "*SOS*", short for "*Son of sevenless*"[2]. Third, one of the problems with biomedical information is the lack of widely recognised terminology standards. New names and terms are created every time a biologist discovers a new gene or other important biological entities, and there often exist several (inconsistent) typographical/lexical variants [14]. That authors also normally have their own writing style [17] further worsens the situation. Fourth, partly as a result of the existence of several term variants, important words and symbols suitable for indexing have often low occurrence frequency, and many of terms appear only once in the entire document collection. While this may, in some cases, be useful since the discrimination effectiveness is often inversely proportional with the word's document frequency, this may also mean high data sparseness, which would, in turn, have negative effects on the retrieval performance [3].

In summary, current biomedical IR systems have to deal with heterogeneous and possibly inconsistent information. This makes it challenging to apply "standard" text IR methods. With static document collection – i.e., no valuable changes over time, the above characteristics would be less problematic. However in recent years, approximately 1000 new citation records are added to MEDLINE every day, making it less straightforward to handle for IR systems. In addition, there is a challenge to measure relevance. While establishing the notion of relevance based on, for example, the vector space model [3, 5, 20] is well-known and works very well for traditional (text) IR, this is not necessarily the case within biomedical IR, mainly because of the characteristics described above. As a result, the notion of relevance must be examined with more care, knowing that for a specific query, what is relevant for one biologist may not necessarily be relevant for another.

1.2 Objectives and Contributions

As can be inferred from the above discussion, we must provide a generic biomedical IR system that can be *adapted* to meet different information needs. A basic requirement for such a system is that it must address the fact that users often

---

[1] MEDLINE is a trade mark of the US National Library of Medicine. See http://www.nlm.nih.gov/pubs/factsheets/medline.html

[2] See http://www.wormbase.org/db/gene/ gene?name=WBGene00004947;class=Gene

have their own view of relevance. Moreover, the heterogeneity of biomedical information has made it important to have a customised system. This means a system that (1) allows the user to specify relevant documents from the returned search results through user relevant feedback (URF), and (2) allows us to specify the similarity/language model and the importance of specific parts in a document. From this point of view, the main objective of this work is to investigate information retrieval methods that provide the best ranking of relevant results. More specifically, the main contribution of this work is improving existing similarity models, such as the BM25 model, by the combination of applying *boolean queries*, *wildcard queries* and *query – documents correlation factor*. We provide an extensive evaluation of our method based on known evaluation principles and a proof-of-concept prototype implementing the method. We also show that we can achieve the improvement without using controlled vocabulary such as MeSH [15].

The remainder of this paper is organised as follows. Section 2 describes the approach we have applied in this work. Then, in Section 3 we present and discusses the results from testing the method and the prototype. Section 4 discusses relation to other work, and finally, in Section 5 we summarise the paper and present future work.

2   The Approach

2.1   Choosing Text Operations

Applying text operations in information retrieval is a process of choosing candidate words or tokens to index [3, 5]. Consequently, they are crucial and can contribute to increase our confidence that the document is indeed relevant to the query. Tokenization and stemming are examples of such operations. While tokenization is straightforward for general English text, this is not necessarily the case with biomedical information due to the characteristics described in Section 1. Existing empirical studies on tokenizing biomedical texts further emphasise this [11, 21].

Now, both of these studies suggest applying conditional stemming as part of the normalization process after the tokenization process. Stemming means that we only index the root or the *stem* of a specific term, while at the same time being able to search all grammatical variants of that term – e.g., `activate` versus variants like `activates, activated` and `activating`. Based on the results from [11, 21], we believe stemming would work if it is customised to biomedical texts. However, because the benefit versus cost of stemming is often debatable [3, 5], especially in applications like ours, we chose to compare the effects of the use against omitting stemming. Our conclusion is that stemming did not give significant benefits in terms of retrieval performance. Further, for some types of queries it could change the semantic or meaning of the query. For example, a query to find all proteins that are *activated* by a specific protein could also include a query finding all proteins that *activate* the actual protein. This would clearly be a different biological process. Ideally, conditional stemming should take such semantic differences into account, but this is beyond the scope of this work.

So instead of stemming, we considered the use of *wildcard queries*. With a wildcard query, we can choose a specific query term as a prefix. Then, we extend the original query with all terms in the index that have the same prefix. For example, a query with `ferroportin*`, will find articles where `ferroportin1` and `ferroportin-1` occur, given that they are in the collection vocabulary or index. From our perspective, this is useful since it, as opposed to stemming, gives the users the freedom to choose when to extend the queries with the term variants. Our experiments also show its usefulness in terms of good retrieval performance.

2.2 Finding Optimal Scoring Scheme towards Optimal Document Rankings

To further address some of the challenges in Section 1, a good ranking method is needed. A sensible question is, thus, what scoring schemes are suitable? Existing scoring schemes are good for general purposes. However, as they are mainly developed for general texts (in natural languages), they may not necessarily meet our needs with biomedical information. When developing our method and prototype, we investigated several different schemes and used these as a starting point towards a more improved scheme. In addition to designating suitable ranking models, we also try to find out how we can influence the ranking by *boosting important parts* in the document and *constraining documents* based on their query matching degree.

Choosing Ranking Models. Several ranking or similarity models have been proposed over the years. One of the earliest, proposed by Salton and Buckley [20] was the Vector Space Model (VSM). This is a similarity model based on cosine similarity between a specific query and the documents in the collection. Basically, the idea is that for all documents in the collection that contain the terms in the query, a ranking is produced by measuring the cosine of the angle between the query and the document vectors. For general text, it has been shown that this model gives good retrieval performance [3]. Because VSM is one of the most used models, we applied it as a baseline for our experiments. In addition, we implemented an extension based on Lucene[3] [8] .

Another similarity model that has been increasingly popular in information retrieval is the Okapi BM25 [19]. In contrast to the VSM, BM25 is a probability-based approach. As with VSM, it has been shown to be effective on general text retrieval [5]. This is also partly why we decided to implement it in this work. Moreover, we want to find out how it performs when used in a highly scientific domain such as the biomedical domain. This means that we first implemented the baseline model as an extension to Lucene. Then, as shown below, we extended it to take into account that parts of the documents have different boosts, which will, as a result, also affect the way the search results are ranked.

Further, in order to be able to compare their performances when using biomedical information, we also implemented Lemur TF-IDF [25], and Divergence From Randomness (DFR) BM25 [2]. These are models that are similar to the BM25

---

[3] See: http://lucene.apache.org/java/docs.

model in that they are probability-based [2, 19, 25]. Due to the limited space available, we refer to the literature for detailed information on how the Lemur TF-IDF and DFR BM25 models are built. Scoring with an extended BM25 is elaborated later in this section.

Boosting Specific Document Part. Boosting specific parts in a document is one way to specify how important one part in a document is, compared to others. By defining this importance, we implicitly specify how the documents in the search results should be ranked. A document part can be a structural part such as the title or the abstract, or it can be specific sentences or terms. Boosting structural parts of documents is not new, per se, and previous studies have shown that information retrieval systems may benefit from exploiting document structures [18, 23].

By default, we perform search on both the *"title"* and the *"abstract"* fields of a document. These fields can be given boosts during index time or search time. Now, we can assume that a title is often chosen to best describe the content of a document. As such, terms in a title can readily be assumed important, and thus given a higher weight than those in other places in the document - e.g., in the abstract. Our experiments have shown that weighting the *"title"* field twice as much as *"abstract"* yields best ranking. Another advantage is that by having different weights for these fields, we also account for the fact that many of MEDLINE documents may only contain a title and no abstract. With the same weight, documents without an abstract would automatically be placed longer down in the list of results, independent of their relevance.

In addition to index time boosting, specific terms can be given higher boosts than other terms during search time. The main advantage of this is that terms that a user considers more important than other terms can be given additional weight, in addition to their statistical information, such as term frequency (tf) and document frequency (df). As an example, say we want to find all articles describing the function of the protein "ferroportin1". To do do this, we could compose a query as `ferroportin1^2.0 protein function`. This tells our search engine that we would like to weight "ferroportin1" as twice as much as the "protein" and "function".

Constraining Documents Based on Their Query Matching Degree

Preliminaries: In general, a document can be given a score based on its similarity to the query - i.e.,

$$Score(q, d_j) = sim(q, d_j) = \sum_{i \in q} w_{ij} \cdot w_{iq}, \tag{1}$$

Here we assume that $\overrightarrow{d_j} = (w_{1j}, w_{2j}, .., w_{sj}), w_{ij} \geq 0$ is the vector of term weights for d_j and $\overrightarrow{q} = (w_{1q}, w_{2q}, .., w_{sq}), w_{iq} \geq 0$ for a query q, where s is the total number of terms in the index.

Now, assume d_j consists of n fields f_{kj}, $k = 1, 2, ..., n$. Taking the boosting values into account, we get

$$\overrightarrow{d_j^*} = \sum_{k=1}^{n} \beta_k \cdot \overrightarrow{f_{kj}}, \tag{2}$$

where β_k denotes the boosting value for field f_{kj}. This means that our special case can be defined as $\vec{d_j^*} = 2.0 \cdot \vec{f_{1j}} + 1.0 \cdot \vec{f_{2j}}$, where f_{1j} and f_{2j} is the title and abstract field, respectively.

Using the Okapi BM25 model [19], each term in d_j and q will have the following weights w_{ij} and w_{iq}, respectively:

$$w_{ij} = \log\left(\frac{N - df_i + 0.5}{df_i + 0.5}\right) \cdot \frac{(k_1 + 1)tf_{ij}}{K + tf_{ij}} \text{ and } w_{iq} = \frac{(k_3 + 1)tf_{iq}}{k_3 + tf_{iq}}, \tag{3}$$

where $K = k_1((1 - b) + b(L_{d_j}/L_{avg}))$, N is the total number of document in the collection, df_i is the document frequency – i.e., the number documents in the collection that a term t_i occurs in, tf_{ij} is the frequency of a term t_i within d_j, L_{d_j} is the length of d_j – i.e., the number of terms in d_j, L_{avg} is the average document length, while k_1, k_3 and b are tuning constants with default values 1.2, 2.0. 0.75, respectively[4].

Now, let w_{ikj} be the weight of a term in f_{ij} of d_j^*. Then, applying this on Eq. 3, we get [18]:

$$w_{ikj} = \log\left(\frac{N - df_t + 0.5}{df_t + 0.5}\right) \cdot \frac{(k_1 + 1)\beta_k tf_{ij}}{K + \beta_k tf_{ij}}, \tag{4}$$

where $K = k_1((1 - b) + b(L_{d_j}/L_{avg}))$.

The query-document correlation factor: In the attempt to improve the ranking of relevant documents, we have added a new factor based on the degree of query matching. The idea is to add a scoring factor based on how well a document matches a query. We call this constraining documents based on their query matching degree, or simply *query-document correlation factor*. Such a constraining processes is in itself not new. Lucene allows a form of document constraining, too [8]. In our approach, however, we apply a slightly modified factor. In addition, we combine it with the similarity model BM25 [19]. To our knowledge, using document query correlation factor with BM25 is new.

Note that this factor does not directly help to increase the *overall* retrieval precision or recall, but it is meant to influence the ranking of already retrieved results. Its main goal is to maximise the number of relevant documents in the top-k hits of the search results.

Inspired by the scoring scheme in Lucene [8], we extended the original BM25 scoring equation by adding a document-query correlation factor, called $\Gamma(q, d_j)$ for a query q and a document d_j. This factor is calculated based on how many terms in q are found in d_j, and is proportional to the overlap between q and d_j. In our approach, $\Gamma(q, d_j)$ is computed as follows:

$$\Gamma(q, d_j) = \left(\frac{n_{over}(q, d_j)}{max_l \, n_{over}(q, d_l)}\right)^\theta = \left(\frac{\sum_{i=1}^n n_{over}(q, f_{ij})}{max_l \, n_{over}(q, d_l)}\right)^\theta \tag{5}$$

Here θ is a natural number, $n_{over}(q, d_j)$ is the number of terms in q that overlaps with document d_j, while for all documents in the result set, $max_l \, n_{over}(q, d_l)$ is the maximum n_{over} for the retrieved documents.

---

[4] The value was set in accordance with the recommendation by Robertson and Jones [19].

Formally, $n_{over}(q, d_j)$ is defined as follows: Assume that t_i is a term index, $i = 0.1, ..., s$, and s is the total number of terms in the index, i.e., $S = \{t_0.t_1, .., t_s\}$ is the set of all distinct terms in the index. The overlap between a document d_j and q is defined as $\forall t \in S \mid t \in d_j \bigcap q$, $n_{over}(q, d_j) = |d_j \bigcap q|$.

Studying the effect of the factor Γ on the retrieval results and the overall evaluation result, we observed that with a small value of θ, the factor is too dominating and thus it has unwanted effects on the ranking – i.e., relevant documents come too late in the result lists. Similarly, with a big value, θ will be too restrictive and the factor will have bad influence on the ranking. Therefore, the value of θ has to be chosen carefully. After executing several experiments, the resulting optimal value of θ is 4. This means that $\theta = 4$ gave the overall best retrieval result.

Using this, Eq. 2 and Eq. 4, the extension of the similarity score from Eq. 1 can now be computed as:

$$Score(q, d_j) = \Gamma(q, d_j) \cdot sim(q, d_j^*) = \Gamma(q, d_j) \cdot \sum_{\forall i \mid t_i \in q} w_{ikj} \cdot w_{iq} \qquad (6)$$

2.3 Applying Boolean Query with BM25

As for the Vector Space Model [20], BM25 was originally designed for keyword-based queries [19]. However, to be able to restrict the search results, thus filtering out unwanted hits, we wanted to investigate the effect of using boolean operations in combination with the BM25. Therefore, we implemented our prototype to allow users to search with boolean operations AND, OR and NOT in combination with the BM25 similarity model.

The boolean query model was implemented in one of the earliest search engines, but is still used today [3, 5]. However, the original model has been seen to be too limited for several reasons. First, it does not rank the retrieved results based on relevance to the query, and retrieves only results that exactly match the query. To address this problem, we investigated the effects of combining boolean queries with BM25. The benefit is that, we can filter the search results based on the boolean operations in the query, and at the same time rank them based on BM25 relevance ranking model. Second, a general criticism against boolean query usage is that users might be unwilling or even lacking the ability to compose this type of query. While we recognise that this is a valid concern, we still believe a system has to provide the possibility of processing boolean queries. In fact, studying a "typical day" pubmed query log [10] with aprox. 3 million queries shows that 36.5 % of the queries were boolean queries. Although many of these queries might be computer generated – e.g. by automatic query extension, in our opinion, this is a strong enough motivation for investigating the effects of boolean queries.

Moreover, although boolean queries do pose some challenges when it comes to finding all relevant documents from the collections, our experiments (see also Section 3.2) has shown that we can improve the average top-100 precision with a 17 % increase compared to the baseline BM25. This means that boolean queries combined with BM25 can have good effect on search precision.

2.4   User Relevant Feedback (URF)

As can be inferred by our previous discussion, there are many ways to involve the user in influencing the ranking of documents. Involving the user through user relevant feedback has been around for a while within traditional and multimedia information retrieval. However, within the biomedical domain it seems still missing. A challenge here is to choose the right strategy. In our work, we have chosen to investigate the use of URF based on the scoring scheme suggested by Robertson and Sparck Jones [19]. In addition, we apply the extended BM25 as described earlier. That is, we also extended the original model with the document-query similarity factor $\Gamma(q, d)$. The scoring scheme equation is similar to the one in Eq. 6, but now the term weight includes the relevance information added by the users. Based on the ideas of Robertson and Sparck Jones [19] and Eq. 4, this weight can be expressed by

$$w_{ikj} = \log \left(\frac{(r + 0.5)(N - n - R + r + 0.5))}{((n - r + 0.5)(R - r + 0.5))} \right) \cdot \frac{(k_1 + 1)\beta_k \mathrm{tf}_{ij}}{K + \beta_k \mathrm{tf}_{ij}}, \qquad (7)$$

where $K = k_1((1 - b) + b(L_d/L_{avg}))$, r is the number of retrieved documents being relevant and R is the number of relevant documents in the collection for a specific query.

Here, the value of R can be derived from the users' click through information in the query log. Click through information may work, in this respect, as relevance judgement information in that we can assuming that all documents that a user has clicked are relevant to a specific query [5]. To be able to evaluate this approach, we simulated the user relevant feedback process using the relevance information from the test collection.

3   Evaluation

3.1   Prototype Implementation

In order to test out our ideas, we have implemented a proof-of-the-concept prototype, called BioTracer. Instead of re-inventing the wheel, we decided to use existing open source libraries to implement the prototype. Because of the requirements for performance, extensibility and simplicity as well as scalability, our choice felt on Java Lucene, which we already mentioned in Section 2.2.

Figure 1 shows the BioTracer architecture. Here, we mainly use Lucene as a basis for indexing documents and handling queries, extended with a graphical user interface (GUI) based on JSP (Java Sever Pages) and AJAX (Asynchronous JavaScript and XML). The index is constructed mainly based on the MEDLINE database which is parsed and handled by the Document Handler. To facilitate the parsing and generation of Lucene-friendly documents, we use Lingpipe[5] MEDLINE parser as a base for implementing the Document Handler. This handler also interacts with both the Language Model Handler and IndexManager to index documents based on chosen language or similarity model.

---

[5] See http://alias-i.com/lingpipe/.

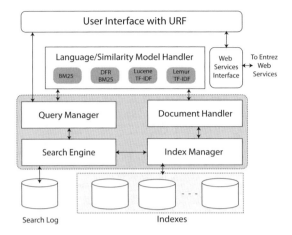

Fig. 1. The BioTracer architecture

All search is logged in the Search Log repository. This is used to "learn from experience", allowing BioTracer to use data from previous searches and user choices/interactions (e.g. URF). The Log is implemented using MySQL[6].

Figure 2 shows the implemented web-based GUI including the search environment. This also illustrates the URF possibility as described above.

Each returned relevant hit can be marked by the user. The system will then use this information to re-rank the results.

Note that due to US National Library of Medicine (NLM) license regulations, BioTracer is not allowed to provide abstracts directly from MEDLINE. However, we have implemented a workaround that still allows the user to browse the abstracts inside BioTracer. The solution is using the Entrez Web Services interfaces in combination with AJAX. This allows us to retrieve a specific abstract from PubMed based on the Pubmed ID (if it is available) and process it. In this way, we are able to allow the user to study the abstracts inside BioTracer, rather than going to an other Web page. Moreover, if the user wants to examine more than one abstracts, our AJAX implementation allows several PubMed abstract windows to be popped up at a time.

3.2 Experimental Results

To test the retrieval performance of the BioTracer prototype we have performed the evaluation based on the TREC 2004 Genomic Track [9] test collection. The main reason for choosing this collection is the number of the topics covered, which spans from gene name searches to disease searches. This allows us to do a comprehensive evaluation of the BioTracer retrieval performance. We also believe this reflects how the intended users do their search.

The TREC 2004 collection originally consists of 4,591,008 MEDLINE documents. Our evaluation was based on a subset of 42,255 documents that were

---

[6] MySQL is a trademark of Sun Microsystems. See http://www.mysql.com.

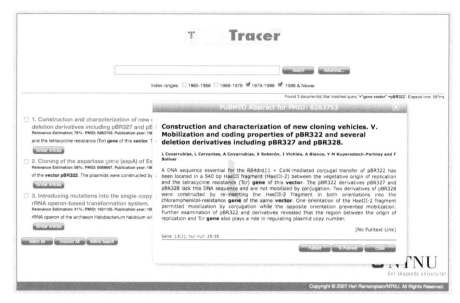

Fig. 2. Screen dump showing the BioTracer search environment

judged against 50 topics. Each topic consists of a *title*, *need* and *context* field. The queries were generated manually from the topics using all the fields. The runs were carried out as follows: First, we tested the generated queries against an off-the-shelf Lucene similarity model. Then, we used the same queries on the extended models that we discussed earlier.

To evaluate the retrieval performance, we use the same approach implemented for Text REtrieval Conference (TREC), that is, by focusing on TREC mean average precision (MAP). For each query, we may get the average precision by computing the average of the precision value for the set of top k documents after each document is retrieved. Thus, MAP is the mean of the average precision values for all queries. MAP has been widely used as the measure to evaluate ad hoc retrieval results [24, 22]. It has also been used in the TREC Genomics Track evaluation [9]. Since MAP is sensitive to the rank of every relevant document, it reflects well the overall ranking accuracy. For this reason, the best results is the one with highest MAP values.

Further, since users are generally most interested in the results within the top 100 retrieved documents, we have stressed measuring the BioTracer's ability to find relevant data among the top 100 hits. Therefore, we measured specifically the precision at 10 retrieved documents (P@10) and precision at 100 (P@100).

To make our evaluation as independent as possible and to be able to compare with previous results, we use the Buckley's **trec_eval** program[7]. Using trec_eval, the maximum number of allowed retrieved documents for each query was, by default, set to 1000. For each run, documents without any specific judgement were treated as non-relevant.

---

[7] See http://trec.nist.gov/trec_eval/

Table 1. Results from running based on pooled TREC 2004 corpus

	Baseline Lucene TFIDF	Custom TFIDF	Baseline BM25	Boolean +BM25	URF BM25
MAP	0.346	0.4975	0.398	0.5122	**0.5129**
R-precision	0.3837	0.5443	0.4547	**0.558**	0.5527
P@10	0.534	0.652	0.594	0.666	**0.712**
P@100	0.3464	0.4552	0.3974	0.469	**0.4734**
Total recall	0.67	0.737	0.637	0.735	**0.738**

Table 1 summarises the results from our evaluation. In this table the first column is the result from running the baseline method using Lucene TFIDF-based similarity model (VSM). The next column shows the results after we modified this model with the same extensions as those for Okapi BM25. Further, column number three contains the result from running the baseline BM25 model. The result from our extensions in Section 2 are presented in the column named "Boolean+BM25", and the results from using user relevance feedback is shown in "URF BM25" column. In addition to Table 1, Figure 3 shows the average precision values with respect to number of retrieved documents and the used method. Note that in addition to these results, we have tested the BioTracer prototype using Divergence From Randomness (DFR) BM25 [2], and Lemur TF-IDF models [25] with boolean and document boosts. However, the results from these runs were not significantly different from Boolean BM25. Therefore, they are not included in this paper.

What we can observe from the results in Table 1 and Figure 3 is that there are only slight differences among the extended runs, although the URF BM25 had the overall best retrieval performance. This were most obvious for the top 15 hits. We can further see that the extended models performed much better than the baseline ones, which also show the effects of applying the extensions we discussed in Section 2. For the TF-IDF model (i.e., the vector space model) the total improvement is 43.8% going from the baseline model to our custom TFIDF, while the total improvements for the BM25-based models are respectively 28% and 29% from the baseline model to extended BM25 and from the baseline model to URF BM25. Focusing on these results, adding the extensions is useful, in terms of retrieval performance. Further, comparing to the results from TREC 2004 Genomic Track [9] and assuming similar experiments, all of our extended models seem to perform better than the best run from this track, where the MAP, P@10 and P@100 were to 0.4075, 0.604 and 0.4196, respectively [9].

Despite the above promising results, there are issues that we have to address. First, our evaluation is based on a somehow "closed" test collection. Although we have argued its comprehensiveness, we recognise that such a collection would hardly cover absolutely all aspects of user's needs in real search environments. This in combination with the fact that the BioTracer prototype can be seen as a highly interactive information search system, the generality/completeness and validity of the collection might be debatable. A way to make our evaluation more general is to involve real users, and study how they interact with BioTracer, as

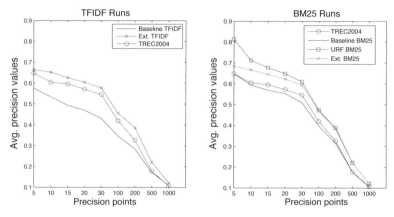

Fig. 3. Graphs for top-k precision values

well as their evaluation of the retrieval performance. However, here it is still not possible to guarantee perfect evaluation [12], since we have to rely on several factors [13] such as the users' willingness to answer the interviews, the completeness of the questionnaire, and the broadness of the users.

4   Relation to Other Work

As previously mentioned, the biomedical information retrieval research domain is no longer new, and there are other methods and systems that have been suggested and developed. Most previous work have been presented in several TREC Genomic Track conferences, including the aforementioned TREC 2004 [9]. Other approaches applying tokenization heuristics were studied by Jiang and Zhai [11]. Their evaluation has shown that these methods can successfully improve the retrieval performance.

Like ours, many existing approaches have focused on expanding queries [1, 9]. However, we have attempted to go further by combining the use of different ranking models that can be adapted to different types of information needs, boosting different parts in the documents, applying query-document correlation factor, using wildcard queries as query extension rather than stemming, using boolean queries with the BM25, and involving the users by user relevance feedback.

Concerning retrieval systems, there are a few systems that our work can be related to. Because these systems mainly use proprietary ranking and indexing strategies, our discussion will focus on the system features and functionality.

First, perhaps the most used retrieval tool is PubMed[8]. Pubmed provides several useful features for searching biomedical abstracts, such as the use of MeSH terms to expand queries and the possibility to access related articles. However, to our knowledge, it does not provide ranking based on document relevance, per se. Instead, PubMed seems to use a proprietary algorithm to order the search results based on publication date, author names and journal. Nevertheless, a more

---

[8] See http://www.pubmed.org

useful web-based GUI extension to PubMed is available, called HubMed [7]. Like BioTracer, HubMed implements the web services facilities for PubMed.

ScienceDirect is another search system[9]. It makes use of the powerful Scirus search facility. Scirus uses a more sophisticated ranking algorithm, which seems to produce more relevant results than PubMed. To our knowledge, the main difference with BioTracer is that ScienceDirect/ Scirus does not allow any kind of user relevance feedback to refine the search. It is also worth noting that SienceDirect is a commercial system that covers a much larger scientific area than BioTracer. Therefore, the search results from this systems often include other than biomedical documents.

A third system worth discussing is Textpresso [16]. Textpresso is also a search engine allowing specialised search of biomedical information. In contrast to Bio-Tracer, however, Textpresso extensively uses ontologies in the retrieval process. For a biomedical text, each word or phrase is marked by a term in the ontology when they are indexed. The ranking algorithm of Textpresso is based on the frequency of queried index terms. This means that the document which contains the largest number of query terms is ranked at the top. To our knowledge, Textpresso does not offer any user relevance feedback feature.

Fourth and finally, BioIE [6] is a rule-based information retrieval system that extracts informative sentences from the biomedical literature such as MEDLINE abstracts. It uses MEDLINE as the main underlying searchable information. In addition, it allows users to upload their own text to be searchable. Both statistical analysis (word distribution, filtered word distribution, N-gram distribution and MeSH term distribution) and sentence extraction can be performed. BioIE extracts informative sentences based on predefined templates for a user-specified category. The ranking algorithms of BioIE are based on the number of occurrences of terms in the query, much like Textpresso. BioIE does not support user relevance feedback.

5   Conclusion and Future Work

This paper has presented our ongoing work towards the development of an information retrieval system, called BioTracer. BioTracer is a search tool prototype that allows customised ranking of search results through boosting specific parts of documents, customising scoring schemes, and allowing users to affect the ranking through user relevance feedback (URF). In summary, we have investigated the effect of using and/or extending existing models like TFIDF-based models and BM25 with support for boolean queries, boosting documents and document parts, as well as enabling URF on retrieval performance and result ranking. Focusing on URF and the ability to customise the retrieval process, users are more flexible to specify their views of relevance, and thus addressing the challenges that we face in searching biomedical information, in general. In this respect, the major contribution of this work has been the development of the BioTracer search tool providing adaptable searching and ranking of biomedical information. Although we have built our tool on existing and partly well-known techniques, to our knowledge, the way we integrated them and extended them is unique.

---

[9] See http://www.sciencedirect.com

Moreover, we have done experiments with the TREC collection to investigate BioTracer's retrieval performance. We believe that these experiments on biomedical information, leading to our comparison of the different ranking models and their retrieval characteristics, are in itself an interesting result. Nevertheless, focusing on BioTracer as a whole, the main conclusion from these experiments is that BioTracer is a tool that is able to retrieve relevant information and that our extensions have helped improving the retrieval performance.

Although the results seem satisfactory, there are still challenges left for further studies. First, the system has only been tested against a TREC corpus. As discussed earlier, the strength and the validity of such a test is debatable. Therefore, we recognise the necessity of doing an extensive empirical study with real users in a realistic environment. This will reveal areas where our work can be improved. Further, we will include NLP - natural language processing methods to further improve the document handling. This would, for instance, allow the system to automatically identify important biological keywords and sentences, thus further improving the way parts of a document can be boosted. Finally, we will include a text classification facility. Our preliminary experiments based the Support Vector Machine (SVM) have, by far, shown good potential in terms of increased search precision.

Acknowledgments

The author would like to thank Jon Olav Hauglid, Roger Midtstraum, Reidar Conradi, and Min-Yen Kan for their suggestions to improve this paper.

References

1. Abdou, S., Savoy, J.: Searching in Medline: Query expansion and manual indexing evaluation. Information Processing & Management 44(2), 781–789 (2008)
2. Amati, G., Rijsbergen, C.J.V.: Probabilistic models of information retrieval based on measuring the divergence from randomness. ACM Transactions on Information Systems 20(4), 357–389 (2002)
3. Baeza-Yates, R.A., Ribeiro-Neto, B.: Modern Information Retrieval. Addison-Wesley Longman Publishing Co., Inc., Boston (1999)
4. Chen, L., Liu, H., Friedman, C.: Gene name ambiguity of eukaryotic nomenclatures. Bioinformatics 21(2), 248–256 (2005)
5. Croft, B., Metzler, D., Strohman, T.: Search Engines: Information Retrieval in Practice, 1st edn. Addison-Wesley, Reading (February 2009)
6. Divoli, A., Attwood, T.K.: BioIE: extracting informative sentences from the biomedical literature. Bioinformatics 21, 2138–2139 (2005)
7. Eaton, A.D.: Hubmed: a web-based biomedical literature search interface. Nucleic Acids Research 34(Web Server issue), W745–W747 (2006)
8. Hatcher, E., Gospodnetic, O.: Lucene in Action. Manning Publications Co., Greenwich (2005)
9. Hersh, W.R., Bhupatiraju, R.T., Ross, L., Roberts, P., Cohen, A.M., Kraemer, D.F.: Enhancing access to the bibliome: the trec 2004 genomics track. Journal of Biomedical Discovery and Collaboration 2006 1(3), 10 (2006)
10. Herskovic, J., Tanaka, L., Hersh, W., Bernstam, E.: A day in the life of PubMed: Analysis of a typical days query log. Journal of the American Medical Informatics Association 14(2), 212–220 (2007)

11. Jiang, J., Zhai, C.: An empirical study of tokenization strategies for biomedical information retrieval. Information Retrieval 10(4-5), 341–363 (2007)
12. Käki, M., Aula, A.: Controlling the complexity in comparing search user interfaces via user studies. Information Processing and Management 44(1), 82–91 (2008); Evaluation of Interactive Information Retrieval Systems
13. Kelly, D., Harper, D.J., Landau, B.: Questionnaire mode effects in interactive information retrieval experiments. Information Processing and Management 44(1), 122–141 (2008); Evaluation of Interactive Information Retrieval Systems
14. Krauthammer, M., Nenadic, G.: Term identification in the biomedical literature. Journal of Biomedical Informatics 37(6), 512–526 (2004)
15. Lowe, H.J., Barnett, G.O.: Understanding and using the medical subject headings (MeSH) vocabulary to perform literature searches. JAMA 271(14), 1103–1108 (1994)
16. Muller, H.-M., Kenny, E.E., Sternberg, P.W.: Textpresso: an ontology-based information retrieval and extraction system for biological literature. PLoS Biol. 2(11), e309 (2004)
17. Netzel, R., Perez-Iratxeta, C., Bork, P., Andrade, M.A.: The way we write. EMBO Reports 4(5), 446–451 (2003)
18. Robertson, S., Zaragoza, H., Taylor, M.: Simple bm25 extension to multiple weighted fields. In: CIKM 2004: Proceedings of the thirteenth ACM international conference on Information and knowledge management, pp. 42–49. ACM, Washington (2004)
19. Robertson, S.E., Jones, K.S.: Simple proven approaches to text retrieval. Technical Report 356, University of Cambridge (1994)
20. Salton, G., Buckley, C.: Term-weighting approaches in automatic text retrieval. Information Processing and Management 24(5), 513–523 (1988)
21. Trieschnigg, D., Kraaij, W., de Jong, F.: The influence of basic tokenization on biomedical document retrieval. In: Proceedings of the 30th international ACM SIGIR conference on Research and development in information retrieval (SIGIR 2007), p. 803 (2007)
22. Voorhees, E.M.: On test collections for adaptive information retrieval. Inf. Process. Manage. 44(6), 1879–1885 (2008)
23. Wilkinson, R.: Effective retrieval of structured documents. In: Proceedings of the 17th International ACM SIGIR Conference on Research and Development in Information Retrieval, SIGIR 1994, pp. 311–317. Springer, New York (1994)
24. Yilmaz, E., Aslam, J.A.: Estimating average precision when judgments are incomplete. Knowledge and Information Systems 16(2), 173–211 (2008)
25. Zhai, C.: Notes on the lemur TFIDF model. note with lemur 1.9 documentation. Technical report, School of CS, CMU (2001)

A Self-organizing State Space Approach to Inferring Time-Varying Causalities between Regulatory Proteins

Osamu Hirose and Kentaro Shimizu

Bioinformation Engineering Laboratory, Department of Biotechnology,
Graduate School of Agricultural and Life Sciences, The University of Tokyo,
1-1-1 Yayoi, Bunkyo-ku, Tokyo 113-8657, Japan

Abstract. A number of methods based on time-dependent state space models have been proposed for inferring time-varying gene regulatory networks. These methods are capable of detecting a relatively small number of topological changes in gene regulatory networks. However, they are insufficient since there is a greater number of changes in the gene regulatory mechanisms; the function of a regulatory protein frequently changes due to post-translational modification, such as protein phosphorylation and ATP-binding. We propose a self-organizing state space approach to inferring consecutive changes in causalities between regulatory proteins from gene expression data. Hidden regulatory proteins are identified using a test-based method from genome-wide protein-DNA binding data. Application of this approach to cell cycle data demonstrated its effectiveness.

1 Introduction

Cells operate extraordinarily many proteins and control gene expressions in order to live, grow, proliferate, and communicate. To understand the elaborate and complex mechanisms of gene regulation, it is essential to elucidate interactions and relations among proteins and genes, as well as their functions. One approach to this challenging task is to develop mathematical models for inferring causality networks from time-course gene expression data, including dynamic Bayesian network models[1,2,3,4], autoregressive models [5,6,7], and state space models [8,9,10,11,12]. However, many of these models are based on time-invariant models and thus lack the ability to track topological changes in a gene regulatory network. A number of models based on time-dependent models have been proposed to overcome this limitation. The dynamic vector autoregressive model, for example, uses a smoothing technique for its evolving autoregressive coefficients [5]. However, this model is unable to take into account regulatory proteins that play key roles in gene regulatory networks since random vectors for only mRNA expression levels are included in this model.

State space models (SSMs) model unobserved activities of regulatory proteins by using hidden state variables [13]. There are several methods that utilize

S. Khuri, L. Lhotská, and N. Pisanti (Eds.): ITBAM 2010, LNCS 6266, pp. 158–171, 2010.

time-dependent SSMs to infer causality networks. All are based on the Markov switching model, which provides several attractive approaches to inferring topological changes in causality networks [12,14]. With these approaches, topological changes in causality networks can be detected for a relatively small numbers of change points. However, such approaches are insufficient since the gene regulatory mechanism changes more frequently; the function of a regulatory protein is dependent on its post-translational modification, e.g. protein phosphorylation, ATP-binding. One way to overcome this limitation is to use an SSM that changes in consecutive times. That is, relaxing the temporal invariance of the Markov switching model might enable, more frequent changes in gene regulatory networks to be detected. However, the maximum likelihood estimation for such an unrestricted setting of the model yields meaningless results because of over-parameterization; the number of parameters is always greater than the length of the time series.

In this paper, we propose a novel method for inferring a time-dependent causality network among regulatory proteins from gene expression data. The over-parameterization problem is avoided by a penalized likelihood approach, which is interpreted as a self-organizing state space approach. Hidden regulatory proteins are identified using a test-based method from genome-wide protein-DNA binding data. We also present an efficient estimation algorithm based on the expectation-maximization (EM) algorithm. The effectiveness of our approach was demonstrated by applying it to to cell cycle data.

2   Methods

2.1   Model

We model gene regulatory networks based on an SSM in a manner similar to that used by Li *et al.* [13]. SSMs are typically defined as two models, the observation model and the system model. Suppose p is the number of genes and k is a positive integer that satisfies $k < p$. Also, suppose $\mathcal{M}$ denotes a set of positive integers representing observation times that are possibly irregularly-spaced. We assume that the observation model describes how gene expressions are controlled by transcription factors (TFs) or other regulatory proteins cooperative with the TFs:

$$y_n = H_n x_n + w_n, \quad n \in \mathcal{M}, \tag{1}$$

where $y_n \in \mathbb{R}^p$ is a data vector, the gth element of which represents the expression level of gene g at time n, and $x_n \in \mathbb{R}^k$ is an unobserved state vector, the ith element of which represents the unobserved concentration of TF i or group i of cooperative regulatory proteins at time n. That is, an expression level of a gene is modeled as a weighted sum of concentrations of k distinct groups of cooperative regulatory proteins. The (g, i)th element of observation matrix $H_n \in \mathbb{R}^{p \times k}$ represents the influence of the ith group of regulatory proteins on the expression level of gene g. Observation noise $w_n \in \mathbb{R}^p$ follows a normal distribution with

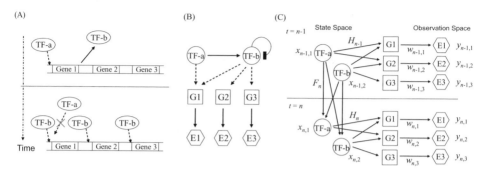

Fig. 1. (A) Example gene regulatory network with negative feedback loop, which comprises two TFs and three genes. TF-a binds to the regulatory region of gene 1, which encodes TF-b and promotes the production of TF-b via transcription and translation. Then TF-b binds to the regulatory region of gene 1 and prevents TF-a from binding to the region. As a result, TF-b interferes with its own production. (B) Symbolic representation of gene regulatory network. 'G' and 'E' represent gene and expression, respectively. Protein-DNA bindings are denoted by broken lines; repressing effect is denoted by rectangle-headed arrow. (C) Schematic illustration of gene regulatory network model based on the state space model.

mean vector 0 and covariance matrix $R \in \mathbb{R}^{p \times p}$. The system model describes how the concentration of regulatory proteins evolve and is defined as

$$x_n = F_n x_{n-1} + v_n \quad n \in \mathcal{N}, \tag{2}$$

where $\mathcal{N} = \{1, \cdots, N\}$. That is, the evolution of concentration vector x_n is modeled as a vector autoregressive model. The (i, j)th element of system matrix $F_n \in \mathbb{R}^{k \times k}$ represents the influence of the jth group of regulatory proteins on the concentration of ith group. System noise $v_n \in \mathbb{R}^k$ corresponds to other unknown effects on the concentration of regulatory proteins and follows a normal distribution with mean vector 0 and covariance matrix $Q \in \mathbb{R}^{k \times k}$. The initial concentration vector $x_0 \in \mathbb{R}^k$ is also assumed to follow a normal distribution with mean vector $\mu_0 \in \mathbb{R}^k$ and covariance matrix $V_0 \in \mathbb{R}^{k \times k}$. Note that the parameters to be estimated are $\mu_0, V_0, H_n, F_n, R_n,$ and Q_n for all $n = 1, \cdots, N$. The gene regulatory network modeling is summarized in Figure 1.

Let us denote a set of parameters $\theta_n = (H_n, F_n, R_n, Q_n)$. In an earlier study of the inference of gene regulatory networks based on the SSM, the parameters of the model were assumed to be time-invariant [10]; that is,

$$\theta_1 = \cdots = \theta_N.$$

In such a time-invariant setting, however, it is not possible to infer time-varying dependencies for genes and regulatory proteins. To overcome this limitation and so as to be able to detect topological changes in gene regulatory networks, Markov switching approaches based on the SSM were developed that relaxed the assumption of time-invariance [12,14]:

$$\theta_1 = \cdots = \theta_{t-1} \neq \theta_t = \cdots = \theta_N.$$

They provided an attractive way to detect topological changes in gene regulatory networks. However, such approaches are not suitable if the gene regulatory mechanism changes more frequently; the functions of a regulatory protein frequently changes in accordance with its post-translational modification such as protein phosphorylation and ATP-binding.

2.2 A Penalized Likelihood Approach

Here, we propose a novel method for inferring time-varying causalities between regulatory proteins from high-dimensional gene expression data. The limitation of the Markov switching model is overcome by further relaxation of the assumption of time-invariance:

$$\theta_1 \neq \cdots \neq \theta_N.$$

With a time-invariant SSM, the parameters can be estimated using the maximum likelihood approach [15]. In our time-dependent approach, however, the maximum likelihood estimator can be ill-posed because of the over-parameterization; the number of parameters is always greater than the length of the time series. In fact, the maximum likelihood estimation of the time-dependent SSM using the EM algorithm always fails if $k > 1$ since estimates of H_n and F_n become singular matrices. Suppose $f_{ij,n}$ is the (i, j)th element of system matrix F_n at time n. To avoid such ill-posed solutions, we define a penalized log-likelihood:

$$L_{\lambda,\eta}(\theta) = \ln p(y_1, \cdots, y_N; \theta) - \lambda \sum_{n=1}^{N} \sum_{i,j}^{k} (f_{ij,n+1} - \eta f_{ij,n})^2, \qquad (3)$$

where η is a parameter that defines the decay rate of the system matrix in a unit time interval while $\lambda > 0$ is a smoothing parameter that represents a trade-off between the fidelity of the data and the smoothness of the solution. Here, the relaxation of the assumption of time-invariance is applied only to system matrix F_n, and the remaining parameters (H_n, R_n, Q_n) are time-invariant in order to avoid meaningless results due to imposing a severe penalty on the maximum likelihood. This penalized likelihood approach is interpreted to be a self-organizing state space model, which provides sophisticated and general approaches to analyzing time-series data [16,17,18].

Once the parameters of the SSM are estimated, time-varying causalities for hidden regulatory proteins within any time interval can be obtained. Suppose that $F_{t_2:t_1} = F_{t_2} F_{t_2-1} \cdots F_{t_1} \in \mathbb{R}^{k \times k}$ is the multiplication of system matrices within the interval t_1 to t_2. Then, the (i, j)th element of $F_{t_2:t_1}$ becomes the $(t_2 - t_1)$-lagged influence of the jth group of regulatory proteins on the concentration of the ith group at time t_1 since the system model (Eq.2) is rewritten by recursive applications of itself:

$$x_{t_2} = F_{t_2:t_1} x_{t_1} + c_{t_2:t_1},$$

where accumulated noise $c_{t_2:t_1} \in \mathbb{R}^k$ is defined as $c_{t_2:t_1} = v_{t_2} + \sum_{n=1}^{t_1} F_{t_2:t_2-n+1} \cdot v_{t_2-n}$.

2.3 Parameter Estimation

We present an algorithm for maximizing the penalized likelihood $L_{\lambda,\eta}(\theta)$. We first explain the parameter constraints imposed on the SSM. A problem with SSMs is their lack of uniqueness; that is, there exist an infinite number of models with equal likelihood [12]. To make the model unique, we impose parameter constraints

- $Q = I$.
- $H^T R^{-1} H = \Gamma \equiv \operatorname{diag}(\gamma_1, \cdots, \gamma_k)$, where $\gamma_1 > \cdots > \gamma_k$.
- Arbitrary sign condition for each column vector of H.

These constraints are sufficient to ensure model uniqueness [12]. With them, the entire estimands of the model become

$$\theta = (\mu_0, H, R, F_1, \cdots, F_N),$$

where covariance matrix R is restricted to be diagonal to avoid over-parameterization. Note that V_0 is not estimated since both μ_0 and V_0 cannot be estimated simultaneously [15]. For brevity, we define two notations:

$$\langle a_n b_n^T; \theta \rangle = E[a_n b_n^T | y_1, \cdots, y_N; \theta],$$
$$\langle a_n b_n^T; \theta \rangle_{\mathcal{M}} = \sum_{n \in \mathcal{M}} \langle a_n b_n^T; \theta \rangle,$$

where a_n and b_n represent either a state vector or an observation vector at time n. The time-varying parameters of self-organizing state space models are usually estimated using sampling techniques whereas the proposed penalized-likelihood can be (locally) maximized using the EM algorithm, which makes it possible to estimate time-varying parameters from high-dimensional time-series data such as gene expression data:

Proposition 1. *Suppose $\chi : \{T, F\} \rightarrow \{0, 1\}$ is a characteristic function which takes one if the logical expression in its argument is true and zero, otherwise. The penalized log-likelihood $L_{\lambda,\eta}(\theta)$ of the SSM can be optimized by iterating the following updating formulae:*

$$H^{new} = \langle y_n x_n^T; \theta \rangle_{\mathcal{M}} \langle x_n x_n^T; \theta \rangle_{\mathcal{M}},$$
$$R^{new} = \langle y_n y_n^T; \theta \rangle_{\mathcal{M}} - \langle y_n x_n^T; \theta \rangle_{\mathcal{M}} \langle x_n x_n^T; \theta \rangle_{\mathcal{M}}^{-1} \langle y_n x_n^T; \theta \rangle_{\mathcal{M}}^T,$$
$$\mu_0^{new} = \langle x_0; \theta \rangle,$$
$$F_n^{new} = \begin{cases} -B_n A_n^{-1} & (n = N) \\ -F_{n+1}^{new} S_{n+1} + T_{n+1} - \chi(n \neq N-1) F_{n+2}^{new} & (o.w.) \end{cases},$$

where S_n, T_n, A_n and B_n are defined as

$$S_n = (2\eta\lambda)^{-1} \langle x_{n-1} x_{n-1}^T; \theta \rangle + \{\chi(n \neq N)\eta + \chi(n \neq 1)\eta^{-1}\}I,$$
$$T_n = -(2\eta\lambda)^{-1} \langle x_n x_{n-1}^T; \theta \rangle,$$

$$A_n = \begin{cases} S_1 & (n = 1) \\ S_{n-1} - A_{n-1}^{-1} & (o.w.) \end{cases},$$

$$B_n = \begin{cases} T_1 & (n = 1) \\ T_{n-1} + B_{n-1}A_{n-1}^{-1} & (o.w.) \end{cases}.$$

Proof. We focus on time-varying parameter $F_1, \cdots, F_N$; derivations of the remaining parameters μ_0, H, and R are omitted because they are exactly the same as derivations for the time-invariant SSMs. The updating equations are obtained using the EM algorithm. By taking the expectation of the penalized complete data log-likelihood L_C over the state vectors and missing data vectors, we obtain

$$2 \cdot \langle L_C \rangle = \text{const.} - \text{tr} \sum_{n \in \mathcal{M}} \langle (x_n - F_n x_{n-1})(x_n - F_n x_{n-1}) \rangle^T$$

$$- 2\lambda \text{tr} \sum_{n=1}^{N-1} (F_{n+1} - \eta F_n)(F_{n+1} - \eta F_n)^T$$

where the parenthesis $\langle \cdot \rangle$ denotes expectation over the state vectors and over the missing data vectors governed by the old parameter $\bar{\theta}$. Next, by taking the derivative of $\langle L_C \rangle$ for each F_n, we obtain

$$\frac{\partial \langle L_C \rangle}{\partial F_n} = \langle x_n x_n^T \rangle - F_n \langle x_n x_{n-1}^T \rangle$$

$$+ 2\lambda \begin{cases} \eta F_{n+1} - \eta^2 F_n & (n = 1) \\ -F_n + \eta F_{n-1} & (n = N) \\ \eta F_{n+1} - (1 + \eta^2)F_n + \eta F_{n-1} & (o.w.) \end{cases}.$$

By setting these derivatives to zero and rearranging these equations, we obtain a recurrence relation of order three:

$$\begin{cases} F_{n+1} - F_n S_n = T_n & (n = 1) \\ F_{n-1} - F_n S_n = T_n & (n = N) \\ F_{n+1} - F_n S_n + F_{n-1} = T_n & (o.w.) \end{cases} \qquad (4)$$

where T_n and S_n are $k \times k$ matrices defined in the statement of the proposition. Sequential elimination of $F_1, \cdots, F_N$ from Eq.4 rewrites the recurrence relation as that of order two:

$$\begin{cases} B_n = -F_n A_n & (n = N) \\ B_n = -F_n A_n + F_{n+1} & (o.w.) \end{cases}$$

where A_n and B_n are $k \times k$ matrices also defined in the statement. This recurrence relation gives the resulting updating equation for F_N. Finally, the backward calculation of F_n using Eq.4 provides the remaining updating formulae for $n = N - 1, \cdots, 1$.

The updating equations we obtained maximize the penalized likelihood much faster than the naive algorithm presented below. Eq.4 can be represented in an equivalent form:

$$(F_1 \cdots F_N) \begin{pmatrix} -S_1 & I & & & & & \\ I & -S_2 & I & & & O & \\ & I & -S_3 & & & & \\ & & & \ddots & & & \\ & & & & -S_{N-2} & I & \\ O & & & & I & -S_{N-1} & I \\ & & & & & I & -S_N \end{pmatrix} = (T_1 \cdots T_N).$$

Thus, it is possible to maximize $\langle L_C \rangle$ by multiplying both sides of the equation by the inverse matrix of the $Nk \times Nk$ tri-block-diagonal matrix, which comprises $S_1, \cdots, S_N$ and unit matrices. The computational cost of the inversion of the tri-block-diagonal matrix is $O((Nk)^3)$ whereas that of the updating equations we derived is $O(Nk^3)$. Since the computational cost of Kalman filtering and smoothing is $O(Nk^3 p)$, the total computational costs of the two algorithms for one step of the EM algorithm is $O(Nk^3(p + N^2))$ and $O(Nk^3 p)$, respectively. Thus, our algorithm drastically reduces the computational burden, especially if N is relatively large.

2.4   Extraction of Co-expressed Genes

As a first step in identifying hidden regulatory proteins, we extract co-expressed genes using the method of Yamaguchi et al. [11]. A cluster of co-expressed genes can be extracted for each coordinate of the state space by mapping noise-removed gene expression vectors to the state space:

$$x_n = D^T (y_{n-1} - w_n),$$

where projection matrix D is defined as $D = R^{-1/2} H \Gamma^{-1}$ [11]. Suppose d_i is the ith column vector of D and r_i is a predefined number of co-expressed genes. They extracted genes, the corresponding elements of d_i of which are among the r_ith highest for each state i. This approach becomes more understandable if one considers the observation model normalized by the covariance matrix of the measurement noise:

$$R^{-1/2} y_n = R^{-1/2} H x_n + w'_n.$$

where $w'_n = R^{-1/2} w_n$ is a normalized noise vector that follows a normal distribution with mean vector 0 and covariance matrix I. Since the extraction procedure is irrelevant to diagonal matrix Γ, the procedure is identical to one that uses normalized observation matrix $R^{-1/2}H$ instead of projection matrix D. More simply, observation matrix H, the (i,j)th element of which represents the normalized causality from TF j to gene i, gives the same result, especially if $R = \sigma^2 I$. Thus, this approach can be interpreted as follows: If the causalities from a TF to specific genes are large enough, such genes are regulated by the TF and thereby co-expressed.

2.5   Identification of Hidden Regulatory Proteins

We identify hidden regulatory proteins using known regulatory information and k clusters of co-expressed genes extracted by the method [11]. The known regulatory information we use is protein-DNA binding data for budding yeast, which provide the binding regions for all TFs on the genome and thus suggest gene regulatory information for the TFs [19]. Suppose p, q_l, r_i, and s_{il} are the numbers of all genes, genes regulated by TF l, genes in the ith cluster of co-expressed genes, and genes regulated by TF l in the ith cluster, respectively. To determine whether any TFs regulate genes in the ith cluster at a frequency greater than that would be expected by chance, we calculate p-value π_{il} using the hypergeometric distribution:

$$\pi_{il} = 1 - \sum_{t=0}^{s_{il}} \binom{q_l}{t} \binom{p - q_l}{r_i - t} \bigg/ \binom{p}{r_i},$$

for all i, l. If π_{il} is less than a predefined cutoff, we conclude that TF l is related to the regulation for the ith cluster of co-expressed genes, *i.e.* TF l is a hidden regulatory protein corresponding to ith coordinate of the state space. Note that the number of extracted TFs for each state is possibly greater than one, which is not surprising since genes with closely-related functions are often regulated by the cooperation of multiple TFs.

3   Application

We applied the proposed method to Spellman's cell cycle gene expression data [20]. We used the dataset based on the cdc15-based synchronization method. We used 4381 genes that had no missing observations to ensure the quality of our analysis. To avoid the problem caused by irregularly-spaced time points $\{10, 30, 50, 70, 90, 100, \ldots, 240, 250, 270, 290\}$, we treated $\{20, 40, 60, 260, 280\}$ minutes as missing observations; *i.e.* we set $\mathcal{N} = \{1, \cdots, 29\}$ and $\mathcal{M} = \{1, 3, 5, 7, 9, 10, \cdots, 25, 27, 29\}$. We compared the prediction error of the proposed method with that of the time-invariant SSM under the above conditions. Suppose that $\hat{\theta}_k^{(-n)}$ is the parameter estimated under a fixed k from the dataset, the nth data vector of which is intentionally removed. Also, suppose that $\hat{y}_n^{(-n;k,\lambda)} = E[y_n | y_1, \cdots, y_{n-1}; \hat{\theta}_k^{(-n)}]$ is the one-step-ahead prediction vector at time n, given

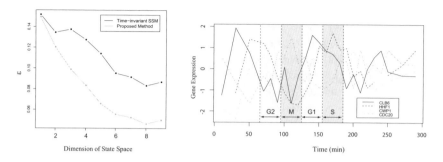

Fig. 2. (Left) Comparison of prediction error ϵ_k between proposed method and time-invariant SSM. (Right) Plot of expression of genes that have phase-specific peaks during cell cycle.

parameter estimate $\hat{\theta}_k^{(-n)}$. For each k, we computed a test-error measure defined as

$$\epsilon_k = (Np)^{-1} \sum_{n \in \mathcal{M}} ||y_n - \hat{y}_n^{(-n;k)}||^2.$$

The left graph of Figure 2 shows the result of the comparison between the time-invariant SSM and the proposed method. The vertical axis represents the prediction error and the horizontal axis represents k. The black solid line shows the plot of ϵ_k calculated using the time-invariant SSM, and the blue broken line shows the plot of ϵ_k for $\lambda = 750$. This result suggests that the proposed method has the better predictive performance than the time-invariant state space model.

Using $(k, \lambda) = (8, 750)$ which minimizes ϵ_k, we inferred phase-specific causality networks that comprise regulatory proteins from the entire dataset. Time intervals corresponding to each phase of the cell cycle were determined based on genes which had phase-specific peaks of expressions. Extracted intervals were $\{70, 80, 90\}$, $\{100, 110, 120\}$, $\{130, 140, 150\}$, and $\{160, 170, 180\}$ for the G2, M, G1, and S phases, respectively. The right graph of Figure 2 shows the plots of the expressions for CLB6, HHF1, CWP1, and CDC20, which are examples of genes that have distinct phase-specific peaks. The regulatory information needed to calculate π_{il} was obtained from the genome-wide protein-DNA binding data for budding yeast [19] with significance level 5%.

We identified the top 3% of the genes as a cluster of co-expressed genes among all 4381 genes for each state by using the method of Yamaguchi *et al.* [11], *i.e.* the number of co-expressed genes r_i was set to 131 for all i. Figure 3 shows images of the eight extracted clusters. The 20 top-ranked genes are displayed for each cluster, revealing that the gene expression patterns in each cluster were clearly correlated.

We then identified TFs for each co-expressed genes using the test-based method presented in Section 2. The cut-off value for the p-values was set to 0.03.

Table 1. Identification of TFs for each coordinate of the state space. TFs with corresponding p-values less than 0.05 are listed. Each p-value is shown in parenthesis.

State	TF name (p-value)
1	Cbf1 (8.85e-03)
2	Gcr1 (4.12e-04), Met4 (5.49e-03)
3	Reb1 (1.11e-02)
4	Fhl1 (2.80e-14), Gat3 (2.09e-05), Rap1 (5.48e-03), Yap5 (3.11e-05), Rgm1 (2.75e-04), Met4 (2.60e-03), Met31 (4.77e-03), Sfp1 (8.42e-03)
5	Arg80 (4.27e-02)
6	Hir2 (2.52e-02), Ash1 (3.82e-02)
7	Ndd1 (1.05e-14), Fkh2 (2.12e-08), Mcm1 (1.37e-04), Hsf1 (1.69e-04), Cin5 (2.92e-04), Hir2 (4.69e-03), Swi4 (8.37e-03), Ino4 (1.22e-02), Ash1 (3.82e-02), Met4 (3.89e-02)
8	Fkh2 (8.15e-06), Swi4 (3.17e-04), Hsf1 (2.13e-03), Swi6 (2.66e-03), Mbp1 (7.08e-02), Stb1 (1.30e-02), Rlm1 (3.20e-02), Rme1 (3.48e-02)

The identified TFs and corresponding π_{il}'s are listed in Table 1. They included known regulatory modules (Ndd1, Mcm1, Fkh2) and (Swi6, Swi4, Stb1, Mbp1) for genes expressed in specific phases of the cell cycle: Swi6 and Swi4 are subunits of the SBF complex, which regulates proteins involved in the initiation of the G1/S transition and progression into the S phase; Stb1 is a stable component of the SBF complex during the G1 phase [21,22]. MBF is a heterodimer of Mbp1 and Swi6, which binds to almost all the promoter regions bound by Mbp1 and Swi4, indicating that it is a co-factor of these two regulators throughout the genome [23]. Mcm1 and Fkh2 form a complex which binds a specific DNA site and regulate genes expressed in the G2/M phase when Ndd1 transiently interacts with the complex in the G2/M phase[24]. Figure 5 summarizes known physical interactions between identified TFs for states 7 and 8.

Figure 4 shows plots of TF concentration estimated using the mean vector of the smoothing distribution, $p(x_n|y_1, \cdots, y_N; \hat{\theta})$ for $n = 1, \cdots, 29$. Each transition of the estimated TF concentration was clearly related to the expression pattern of the corresponding cluster of co-expressed genes. These results suggest that the concentration of Ndd1 and Swi6 peaked in intervals $\{90, 100, 110\}$ and $\{150, 160, 170\}$, respectively. This is consistent with the findings in related studies: Swi6 and Ndd1 activate genes expressed in late G1 and early S, and in late G2 and early M, respectively [24,23].

Figure 6 shows the resulting causality networks for the identified TFs. To track the changes in the networks during each phase of the cell cycle, we calculated the lagged-causality matrices ($\hat{F}_{9:7}, \hat{F}_{12:10}, \hat{F}_{15:13}$ and $\hat{F}_{18:16}$), corresponding to those for phases G2, M, G1, and S, respectively. We identified significant causalities: the corresponding elements were the highest 10% among all elements of the lagged-causality matrices. The resulting network included time-varying causalities that suggested known interactions among the identified TFs. Arg80 and Mcm1 combine in a complex with Arg81, and this complex acts as an arginine

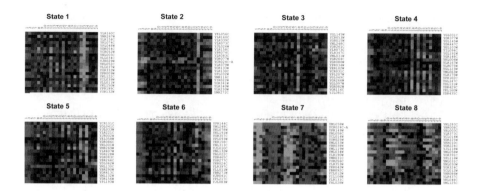

Fig. 3. Extracted co-expressed genes. Twenty top-ranked genes for each state are displayed in decreasing order of clustering score from top to bottom. Red and green squares represent over- and under-expressed, respectively.

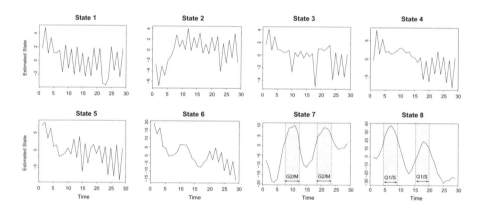

Fig. 4. Time-series plots of transcription factor concentrations suggested by smoothing distribution $p(x_n|y_1, \cdots, y_N; \hat{\theta})$

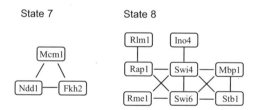

Fig. 5. Identified TFs for states 7 and 8; they include many cell-cycle regulated genes for each of the extracted co-expressed genes. Solid lines show known physical contacts.

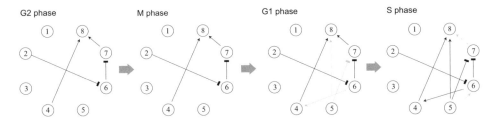

Fig. 6. Estimated time-varying causalities between identified TFs during each phase of cell cycle. Arrow-headed lines represent stimulatory effects while rectangle-headed lines represent suppressing effects. Newly-appeared and disappeared lines are shown in blue and are represented by solid and broken lines, respectively.

sensor that regulates the expression of arginine-anabolic and -catabolic genes [25]. This relationship was suggested by the edge between states 6 and 7 during phases G1 and S. Furthermore, many of the estimated causalities among states 5, 6, 7, and 8 were supported by indirect relationships suggested by protein-interaction maps [26]. For example, the edges from state 6 to 4, 6 to 7, and 7 to 8 were supported by indirect pathways Hir2–Hhf1–Fhl1, Hir2–Hhf1–Fkh1–Mbp1, and Fkh2–Fkh1–Mbp1, respectively.

4   Conclusion

We have described a method for inferring time-varying causalities between regulatory proteins from high-dimensional gene expression data. This method is based on a state space model, unknown system parameters of which change at successive time points. To avoid over-parameterization of the model, we developed a penalized likelihood approach defined by the differences between two successive system matrices. This method can be interpreted as a self-organizing state space model. Many of the self-organizing state space methods that have been developed in the field of time-series analysis are targeted at the analysis of a one-dimensional time series. In contrast, our method is targeted at the analysis of gene expression data with more than ten-thousands dimensions. We presented an efficient algorithm for estimating the unknown system parameters, which are difficult to estimate with the sampling techniques commonly used in the self-organizing state space approaches [16,17,18].

The numerical example suggests that our method improves prediction accuracies for cell cycle gene expression data. Our method successfully identified co-expressed genes and hidden regulatory proteins. Furthermore, the estimated network included time-varying causalities that suggested known interactions or indirect relationships among key regulatory modules. One limitation of our approach is that the expected speed of causality changes is constant. Therefore, it is difficult to track rare and drastic changes in causalities that may occur, for example, at cell differentiation. If the expected speed of causality changes is time-dependent, a more attractive approach might be to infer both slow and drastic changes in causalities between regulatory proteins. An extension to relax the assumptions is under consideration.

References

1. Friedman, N., Linial, M., Nachman, I., Pe'er, D.: Using ayesian networks to analyze expression data. J. Comput. Biol. 7, 601–620 (2000)
2. Friedman, N.: Inferring cellular networks using probabilistic graphical models. Science 303, 799–805 (2004)
3. Imoto, S., Goto, T., Miyano, S.: Estimation of genetic networks and functional structures between genes by using bayesian networks and nonparametric regression. In: Proceedings of Pacific Symposium of Biocomputing, pp. 175–186 (2002)
4. Tamada, Y., Imoto, S., Tashiro, K., Kuhara, S., Miyano, S.: Identifying drug active pathways from gene networks estimated by gene expression data. Genome Inform. 16, 182–191 (2005)
5. Fujita, A., Sato, J.R., Garay-Malpartida, H.M., Morettin, P.A., Sogayar, M.C., Ferreira, C.E.: Time-varying modeling of gene expression regulatory networks using the wavelet dynamic vector autoregressive method. Bioinformatics 23, 1623–1630 (2007)
6. Shimamura, T., Imoto, S., Yamaguchi, R., Fujita, A., Nagasaki, M., Miyano, S.: Recursive regularization for inferring gene networks from time-course gene expression profiles. BMC Syst. Biol. 3, 41 (2009)
7. Kojima, K., Fujita, A., Shimamura, T., Imoto, S., Miyano, S.: Estimation of nonlinear gene regulatory networks via L1 regularized NVAR from time series gene expression data. Genome Inform. 20, 37–51 (2008)
8. Beal, M.J., Falciani, F., Ghahramani, Z., Rangel, C., Wild, D.L.: A Bayesian approach to reconstructing genetic regulatory networks with hidden factors. Bioinformatics 21, 349–356 (2005)
9. Rangel, C., Angus, J., Ghahramani, Z., Lioumi, M., Sotheran, E., Gaiba, A., Wild, D.L., Falciani, F.: Modeling T-cell activation using gene expression profiling and state-space models. Bioinformatics 20, 1361–1372 (2004)
10. Wu, F.X., Zhang, W.J., Kusalik, A.J.: Modeling gene expression from microarray expression data with state-space equations. In: Proceedings of Pacific Symposium on Biocomputing, pp. 581–592 (2004)
11. Yamaguchi, R., Yoshida, R., Imoto, S., Higuchi, T., Miyano, S.: Finding module-based gene networks with state-space models. IEEE Signal Processing Magazine 24, 37–46 (2007)
12. Yoshida, R., Imoto, S., Higuchi, T.: Estimating time-dependent gene networks from time series microarray data by dynamic linear models with markov switching. In: Proceedings of Computational Systems Bioinformatics, pp. 289–298 (2005)
13. Li, Z., Shaw, S.M., Yedwabnick, M.J., Chan, C.: Using a state-space model with hidden variables to infer transcription factor activities. Bioinformatics 22, 747–754 (2006)
14. Rao, A., Hero, A.O., States, D.J., Engel, J.D.: Using directed information to build biologically relevant influence networks. In: Comput. Syst. Bioinformatics Conf., vol. 6, pp. 145–156 (2007)
15. Shumway, R.H., Stoffer, D.S.: An approach to time series smoothing and forecasting using the EM algorithm. Journal of Time Series Analysis 3, 253–264 (1982)

16. Kitagawa, G.: A self-organizing state-space model. Journal of the American Statistical Association 93, 1203–1215 (1998)
17. Higuchi, T., Kitagawa, G.: Knowledge discovery and self-organizing state space model. IEICE Transactions on Information and Systems E Series D 83, 36–43 (2000)
18. Yano, K.: A self-organizing state space model and simplex initial distribution search. Computational Statistics 23, 197–216 (2008)
19. Lee, T.I., Rinaldi, N.J., Robert, F., Odom, D.T., Bar-Joseph, Z., Gerber, G.K., Hannett, N.M., Harbison, C.T., Thompson, C.M., Simon, I., Zeitlinger, J., Jennings, E.G., Murray, H.L., Gordon, D.B., Ren, B., Wyrick, J.J., Tagne, J.B., Volkert, T.L., Fraenkel, E., Gifford, D.K., Young, R.A.: Transcriptional regulatory networks in Saccharomyces cerevisiae. Science 298, 799–804 (2002)
20. Spellman, P.T., Sherlock, G., Zhang, M.Q., Iyer, V.R., Anders, K., Eisen, M.B., Brown, P.O., Botstein, D., Futcher, B.: Comprehensive identification of cell cycle-regulated genes of the yeast Saccharomyces cerevisiae by microarray hybridization. Mol. Biol. Cell. 9, 3273–3297 (1998)
21. Costanzo, M., Schub, O., Andrews, B.: G1 transcription factors are differentially regulated in Saccharomyces cerevisiae by the Swi6-binding protein Stb1. Mol. Cell. Biol. 23, 5064–5077 (2003)
22. de Bruin, R.A.M., Kalashnikova, T.I., Wittenberg, C.: Stb1 collaborates with other regulators to modulate the G1-specific transcriptional circuit. Mol. Cell. Biol. 28, 6919–6928 (2008)
23. Simon, I., Barnett, J., Hannett, N., Harbison, C.T., Rinaldi, N.J., Volkert, T.L., Wyrick, J.J., Zeitlinger, J., Gifford, D.K., Jaakkola, T.S., Young, R.A.: Serial regulation of transcriptional regulators in the yeast cell cycle. Cell 106, 697–708 (2001)
24. Koranda, M., Schleiffer, A., Endler, L., Ammerer, G.: Forkhead-like transcription factors recruit Ndd1 to the chromatin of G2/M-specific promoters. Nature 406, 94–98 (2000)
25. Amar, N., Messenguy, F., Bakkoury, M.E., Dubois, E.: ArgRII, a component of the argr-mcm1 complex involved in the control of arginine metabolism in saccharomyces cerevisiae, is the sensor of arginine. Mol. Cell. Biol. 20, 2087–2097 (2000)
26. Ho, Y., Gruhler, A., Heilbut, A., Bader, G.D., Moore, L., Adams, S.L., Millar, A., Taylor, P., Bennett, K., Boutilier, K., Yang, L., Wolting, C., Donaldson, I., Schandorff, S., Shewnarane, J., Vo, M., Taggart, J., Goudreault, M., Muskat, B., Alfarano, C., Dewar, D., Lin, Z., Michalickova, K., Willems, A.R., Sassi, H., Nielsen, P.A., Rasmussen, K.J., Andersen, J.R., Johansen, L.E., Hansen, L.H., Jespersen, H., Podtelejnikov, A., Nielsen, E., Crawford, J., Poulsen, V., Srensen, B.D., Matthiesen, J., Hendrickson, R.C., Gleeson, F., Pawson, T., Moran, M.F., Durocher, D., Mann, M., Hogue, C.W.V., Figeys, D., Tyers, M.: Systematic identification of protein complexes in Saccharomyces cerevisiae by mass spectrometry. Nature 415, 180–183 (2002)

Retrieving Samples from Biobanks*

Claus Dabringer and Johann Eder

Alps Adria University Klagenfurt, Department of Informatics Systems
{Claus.Dabringer,Johann.Eder}@uni-klu.ac.at

Abstract. Biobanks are extremely important resources for medical research: they collect biological material (samples) and data describing this material. Biobanks provide medical researchers with material and data they need for their studies. Data availability varies greatly among samples and makes the retrieval of data and identification of relevant samples a strenuous task. We show the challenges and limitations when using pure SQL statements for querying a relational database. To tackle the problem of locating interesting material we present a novel approach which automatically generates approximate queries with ranking capabilities. Medical researchers use a Query By Example interface to specify desired attributes and restrictions and assign weights to them to influence the ranking function.

Keywords: searching in biobanks, approximate querying, result ranking, query generation.

1 Introduction

Biobanks are collections of biological material (tissue, blood, cell cultures, etc.) together with data describing this material and their donors and data derived from this material [13]. Biobanks are of eminent importance for medical research - for discovering the processes in living cells, the causes and effects of diseases, the interaction between genetic inheritance and life style factors, or the development of therapies and drugs. Information systems are an integral part of any biobank and efficient and effective IT support is mandatory for the viability of biobanks.

For example: A medical researcher wants to find out why a certain liver cancer generates a great number of metastasis in some patients and in others not. This knowledge would help to improve the prognosis, the therapy, the selection of therapies and drugs for a particular patient, and help to develop better drugs. For such a study the researcher needs besides biological material (cancer tissue) an enormous amount of data: clinical records of the patients donating the tissue, lab analysis, microscopic images of the diseased cells, information about the life style of patients, genotype information (e.g. genetic variations), phenotype information (e.g. gene expression profiles), etc. Gathering all these data in the

---

* The work reported here was partially supported by the European Commission 7th Framework program - project BBMRI and by the Austrian Ministry of Science and Research within the program GEN-AU - project GATIB II.

S. Khuri, L. Lhotská, and N. Pisanti (Eds.): ITBAM 2010, LNCS 6266, pp. 172–185, 2010.
© Springer-Verlag Berlin Heidelberg 2010

course of a single study would be highly inefficient and costly. A biobank is supposed to deliver the data needed for this type of research and share the data and material among researchers.

One of the major problems of the data stored in biobanks is that available attributes vary tremendously between cases, because these data depend on the tests made on a patient or on the tissue harvested from a patient, the follow-up analysis, the availability of questionnaires, the use of the material in studies generating additional information like gene sequencing or gene expression profiling. Additionally the data might be in different qualities, e.g. the age of a patient could be given exactly or in age groups.

All of this makes retrieval of relevant material for a study a strenuous activity, which currently usually involves browsing through a huge number of potentially relevant samples. The goal of the techniques presented in this paper aim at reducing this effort by orders of magnitude and significantly improving the quality and suitability of the data and material used in medical studies.

The rest of this paper is organized as follows: Section 2 deals with the problems of searching for biobanks, subjects and samples. In section 3 we show a simplified data-model for storing biobanks, subjects and related attributes. Further on we give a definition of supported queries and show how a researcher can influence the ranking. The formal definition of the generated query and the calculation of the final rank for each result tuple is also shown in section 3. Experimental results achieved when posting the generated queries and a comparison to posting plain SQL statement is shown in section 4. An outline of some important related work is given in section 5.

2   Searching for Biobanks, Subjects and Samples

Medical researchers are frequently faced with two major questions. First of all it is important to know *which biobank(s) store interesting material for a certain study?* Second the researcher needs to obtain *relevant material and/or data* from that given biobank.

According to our experience, currently the retrieval of data and material is a great effort for several reasons:

- The databases for biobanks are mostly semistructured (respectively, full of null values). This means that for a case very different information is available. This stems partly from different data needed for different types of medical diagnosis and therapy, different tests made by the doctors or by researchers who already used this material. Questionnaires e.g. about life style data might be available, if a patient was included in a medical study.
- Data is of different quality and granularity.
- Researchers have to face the typical recall/precision problem of information retrieval [8]. Queries may be restricted too tightly or too loosely. On one hand it may happen that the query restrictions are under-specified. This leads to the fact that the researcher is confronted with very many results which have to be browsed to find relevant items. On the other hand the

query restrictions may be over-specified. In this case there may be zero or only a few entries in the result set. This leads to iterating queries with small variations. Both situations are not satisfying since the searched material is not in the result set immediately. As a result researchers have to go through all identified elements or reformulate the query and post it again.

- Researchers typically come up with a list of important attributes and constraints concerning their project. This list contains attributes and restrictions *absolutely necessary* for their research project as well as *desired* and also several *minor important attributes and restrictions*. E.g. They are often interested in the availability of certain data (e.g. gene expression profile, therapy description or tumor staging available), as their availability reduces the effort necessary in the actual study or in the value of other attributes (e.g. a person diagnosed with liver cancer). Therefore, it is necessary to express the importance of an attribute or a constraint.
- Frequently there are preferred attribute values in search conditions which are not strict restrictions. E.g. a researcher needs samples from patients with a body mass index of 25. However, he can also take material from persons with a BMI of 24 or 26, but would prefer them to samples from persons with a BMI of 22. To avoid query iteration the posing approximate queries would be an advantage.
- Biobanks are highly heterogenous data sources[23,15]. Different biobanks store attributes and values in different formats, languages, encodings etc. Their data comes from different sources and are collected over longer periods of time where medical standards change, new procedures and machinery becomes available with greater accuracy in test, etc.

All these facts together lead to an ongoing reformulation of the posted query until a satisfying result can be found and to sequential browsing of large result sets. The reformulation process is very time consuming for a researcher, not only in the case of rare diseases. Researchers commonly use a trial and error technique to find interesting biobanks and materials for their studies.

Ways out. To cope with the mentioned problems we developed a technique that automatically generates approximate queries which reflect the researchers' needs. The generated queries can be used for querying semi-structured data and they return a ranked result with the most interesting biobanks, samples etc. on the top-most position(s). Our approach helps researchers to reflect a given list of required attributes and constraints and lets them assign weights to each of them. The recall/precision problem is tackled with the help of approximate query answering and result ranking. With the use of this technique we are able to include also partial and near matches in the result set. Our proposed technique is shown on the case of biobanks but is fully generic and can be used within any other field of application. The aim of this work is to minimize the query posting effort for medical researchers by providing means (i.e. the generated queries) to rank tuples that are not a full match for a given input query.

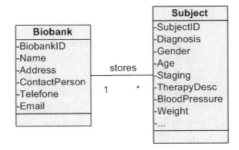

Fig. 1. Light-weight data model for storing biobanks, subjects and their describing attributes

3   Query Processing

The Underlying Data Model. The simplified data model shown in figure 1 is used for explanatory purposes. It is significantly simplified for the purpose of this paper but gives a good basis to formulate and understand queries in the rest of the paper. This data model allows to store different biobanks, each of which stores an arbitrary number of subjects which are further described by some attributes. In our case these attributes are the diagnosis, gender, age, etc. Choosing an upper-bound schema regarding the attributes allows heterogeneous biobanks to store their data in such a data-model. In case a biobank does not store a given attribute of such a data model the field is left blank (i.e. null) in the database. These *null-values* make query processing hard if choosing plain SQL. For the sake of simplicity we assume that for every subject stored in a biobank there are samples available to share.

Example queries that can be posted against this data model are: Find interesting biobanks that store subjects

1. ... with diagnosis C50.8 (breast cancer) which have been taken from a female person aged 50 years and where tumour staging and a therapy description are available.
2. ... with diagnosis C34.0 (lung cancer), systolic blood pressure of 160 and a weight greater than 110 kg.

With the help of those two example enquiries we are showing how our approach can support the medical researcher in locating interesting biobanks and samples for a certain research project.

Supported Queries. Our prototype is able to generate queries for a very broad field of use. We show its application in the field of biobanks but the prototype is generic and contains no biobanks specific operations etc. From a meta-perspective point of view the supported queries can be written as follows:

$$select\ a_1,\ a_2,\ ...\ a_n$$
$$from\ t_1,\ t_2,\ ...\ t_t$$

$$where\ join_1\ ...\ AND\ join_j$$
$$AND\ restriction_1$$
$$AND\ restriction_2\ ...$$
$$AND\ restriction_r$$

The generated queries may contain an arbitrary number of attributes from different tables as well as restrictions affecting attributes from different tables. The restrictions can be very versatile e.g. we are supporting any binary operator available in standard SQL as well as range operators like *BETWEEN*. Restrictions composed of binary operators consist of a left-hand attribute, an operator and a right-hand attribute or value. An example restriction would be: *age = 50*. Posting query-1 of our example queries would result in the following SQL statement:

$$select\ b.name$$
$$from\ biobank\ b,\ subject\ s$$
$$where\ b.BiobankID\ =\ s.BiobankID$$
$$AND\ s.Diagnosis\ =\ 'C50.8'$$
$$AND\ s.Gender\ =\ 'female'$$
$$AND\ s.TherapyDesc\ =\ true$$
$$AND\ s.Staging\ =\ true$$

With this example SQL statement we can easily see that there are a lot of restrictions even if the requirements of query-1 could be stated in just two lines of natural language. Since the wish list of a medical researcher is typically much longer we can conclude that there will be very few or even zero answers in the result set.

Influencing the Ranking. In order to allow the researcher to influence the final ranked result of the query we provide the possibility to specify weights on

- the *availability* of each of the attributes.
- each of the *restrictions*.

The available weights reach from *1 (nice to have)* up to *5 (must have)*. Giving the user the possibility to specify importance weights for the *fulfillment of a restriction* and for the *availability of an attribute* we can directly support a user driven selection of result tuples. Testing for the availability of a certain attribute can be very useful in cases where the exact value of an attribute is not stored in the biobank or where the user can not specify the exact search criteria. E.g. researchers typically ask for the availability of a *therapy description*, a *follow up* or *x-ray images*. Values for those attributes are often not directly searchable in the biobanks since they are free text, etc. But providing the possibility to ask for their availability is very useful. The selection of attributes, defining of restrictions and assignment of corresponding weights is realized using a *Query by Example* front-end.

3.1   Formal Query Definition

Input. Formally the generated approximate query is specified with the help of two sets. Set-1 contains all the attributes that should be checked for their availability. Each of the attributes also has an attached weight which is used for calculating the rank for the result tuples: S1: { $(attr_1, weight_1)$, ... $(attr_n, weight_n)$ }. Set-2 contains all restrictions and their corresponding weights: S2: { $(restriction_1, weight_1)$, ... $(restriction_r, weight_r)$ }. Those two sets together form all needed information for the *automatic query generation* process. Query-1 of our example queries could be formulated by the researcher as follows:

- S1: { (Staging, 3), (TherapyDesc, 4) }
- S2: { (Diagnosis=C50.8, 4), (Gender=female, 5), (Age=50, 3)}

Specifying these preferences means that the searched person *must be* female, the diagnosis *should be* closely related to mamma carcinoma. The age can have a greater *deviation around 50*, a therapy description is *very important* and the tumour staging is *medium relevant.*

Output. Formally the returned result-set of the generated query can be written as R: { $(tuple_1, rank_1)$, ... $(tuple_n, rank_n)$ } where $\forall$ tuples in R: $t.attr_1$ ~fulfills $q.restriction_1$ ... AND $t.attr_r$ ~fulfills $q.restriction_r$. The grade of fulfillment (~fulfills) between an attribute and a given restriction is either 0, *no fulfillment* to 1, *total fulfillment*. How the grade of fulfillment influences the final rank is shown in section 3.3. Due to the approximate query answering support it could also be the case that a resulting tuple does not fulfill any of the given restrictions. E.g. the algorithm could find resulting tuples for our example query-2 with the following values: Diagnosis C34.*3* (Malignant neoplasm: lower lobe, bronchus or lung), systolic blood pressure of *140* and a weight greater than *115 kg*. This result tuple of course has a lower rank attached than a result tuple that totally fulfills all restrictions.

3.2   Automatic Query Generation

Our algorithm is able to automatically generate queries from the chosen attributes, restrictions and the according weights. During the generation process of the query we have to consider how to generate selections as well as projections. The automatic query generation can be separated into different steps:

- The projections are directly taken from the *Query by Example* input of the user. The chosen attributes are rendered into the SQL statement at the corresponding positions. Taken the example query-2 from before that would be the attributes named diagnosis, blood pressure and weight.
- After the projection is rendered properly the SQL statement is augmented by the call of the *ranking function*. The parameter list of the function contains user defined types (UDTs) to pass the sets of attributes and restrictions to the function. UDTs and the passing of UDTs to functions is possible in the

most commonly used database management systems such as Oracle, SQL
Server and DB2. Further on this step introduces an alias for the ranking
function. The alias can be hard coded since it does not change over time.

- The generated SQL statement is then extended by the *from clause* and the
  join statements which can be easily derived from the underlying data model
  of the Query by Example tool.
- The last step in generating the SQL statement is adding the *order by clause*.
  Here we make use of the alias introduced for the ranking function. The order
  by clause only contains the alias of the ranking function. This step leads to
  a query result set ordered by the *ranking function*.

The following piece of pseudo-code shows the process of automatic query generation. The input parameters are the two sets described in section 3.1. The
output parameter is an SQL statement which can be directly posted against
a relational database management system like Oracle, SQLServer or DB2. The
result set produced by issuing this query is formally described in section 3.1.

```
program GenerateQuery (IN Set attrs, IN Set restrictions,
OUT SQLStmt sql)
    var i: Integer
    var ranking: RankFunction
begin
        sql.AddProjections(attrs)

        i := 0
        repeat
            i := i + 1
        ranking.AddAttribute (attrs[i])
        until i = attrs.Count

        i := 0
        repeat
        i := i + 1
        ranking.AddRestriction (restrictions[i])
        until i = restrictions.Count

        sql.AddRankingFunction(ranking)
        sql.AddFromClause()
        sql.AddJoinStatements()
        sql.AddOrderBy(ranking.FunctionName)
end.
```

An example output of the automatic query generation process is shown in the
following. The generator received the restrictions from query-1 as input parameters. Further on we defined the same weights as in section 3.1 on each of the
attributes and restrictions. We can also see that all restrictions in the where
clause are omitted. Only the join conditions remained unchanged.

```
select s.TherapyDesc, s.Staging, s.Diagnosis, s.Gender, s.Age,
    ranking
    (
      attr_list(
        attr_imp( attr('TherapyDesc', val(s.TherapyDesc)), 4),
        attr_imp( attr('Staging', val(s.Staging)), 3)
                 ),
      restrictlist(
        restrict_imp( rest( attr('Diagnosis', val(s.Diagnosis)),
                    val('C50.8'), '='), 4),
        restrict_imp( rest( attr('Gender', val(s.Gender)),
                    val('f'), '='), 5),
        restrict_imp( rest( attr('Age', val(s.Age)),
                    val('50'), '='), 3)
                 )
    ) as rank
      from biobank b, subject s
      where b.BiobankID = s.BiobankID
      order by rank desc;
```

This automatically generated sql statement is then executed against our
database by the *Query by Example* tool in order to retrieve the most relevant
tuples for a given research enquiry. Grouping the result by the biobank and summing up the rank of each result tuple gives the most interesting biobank on the
topmost position.

3.3   Calculating the Rank

The calculation of the rank is done in an embedded function inside the database.
The objective function used for ranking each particular tuple is discussed in
the following. Calculating the rank incorporates several user given aspects (i.e.
attributes, restrictions and weights) as well as similarity measures between different attribute values. Here we especially calculate the similarity between the
attribute values in a result tuple and the values in the restriction of the posted
query. The similarity measures used within our algorithm are adapted versions of
the well known Inverse Document Frequency (IDF) [24,11,22] and IDF-Similarity
[5] often used in Information Retrieval. When measuring the similarity between
attribute values we distinguish between numerical values and categorical data.
For categorical data we are also able to incorporate *Ontologies* which describe
the similarity between different terms. I.e. we provide auxiliary tables for integration of such information. The calculation of the final rank for a single
tuple is stated in equation 1. A tuple T is defined as a set of attributes, namely
$\langle a_1, a_2, ... a_m \rangle$.

$$Rank_{final} = \sum_{i=1}^{n} Avail(a_i, t, w_{a_i}) + \sum_{j=1}^{m} w_{r_{a_j}} * (Fulfills(a_j, r_{a_j}) + Sim(a_j, val_{r_{a_j}}))$$

(1)

Equation 2 defines the function *Avail*. With the help of this function the availability of certain attributes influences the final rank. It returns the user chosen weight w_a for the given attribute a in the case that this attribute is present in tuple t and 0 otherwise.

$$Avail(a, t, w_a) = \begin{cases} w_a, & \text{if attribute } a \in \text{tuple } t \\ 0, & \text{otherwise} \end{cases} \qquad (2)$$

The definition of function *Fulfills* is shown in equation 3. This function evaluates to 1 if the value of the given attribute a fulfills the restriction r and to 0 otherwise.

$$Fulfills(a, r) = \begin{cases} 1, & \text{a fulfills restriction r} \\ 0, & \text{otherwise} \end{cases} \qquad (3)$$

Equation 4 shows how the similarity between two attribute values is calculated. The first parameter (a_j) passed to *Sim* is the attribute value of the tuple, the second parameter $(val_{r_{a_j}})$ is the attribute value given by the user in the restriction. We distinguish between three cases. The most complex case deals with the similarity between two numerical values. The similarity between numerical values a and v is calculated as the density at a of a Gaussian distribution centered at v and scaled by *IDF(v)*. Equation 5 [5] shows the definition of the *NumericalSim(a, v)* used to calculate the similarity between the two given values.

$$Sim(a, v) = \begin{cases} NumericalSim(a, v), & \text{if a is numerical} \\ OntologySim(a, v), & \text{if a and v in ontology} \\ CategoricalSim(a, v), & \text{otherwise} \end{cases} \qquad (4)$$

$$NumericalSim(a, v) = e^{-\frac{1}{2}(\frac{a-v}{h})^2} * IDF(v) \qquad (5)$$

A robust definition of *IDF(v)* is given in equation 6 [5]. We are assuming that $\langle v_1, v_2, ...v_n \rangle$ are the values of a certain *attribute A* in the database. For any of those values we calculate the IDF upfront and store it in auxiliary tables. This tables are not complex since they only map a numerical value t_i to another numerical value which is the IDF. The numerator of equation 6 is the number of different attribute values of *attribute A*. The denominator models the sum of contributions to v from every other possible value v_i of *attribute A*. This models the fact that values v_i farther away from v contribute fewer. The constant h is the bandwidth parameter often defined as: $h = 1.06 * \sigma * n^{-\frac{1}{5}}$, with σ defined as the standard deviation of all values from *attribute A*.

$$IDF(v) = \log \frac{n}{\sum_{i=1}^{n} e^{-\frac{1}{2}(\frac{v_i-v}{h})^2}} \qquad (6)$$

The similarity function used for categorical data is shown in equation 7. It returns either 0 or 1 depending whether the values are equal or not.

$$CategoricalSim(a, v) = \begin{cases} 1, & \text{if a equals v} \\ 0, & \text{otherwise} \end{cases} \qquad (7)$$

	NAME	DIAGNOSIS	GENDER	AGE	BLOODPRESSURE	WEIGHT
1	BB-1	C50.8	female	50	(null)	(null)
2	BB-1	C50.8	female	50	120	60
3	BB-2	C50.8	female	50	110	83

Fig. 2. Resulting tuples of the *initial query* against our testing database

The function *OntologySim* is not described here in a mathematical way since it results in a read-once database access. The similarity between two terms is read from an auxiliary table in the underlying database. This feature can be used to map the similarity of two terms e.g. *breast cancer* and *mamma carcinoma*. With the function *OntologySim* we can further support the similarity definition of terms hierarchically related to each other e.g. terms in the ICD10 or ICD-O coding system [3]. Last but not least our auxiliary tables can also be used to define the similarity of terms described in different vocabularies e.g. how similar is a term in the ICD10 coding system to a term in the *SNOMED* coding system [2].

4   Experimental Results

Within this section we want to give an impression how supportive our prototype can be for medical researchers. The database used during the examination was an *Oracle 10g*. As the underlying data model we used the one described in section 2. The test database was filled with three different biobanks and scrambled real data from those biobanks.

A researcher typically starts with the formulation of the needs for a certain research project. The aim is to find *a biobank* that stores interesting subjects and samples. Once more we take query-1 from section 2 as the basis for our explanations. An SQL statement reflecting those needs could be stated as follows:

> *select b.name, s.diagnosis, s.gender,*
> *s.age, s.bloodpressure, s.weight*
> *from biobank b, subject s*
> *where b.BiobankID = s.BiobankID*
> *AND s.Diagnosis = 'C50.8'*
> *AND s.Gender = 'female'*
> *AND s.TherapyDesc = true*
> *AND s.Staging = true*

The result of posting this query against our data model is shown in figure 2. Since the query is rather restrictive it does not result in the desired output. We can see that the query identified three appropriate cases in two different biobanks, namely *BB-1* and *BB-2*.

Since a researcher typically needs more subjects and thus samples for his research project the query reformulation process starts. The next step is a

	NAME		DIAGNOSIS		GENDER		AGE		BLOODPRESSURE		WEIGHT
1	BB-1		C50.8		female		50		(null)		(null)
2	BB-2		C50.8		female		53		(null)		(null)
3	BB-3		C50.8		female		52		(null)		(null)
4	BB-3		C50.8		female		55		110		65
5	BB-3		C50.8		female		53		115		78
6	BB-1		C50.8		female		50		120		60
7	BB-2		C50.8		female		50		110		83

Fig. 3. Resulting tuples after relaxing the searching criteria from 50 year old subjects to persons aged from 50 years upwards

relaxation of the originally posted query. The researcher relaxes the restriction on the *age* and asks for subjects that are aged from 50 years upwards. The result for posting this adapted query is shown in figure 3.

We can observe that there appeared four new subjects, three of them in a new biobank namely *BB-3*. To gather still more subjects another adaption of the searching criteria must be performed. Removing the needs for the availability of a *therapy description* and *tumour staging* could be one of the next alternatives. Posting this minimalistic query only adds one new subject to the existing result set and therefore the researcher has to continue the adaption process.

The description of the process for locating interesting biobanks and subjects from the researchers perspective shows the needs for an intelligent support in searching interesting material. With the use of our automatically generated query we can heavily support the researcher in his project start-up phase by providing

	NAME		DIAG...		GEN...		AGE		BLOO...		RANK
1	BB-1		C50.8		female		50		(null)		21,12
2	BB-1		C50.8		female		50		120		21,12
3	BB-2		C50.8		female		50		110		21,12
4	BB-3		C50.8		female		52		(null)		17,4
5	BB-3		C50.8		female		47		120		16,83
6	BB-3		C50.8		female		53		115		16,83
7	BB-3		C50.8		female		55		110		16,16
8	BB-3		C50.8		female		45		105		16,16
9	BB-2		C50.8		female		53		(null)		13,83
10	BB-3		C50.8		female		43		115		12,01
11	BB-2		C50.8		female		(null)		160		12
12	BB-2		C50.8		female		48		135		10,4
13	BB-3		C50.8		female		46		100		9,4
14	BB-3		C50.8		female		45		150		9,16

Fig. 4. Resulting tuples with *additional ranking information* returned from our generated approximate query

valuable information where subjects of desire are located. Posting a generated query (like the one in section 3.1) results in a much higher number of interesting subjects with attached ranking information. A *shortened* example output of the generated approximate query is shown in figure 4.

Grouping the result tuples by the *Biobank* and summing up the attached ranks gives the researcher a good hint which biobank to contact first. The best starting point according to our algorithm would be *BB-3* which did not even appear in the first result set in figure 2.

5 Related Work

Our work has been inspired by several different research areas, namely dealing with approximate query answering techniques, ranking query results, definition of similarity measures and of course with query rewriting. Ranking of database query results is very popular in *Information Retrieval Systems* and has been studied extensively. There exist several approaches to deal with the empty- and too-many-answers problem [10,5,9,25,4]. In [10,9] the ranking functions are formulated with the help of probabilistic models. The authors of [5] introduce an adaption of the IDF used in information retrieval and use workload analysis methods to learn more about attribute similarities. The adapted *IDF-Similarity* measure has been used within our approach to calculate similarity between numeric values. The many- and empty-answer set problem is tackled with the help of fuzzy arithmetics in [7].

In contrast to our automatic query generation support the authors of [20] show a query refinement approach where the users can specify similarity queries. The system can be used iteratively to adapt the scoring rules until an adequate result is achieved. Also in [21] query rewriting techniques are applied to retrieve heterogeneous data. An approach for generating queries and attaching ranks to them is shown in [18]. Ranking functions for approximate queries have been previously addressed in [19,12]. Most of them use weighted similarity measures to derive an overall rank. [19] focuses on highly heterogeneous web-databases and presents strategies to efficiently retrieve the top-k answers. In [12] the selection of ordering attributes and tuples is decided upon multiplicative and additive ranking functions.

Also in the context of XML documents the retrieving and ranking of information is very popular [17,14,16,6]. In [16] the weighted term frequency and an inverted element frequency are used to formulate promising ranking functions. The definition of a query language that enables the collection and ranking from different XML data sources is given in a recent publication [14].

6 Conclusion

Searching for interesting biobanks, subjects and samples is a very demanding task for medical researchers. We have shown where the intrinsic problems of retrieving samples and data from biobanks are and have shown that it is basically an optimization problem which requires that researchers formulate the specific requirements of their studies to overcome the recall/precision problem. We presented a solution which automatically generates *approximate queries* based on the definition of the requirements. With the help of a *Query by Example* prototype we allow the definition of weights for the *fulfillment of a restriction* and for the *availability of an attribute*. These weights directly influence our *objective function* used for calculating the *final rank* of each tuple in the result set. We compared our approach of automatically generating queries with an approach of consecutive adaption of the query restrictions. These first experimental results show that the effort for retrieving relevant data from biobanks can be reduced significantly with the presented techniques. To cope with the federated nature of biobanks all over Europe [1] our next steps will be to enhance the presented prototype for the work in a distributed environment.

References

1. Biobanking and biomolecular resources research infrastructure, http://www.bbmri.eu
2. Systematized nomenclature of medicine-clinical terms, http://www.ihtsdo.org
3. Unified global medical coding system, http://www.icd10codes.com
4. Agichtein, E., Brill, E., Dumais, S.: Improving web search ranking by incorporating user behavior information. In: SIGIR 2006: Proceedings of the 29th annual international ACM SIGIR conference on Research and development in information retrieval, pp. 19–26. ACM, New York (2006)
5. Agrawal, S., Chaudhuri, S.: Automated ranking of database query results. In: CIDR, pp. 888–899 (2003)
6. Amer-Yahia, S., Koudas, N., Marian, A., Srivastava, D., Toman, D.: Structure and content scoring for xml. In: VLDB 2005: Proceedings of the 31st international conference on Very large data bases, pp. 361–372. VLDB Endowment (2005)
7. Bosc, P., Hadjali, A., Pivert, O.: Empty versus overabundant answers to flexible relational queries. Fuzzy Sets and Systems 159(12), 1450–1467 (2008); Advances in Intelligent Databases and Information Systems
8. Buckland, M., Gey, F.: The relationship between recall and precision. J. Am. Soc. Inf. Sci. 45(1), 12–19 (1994)
9. Chaudhuri, S., Das, G.: Probabilistic information retrieval approach for ranking of database query results. ACM Trans. Database Syst. 31(3), 1134–1168 (2006)
10. Chaudhuri, S., Das, G., Hristidis, V., Weikum, G.: Probabilistic ranking of database query results. In: VLDB 2004: Proceedings of the Thirtieth international conference on Very large data bases, pp. 888–899. VLDB Endowment (2004)
11. Church, K., Gale, W.: Inverse document frequency (idf): A measure of deviations from poisson
12. Das, G., Hristidis, V., Kapoor, N., Sudarshan, S.: Ordering the attributes of query results. In: SIGMOD 2006: Proceedings of the 2006 ACM SIGMOD international conference on Management of data, pp. 395–406. ACM, New York (2006)
13. Eder, J., Dabringer, C., Schicho, M., Stark, K.: Information systems for federated biobanks. Transactions on Large Scale Data and Knowledge Centered Systems (2009)

14. Fazzinga, B., Flesca, S., Pugliese, A.: Retrieving xml data from heterogeneous sources through vague querying. ACM Trans. Internet Technol. 9(2), 1–35 (2009)

15. Litwin, W., Mark, L., Roussopoulos, N.: Interoperability of multiple autonomous databases. ACM Comput. Surv. 22(3), 267–293 (1990)

16. Liu, S., Zou, Q., Chu, W.W.: Configurable indexing and ranking for xml information retrieval. In: SIGIR 2004: Proceedings of the 27th annual international ACM SIGIR conference on Research and development in information retrieval, pp. 88–95. ACM, New York (2004)

17. Mandreoli, F., Martoglia, R., Tiberio, P.: Approximate query answering for a heterogeneous xml document base (2004)

18. Mandreoli, F., Martoglia, R., Tiberio, P.: Approximate query answering for a heterogeneous xml document base. LNCS. Springer, Heidelberg (2004)

19. Marian, A., Bruno, N., Gravano, L.: Evaluating top-k queries over web-accessible databases. ACM Trans. Database Syst. 29(2), 319–362 (2004)

20. Ortega-Binderberger, M., Chakrabarti, K., Mehrotra, S.: An approach to integrating query refinement in sql (2002)

21. Papakonstantinou, Y., Vassalos, V.: Query rewriting for semistructured data. In: SIGMOD 1999: Proceedings of the 1999 ACM SIGMOD international conference on Management of data, pp. 455–466. ACM, New York (1999)

22. Robertson, S.: Understanding inverse document frequency: on theoretical arguments for idf. Journal of Documentation 60, 503–520 (2004)

23. Sheth, A.P., Larson, J.A.: Federated database systems for managing distributed, heterogeneous, and autonomous databases. ACM Comput. Surv. 22(3), 183–236 (1990)

24. Sparck Jones, K.: A statistical interpretation of term specificity and its application in retrieval, pp. 132–142 (1988)

25. Stojanovic, N., Studer, R., Stojanovic, L.: An approach for the ranking of query results in the semantic web. In: Fensel, D., Sycara, K., Mylopoulos, J. (eds.) ISWC 2003. LNCS, vol. 2870, pp. 500–516. Springer, Heidelberg (2003)

Logical Knowledge Representation of Regulatory Relations in Biomedical Pathways

Sine Zambach[1] and Jens Ulrik Hansen[1,2]

[1] Computer Science, Roskilde University
Universitetsvej 1, DK-4000 Roskilde, Denmark
{sz,jensuh}@ruc.dk
[2] Philosophy, Roskilde University, Universitetsvej 1, DK-4000 Roskilde, Denmark

Abstract. Knowledge on regulatory relations, in for example regulatory pathways in biology, is used widely in experiment design by biomedical researchers and in systems biology. The knowledge has typically either been represented through simple graphs or through very expressive differential equation simulations of smaller sections of a pathway.

As an alternative, in this work we suggest a knowledge representation of the most basic relations in regulatory processes *regulates*, *positively regulates* and *negatively regulates* in logics based on a semantic analysis. We discuss the usage of these relations in biology and in artificial intelligence for hypothesis development in drug discovery.

Keywords: Formal relations, semantic analysis, biomedical ontologies, knowledge representation, knowledge discovery, applied logic, formal ontologies.

1 Introduction

Regulatory networks are used for simple modeling of varying complexity, for example within biology, economy and other fields which apply dynamic systems.

In biomedicine, regulatory networks are widely used to model regulatory pathways, which, in short, are characterized by processes containing gene products and smaller molecules that regulate each other through different mechanisms through different paths. The relations among the building blocks of these networks are typically modeled either very expressively in *e.g.* linked differential equations within the area of physical chemistry as in [1,2], or very simply in graphs in information systems as in KEGG and Reactome [3,4].

In this paper, we take another approach and discuss an initial framework for knowledge representation semantically based on logics. This approach is widely used within knowledge representation and we apply it on an abstraction of the biological notion of regulatory pathways. Our focus is on the relations *positively regulates* and *negatively regulates* as well as neutrally *regulates*, which we assume is a super relation of the two others. We call the three relations "regulatory relations" and we use the terms *stimulates* and *inhibits* interchangeably with *positively-* and *negatively regulates*.

S. Khuri, L. Lhotská, and N. Pisanti (Eds.): ITBAM 2010, LNCS 6266, pp. 186–200, 2010.

The aim of a logical knowledge representation is to capture the formal semantics of the relations. Furthermore, logic implementations offer an opportunity to reason automatically (in a qualitative way) with the goal of obtaining new knowledge. This representation can be utilized in further work on lexical-semantical annotation to be used in information retrieval systems for example. Additionally, the representation can be a part of simulating regulatory networks in biology in a relatively simple manner.

The use of logic in knowledge representation is not a new thing. For instance, the popular tool for semantic web, OWL, has a semantic based on logic. The logic is a variant of a description logic, a family of logics that also have been very popular for knowledge representation. Another classical logic for knowledge representation is first-order logic, which description logic can be seen as a fragment of. We will use first-order logic since it is more expressive, but we will also discuss the possibility of using description logic.

In this paper we will first discuss related work on knowledge representation in the biomedical area in section 2. In section 2.2, we present examples of knowledge on biomedical regulatory pathways. To represent the kind of knowledge described by these examples, the domain in question must be investigated deeper ontologically, and the clarification of the ontology furthermore displays which underlying assumptions are involved in the knowledge we aim to represent. These issues will be discussed in section 3. In section 4, we use First-order Logic to specify a formal semantics of regulatory relations. Next, we analyze the entities involved in regulatory relations, which allows us to clarify regulatory relationships even further. In addition, we discuss the possibilities of representing the relations in Description Logic. Finally, we discuss the biological usage of our formalization of the regulatory networks and further work.

2   Related Work and Examples

2.1   Related Work

Knowledge representation of biomedical pathways typically spans from simple graph representations among gene products to the more sophisticated linked differential equations, as already mentioned.

Graph representations are mostly informal and constructed to illustrate a regulatory path. In more formal graphs like KEGG [3] (in figure 1), Reactome [4], and MetaCyc [1], regulation among entities like small molecules and gene products are formalized into a database, to which you can have simple queries. For example, in the network of figure 1, the legend tells us that "PP1 activates GYS" (because of the arrow) and "PP1" is a gene product (because of the box around "PP1"), which is information stored in the relatively simple structure of KEGG.

At the other end of the scale, regulatory pathways can be represented using linked differential equations expressed in the formula:

$$dS_i/dt = f_i(S_j, p_k) = f_i^+ + f_i^- \quad \begin{array}{l} i, j = (1, ..., n) \\ k = (1, ..., m). \end{array} \tag{1}$$

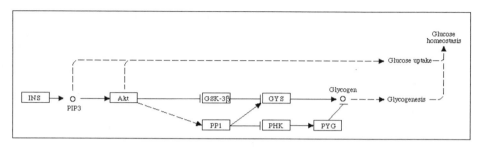

Fig. 1. A chain of inhibitions and stimulations in the insulin signaling pathway (simplified). The figure is a modified picture from KEGG [3].

For our purpose, the two most important parameters are f_i^+, the sum of the incoming flux (leading to positive regulation), and f_i^-, the sum of the outgoing flux leading to negative regulation [2]. This representation is very expressive and will be difficult if not impossible to implement on the almost 10,000 reactions that are represented in KEGG [1].

Additionally, the problems of acquiring such detailed information and the computationally higher complexity in these models, have lead to suggest less complex models, as for instance in [5]. This simpler model makes it possible to reason qualitatively about existing pathways leading to a rough flux-balance analysis similar to MetaCyc [1] and BioSim [6], which uses Prolog and qualitative constraints.

During the last decade a movement towards formalizing biomedical ontologies and the relations the ontologies contain, has progressed. For example, the widely used Gene Ontology [7,8] has been ontologically "cleaned up" and initiatives like OBO have provided a framework for the work on formal relations and cooperative ontology modeling [9,10]. Moreover, concerning properties of relations, the Role Ontology has been developed within the OBO foundry [11]. In the pathway modeling especially concerning regulation, ontologies and formalized systems like the Gene Regulation Ontology [12], EcoCyc/MetaCyc [1] and Pathway Logics [5] have suggested different approaches to logic representation. Furthermore, in the work on the Gene Regulation Ontology(GRO), regulation is present as a concept. The purpose of that work is to formalize the concepts related to gene regulation used in for example the Gene Ontology [8].

This work introduces First-order Logic in the representation in line with [11], for example.

2.2   Examples of Regulation

To be able to argue for the the ontological assumptions in section 3 and the logical semantic presented in section 4, in this section, we will present examples of the knowledge our simple model is supposed to capture.

The regulates-relations *positively regulates* and *negatively regulates* - are central in for example economics and biochemical pathways. In biomedical pathways, which we will concentrate on in the rest of this paper, it is typical gene products and smaller molecules that interacts with each other in complex processes.

A commonly used example of regulation is the insulin response mechanism. Insulin stimulates through a regulatory path, uptake of glucose through cell walls, protein synthesis and glucogenesis, for example. These stimulations occur via for example an activation of PIP3 and the glucogenesis is triggered for example through an activation of the Akt-protein and inhibition of PHK as shown in figure 1. Note here, that most of the regulatory paths are between the biological entities, gene products and small molecules. This typically means that one biological entity regulates the level (by regulating the production/secretion process) or function of another biological entity.

Another example of how regulation in a biological pathway has been represented semi-formally for use in hypothesis testing, is the presentation of the damage response pathway in yeast, which has been investigated and characterized by for example [13]. This work is an usage of a strategy for a longer pathway-traveling concerning gene products that regulates the production of other gene products. The work uses the notion of "deletion-buffering". The meaning of this is: When you remove a transcription factor, X, of the gene product, G, the result is that the production of another protein, P, cannot be regulated anymore by G, if G interacts directly with P. This typically results in an activation of P if G is an inhibitor and an inhibition of P if G is an activator.

There will of course be examples that are non-trivial compared to the above mentioned examples. An example is predicted inhibition in the recently discovered miRNAs, which are small regulating transcripts. miRNAs typically regulates gene products by binding to the mRNA of the gene product. However, often the regulation is just predicted *in silico* by sequence analysis until the experimental data has verified (or falsified) the interaction. This information is difficult to model by a simple regulates-relations since the meaning is rather "predicted to inhibit". We will return to this issue in section 4.3.

3   Ontological Clarifications

Based on the previous presented examples, we investigate in more details the ontological aspects of regulatory relations as they present themselves in biomedical research. We clarify which entities are subjects to relationships and make a distinction between general concepts or classes and individuals instantiating these classes.

3.1   Research Practice and Granularity

When creating models of knowledge to be used in biomedical hypothesis development, inspiration can be obtained by the practice in the biomedical laboratory. Before the validation of a hypothesis is to be carried out in the laboratory, the precise rates and levels of the involved substances are not necessary the first thing to consider. Rather we consider a qualitative overview of the processes to be the primary instrument in this stage of discovery. Thus we ignore the precise levels of substances and only care whether their levels are affected positively or negatively, leaving us with a higher level of abstraction (as in [5]).

Likewise, talking about "insulin positively regulates glucose transport", what is really meant is that an amount (or pool) of insulin causes an amount of glucose molecules to be transported. Or, expressed more precisely: When the level of insulin rises, this rise causes a higher frequency of glucose molecules to be transported (through cell walls). This rise is typically directly or indirectly caused by external addition of substance - either by intake of nutrition, medicals or even by lack of intake of the necessary nutrition to make the system work properly. Hence "amounts" or "pools" of substances are the basic entities, which are subject to possible relations.

3.2   Underlying Ontological Assumptions – Instances and Classes

The former subsection suggests that amounts of molecules rather than single molecules are the central concern of biomedical researchers. In laboratory context, researchers operate with certain amounts or batches of fluids containing multiple molecules. Also, the organs of the human body secrete an amount of molecules for regulating processes. Nothing really happens if the beta cell secretes *one* insulin molecule.

The ontological assumptions we make are virtually in line with the one presented in [11] and [14]. As in [11], we will distinguish between classes and instances. Classes (or concepts or types) refers here to what general exists, such as insulin, glucose, glucose transport, stem cell *etc.* In the following, names of classes will be italicized and begin with a capital letter, for instance *Insulin* and *Glucose_transport*. On the other hand, instances (or individuals, particulars, or tokens) are entities that exist in space and time as instances of a class, such as a particular quantity of insulin or beta cells. We will use $x, y, z, ...$ as variables ranging over arbitrary instances.

The distinction between classes and instances allows us to analyze a natural language expression such as "insulin positively regulates glucose transport" in more details; the sentence does not claim that the class *Insulin* positively regulates the class *Glucose_transport*, but that a certain relation between individuals of these classes exists as presented in section 3.1. Thus we assume that relations between the instances are given, for example by experimental evidence in the laboratory, and on the basis of these we define relations among classes or concepts. For instance, "positive regulation" relations may exists among particular amounts of insulin and particular glucose transports, and on the basis of these we define a relation between the classes *Insulin* and *Glucose_transport*. This we will do in the next section. Names of relations among individuals will be in bold face, *e.g.* "x **stimulates** y", whereas names of relations among classes will be in italic, *e.g.* "*Insulin stimulates Glucose_transport*".

4 Analysis of the Formal Semantic

In this section we provide a thorough semantic analysis of the regulatory relations based on First-order Logic. Finally, we mention the possibilities for an analysis in Description Logic and OWL.

4.1 A Logic Formalization of Regulatory Relations

Given the ontological assumptions, we will now discuss the possible relations between classes involved in the knowledge we aim to represent. In the definition of relations among these classes we will use First-order Logic. First-order Logic is used to reason about individuals and their properties, and allows for quantification over these individuals. The language of First-order Logic is build from propositional connectives such as "and" ($\wedge$), "or" ($\vee$), "not" ($\neg$), predicate symbols involved in $P(x)$ or $Q(x, y)$, variables $x, y, z, \ldots$, and quantifiers $\forall$ and $\exists$ (reading "for all" and "there exists"). We have chosen First-order Logic because of its simple reading and generality.[1]

A first example of a formalized relation between classes is the "part of" relation present in many biological ontologies. One can state that $Cell\_membrane$ is "part of" $Cell$, which expresses the fact that every particular cell membrane is the membrane of a particular cell. In other words, "for every cell membrane there exists a cell of which it is part of". Assuming a **part_of** relation between individuals, one can define a $part\_of$ relations among classes C_1 and C_2 in the following way [14]:

$$C_1 \; part\_of \; C_2 \quad \text{iff} \quad \forall x(C_1(x) \rightarrow \exists y(x \; \textbf{part\_of} \; y \wedge C_2(y))). \qquad (2)$$

A relation between classes defined this way will for easy reading be called "$\forall\exists$". Generally we define a $\forall\exists$ relation $rel_{\forall\exists}$ between two classes, C_1 and C_2, based on a relation **rel** between individuals, by:

$$C_1 \; rel_{\forall\exists} \; C_2 \quad \text{iff} \quad \forall x(C_1(x) \rightarrow \exists y(x \; \textbf{rel} \; y \wedge C_2(y))). \qquad (3)$$

The two classes C_1 and C_2 are also called the *relata* of the relation. Another example of a concrete relation between classes is the one exemplified by the term "enzymes stimulate processes". Even though it may not be visible on the surface, what we have here is an even stronger tie between the two classes than expressed by a $\forall\exists$ relation. The relation between enzymes and process is such that whatever an enzyme stimulates, it is a process. A relation of this kind will be called "$\forall only$" (inspired by the Machester syntax). Formally we define the $\forall only$ relation by:

$$C_1 \; rel_{\forall only} \; C_2 \quad \text{iff} \quad \forall x(C_1(x) \rightarrow \forall y(x \; \textbf{rel} \; y \rightarrow C_2(y))). \qquad (4)$$

---

[1] A commonly used logic for knowledge representation such as Description Logic can be viewed as a fragment of First-order Logic. We will return to the possibilities of given the semantic in terms of Description Logic later in section 4.4.

We now consider the case *positively_ regulates* as exemplified by a phrase such as "insulin positively regulates glucose transport", which exemplifies the kind of knowledge we aim to represent. As previously discussed in section 3.1, a sentence like this should be read as "for all amounts of insulin and all glucose transports, the insulin can potentially positively regulate the glucose transport". To express a relation like this we introduce the "∀∀" relation between classes in the following way:

$$C_1 \; rel_{\forall\forall} \; C_2 \quad \text{iff} \quad \forall x(C_1(x) \rightarrow \forall y(C_2(y) \rightarrow x \; \textbf{rel} \; y)). \tag{5}$$

The reason for choosing the ∀∀ relation instead of the ∀*only* to represent knowledge such as "insulin positively regulates glucose transport", is that Insulin also has the possibility to stimulate other processes such as glycogen production. This possibility is excluded if the knowledge is represented as a ∀*only* relation.

4.2   The Relata of Regulatory Relations

A deeper ontological analysis of the entities involved in regulatory relations reveals that a distinction between continuants and processes has ontological significance. Thus relations between individuals have to be divided into cases depending on whether the individuals are continuants or processes. However, in this section we show that this division can be collapsed using operators for production and output.

In line with [11] we distinguish between continuants and processes. Continuants are entities that continue to exists over time and may undergo changes, contrary to processes, which are events. Continuants are entities that can change and the changes themselves are processes. We will use $c, c_1, c_2, ...$ to range over continuants and $p, p_1, p_2, ...$ to range over processes. An example of a continuant in our domain could be an amount of insulin, whereas a glucose transport is a process.

In case of regulation, continuants can regulate other continuants or processes, but processes can also regulate other processes or continuants. Thus there seems to be four possible regulatory relations depending on whether the related individuals are continuants or processes. Focusing on the relation "stimulates" there are therefore four possible relations among individuals. We name these **stimulates$_{cc}$**, **stimulates$_{cp}$**, **stimulates$_{pc}$**, and **stimulates$_{pp}$**, where for instance the subscript "cc" means that it is a relation that can only hold between two continuants. However, introducing a "production of" and a "output of" operator makes us capable of reducing these four relations to only one.

The *production_of*(...) operator works on a continuant c by transforming it to the process that is the production of c. Similarly the *output_of*(...) operator transforms a process p to the continuant that is the output of p. [2]

---

[2] However, this is not necesarily simple. Some processes may of course have several outputs. In larger regulatory pathways processes may regulate other processes, but this is always through outputs of the first process. These outputs can be unknown or it can be unknown which of the outputs that actually regulates the second process. This will be touched upon in the discussion.

With these operators the instance relations **stimulates$_{cc}$**, **stimulates$_{pc}$**, and **stimulates$_{pp}$** can be reduced to the **stimulates$_{cp}$** relation. These reduction are given by:

c_1 **stimulates$_{cc}$** c_2 reduces to c_1 **stimulates$_{cp}$** $production\_of(c_2)$

p **stimulates$_{pc}$** c reduces to $output\_of(p)$ **stimulates$_{cp}$** $production\_of(c)$

p_1 **stimulates$_{pp}$** p_2 reduces to $output\_of(p_1)$ **stimulates$_{cp}$** p_2

These reductions reflects how the relations are used as verbs in senteces in biological texts, for example: "Insulin **stimulates$_{cc}$** glycogen", "insulin **stimulates$_{cp}$** the glycogenesis", and "insulin **stimulates$_{cp}$** the production of glycogen (through the glygonenesis)" where the process glycogenese is equal to "the production of glycogen". Likewise you can formulate the sentences: "beta cell secretion **stimulates$_{pp}$** glycogenese" that can be reduced to "outout of beta cell secretion **stimulates$_{cp}$** production of glycogen", where the output of beta cell secretion is insulin.

4.3   Modal, Temporal and Spatial Aspect of Regulatory Relations

In the reading of "Insulin stimulates glucose transport" as "for all amounts of insulin and all glucose transports, the insulin can potentially positively regulate the glucose transport" the term "*can potentially*" plays a considerable role. It is a vague modal term, and in this section we will attempt to make it more precise.

When representing "Insulin stimulates glucose transport" as

$$\forall x(Insulin(x) \rightarrow \forall y(Glucose\_transport(y) \rightarrow x \textbf{ stimulates}_{\textbf{cp}} \ y)),$$

the term "can potentially" is implicit in the relation "**stimulates$_{cp}$**". In other words "x **stimulates$_{cp}$** y" is read as "x can potentially stimulate y". This seems sensible since "Insulin stimulates glucose transport" does not express that all amounts of insulin *actually* stimulates all glucose transports, but that they potentially can. Using modal logic formalisms [15] we can replace "x **stimulates$_{cp}$** y" by "$\Diamond(x$ **stim** $y)$", where the "$\Diamond$" is a modal operator representing "potentiality" and "**stim** " is the primitive name of a relation of actual stimulation. Thus "c **stim** p" means that the continuant c actively stimulating the process p. A semantics for this elaborated formula can the be given in the framework of first-order modal logic [16].

The potentiality represented by the $\Diamond$ operator can, however, be analyzed even further in the case of the stimulation relation. There are two kind of vagueness involved in the "can potentially stimulate" expressed in "$\Diamond(...$**stim**$...)$". The first one is due the fact that stimulation only takes place if the substance is actively participating in the process. If the process and substance are separated in space and time, stimulation can of course not take place. The relation of a continuant taking actively part in a process at a given time, is a basic relation and in [11] it is assumed as a primitive relation. Using their notation "p **has$\_$agent** c **at** t"

expresses that the continuant c is causally active in the process p at time t. Together with the **stim** relation, "x **stimulates$_{cp}$** y" can thus be expanded as:

$$\forall t(p \text{ has\_agent } c \text{ at } t \to c \text{ stim } p),$$

hence the $\Diamond$ operator is unnecessary.

The other vagueness involved in "can potentially stimulate" is due to the fact that other substances may interfere with the process, in which case a stimulation may not take place. Thus, in the above formula, x **stim** y should be read as "if no other substances interfere an actual stimulation between x and y takes place". If we use the formalization with the *Diamond* operator, we can include this *ceteris paribus* clause the reading of the $\Diamond$.

In non-trivial examples as the predicted regulation by miRNAs as described in section 2.2 there is an additional vagueness. This is due to the stimulation only being *predicted*. For example, $miRNA$ **stimulates$_{cc}$** c (predicted *in silico*), and c **stimulates$_{cp}$** p should lead to a weaker inference between $miRNA$ and p than if the $miRNA$ was experimentally shown to stimulate c.

4.4   Description Logic Representation of Class Relations

In section 4.1 we used First-order Logic to present a formal semantics for regulatory relations. This was motivated by the easy reading of First-order formulas that also made the difference between the class relations $rel_{\forall only}$ and $rel_{\forall\forall}$ visible. In this section we discuss the possibility of defining the relations in Description Logic.

Description Logic is a family of logics widely used for knowledge representation, and in several of the logics reasoning can be done in low complexity contrary to First-order Logic which is undecidable (for more on the complexity of Description Logic see chapter 3 in [17] . Furthermore, Description Logic is also implemented in several modern tools such as OWL [18]. Protegé-OWL is a popular language for knowledge representation and it can implement most flavours of Description Logics although the OWL-full version of OWL.1 is undecidable.

The two class relations $rel_{\forall\exists}$ and $rel_{\forall only}$(defined in (3) and (4)) can easily be formalized in Description Logic by:

$$C_1 \ rel_{\forall\exists} \ C_2 \quad \text{iff} \quad C_1 \sqsubseteq \exists\textbf{rel}.C_2,$$
$$C_1 \ rel_{\forall\forall_r} \ C_2 \quad \text{iff} \quad C_1 \sqsubseteq \forall\textbf{rel}.C_2.$$

However, the class relation $rel_{\forall\forall_c}$ is not expressible in a majority of Description Logics. Although in very expressible Description Logics including full concept negation and role negation [19,20], the $rel_{\forall\forall_c}$ relation can be formalized by:

$$C_1 \ rel_{\forall\forall_c} \ C_2 \quad \text{iff} \quad C_1 \sqsubseteq \forall(\neg\textbf{rel}).\neg C_2.$$

Alternatively a new operator in line with the "$\exists\textbf{rel}$" and "$\forall\textbf{rel}$" operators could be added to a Description Logic. Such an operator has already been added to similar modal logics and goes under the name "the window operator". However, a minimal Description Logic with this operator appears not to have been investigated. Thus, there is still work left to be done in the field of Description Logic before knowledge on regulatory relations can be optimally represented.

5   Discussion

Based on an analysis of the biomedical examples and our declaration of the ontological assumption, we have suggested that the correct formalizations of *positively* and *negatively regulates* in First-order Logic are represented by the formula $\forall x(C_1(x) \rightarrow \forall y(C_2(y) \rightarrow x \ rel \ y))$. A description of the relata, the First-order formulas, and examples of *regulates, positively_regulates* and *negatively_regulates* are displayed in table 1.

Table 1. Definitions of three regulatory relations. They are expressed as class-level relations in a format similar to that of OBO Relation Ontology [11]. *Relation and relata* capture the representation in e.g. KEGG, *Definitions* displays the First-order Logic formalizations, and *Examples* contributes with examples taken from pubmed-abstracts [21].

A. Regulates

Relations and relata	$C_1 \ regulates_{\forall\forall} \ production\_of(C_2)$; C_1 and C_2 are continuants.
Definitions	$\forall x(C_1(x) \rightarrow \forall y(production\_of(C_2(y)) \rightarrow x \textbf{ regulates } y))$.
Examples	...nitric oxide pathway regulates pulmonary vascular tone... ...non-histone chromosomal proteins may modify gene expression ... ...CREB regulates cyclic AMP-dependent gene...

B. Positively Regulates

Relations and relata	$C_1 \ positively\_regulates_{\forall\forall} \ production\_of(C_2)$; C_1 and C_2 are continuants.
Definitions	$\forall x(C_1(x) \rightarrow \forall y(production\_of(C_2(y)) \rightarrow x \textbf{ positively\_regulates } y))$.
Examples	...IPA stimulates insulin release... ...Ca(2+) influx stimulates exocytosis of secretory granules... ...MMP-7 activates the epidermal growth factor...

C. Negatively Regulates

Relations and relata	$C_1 \ negatively\_regulates_{\forall\forall} \ production\_of(C_2)$; C_1 and C_2 are continuants.
Definitions	$\forall x(C_1(x) \rightarrow \forall y(production\_of(C_2(y)) \rightarrow x \textbf{ negatively\_regulates } y))$.
Examples	...GLP-1inhibits glucagon release... ...lithium inhibits the enzyme glycogen synthase kinase-3... ...RSBX negatively regulates an extension of the RSBV-RSBW pathway... ...insulin secretion from the β-cell to reduce IRI responses...

Thus, our contribution to the field of knowledge representation and biomedical informatics is a logical analysis and representation of regulatory relations. One

of the main advantages of modeling knowledge in a formal framework as logic
is that it makes entire knowledge bases more complete and allows for the use of
reasoning tools to gain new knowledge. This is particularly useful in for instance
artificial intelligence and information retrieval.

In relation to the related work of section 2, this formalization is in the middle
of a complexity scale. It is not as expressive as the linked differential equations
[2], but much better suited for automatic reasoning than simple graphs [3]. In
expressivity and tractability it is close to work like [5,1]. However, this work
provide a semantic and uses First-order Logic formalization, which provides more
information to the relations than the before mentioned due to the quantifications.

5.1   Applications in the Biomedical Domain

From a biological point of view, the main purpose of our formalization of the
regulatory relations is to assist knowledge discovery, hypothesis development,
and, in a broader perspective, lexical resource integration of the semantics of
the words representing the relations.

Inferences and reasoning rules. Proposing rules for reasoning in a logical
framework allows us to obtain new knowledge from an existing knowledge base.

First, we have the inferences that are given from the semantics of the First-
order Logic. For the relation *regulates* defined as in equation (5) we will have
the following inferences:

$$is\_a \circ regulates \rightarrow regulates$$
$$regulates \circ is\_a^{-1} \rightarrow regulates$$

The $\circ$-operator is a common notation for 'composition of'' and the *is_a* relation is interpreted as the subset relation.

Additionally, you can create domain- or application-specific reasoning rules
depending on the amount of knowledge you want from your system. In implementing artificial intelligent systems in biomedical informatics several reasoning
rules have been suggested [22,7].

A list of proposed rules can be found in [22][3] and in [7], and an example of
one of these is:

$$negatively\_regulates \circ negatively\_regulates \rightarrow positively\_regulates$$

From the reasoning rules we can deduce additional relationships from existing
ones, and we can make inferences such as: "if insulin stimulates glucose transport and if the glucose transport inhibits glyconeogenesis, then insulin inhibits
glyconeogenesis". Thus, if you want to find novel gene products and molecules
that regulate a given process or a given molecule in a certain way, you can use
reasoning rules to predict such. Another perspective of this automated reasoning
is the prediction of the side effects of a drug or extra molecule functions.

---

[3] Although the rules above are meant to hold throughout the biomedical domain,
they might not always reflect reality. Instead, they are rules of thumb, used to infer
possible knowledge in drug discovery and hypothesis development.

Furthermore, you can potentially place a new unfamiliar molecule correctly in a regulatory pathway due to its regulatory properties. These functions can be an advantage in drug discovery, identification of adverse effects and in knowledge expansion for more fundamental research purposes. These are just some of the many advantages a logic based knowledge representation, as the one presented here, provides when fully implemented.

Towards implementation of a prototype. The most straightforward evaluation would obviously be an implementation of a prototype system for information retrieval and/or for hypothesis generation that would use the suggested formalisation. A comparison with similar systems not using the same formal representation of regulatory relations, would then make the contribution of the semantical representation clear.

To illustrate the effects and properties of the relations we have constructed a small example in the logical programming language Prolog. We have implemented a small part of the KEGG database from figure 2.1 containing 21 classes and the relations: *is a*, *stimulates* and *inhibits*. Besides the relations in the figure, a small taxonomy is created such that we are able to separate continuants such as (*small_molecule* and *gene_product*) and processes in correspondence to the way KEGG names the entities.

The toy-implementation can be used to infer fundamental inheritances in taxonomies of classes (ontology consisting of pure ISA-relations) as mentioned in the former subsection and can be downloaded and tested from: *www.ruc.dk/sz/Regrel*. Further work needs to be done to prove that the semantics of the implemented relations are actually equal to the semantics we have suggested in this paper.

Another possibility is to implement the system in DL using the suggestion in section 4.4. However, this will require both full role-negation and full concept negation and the tractability of this is to be investigated further.

Ontological aspects of regulation. In section 4.2 we made a distinction between continuants and processes, leading us to a characterization of 4 different basic relations among individuals. For stimulation these where the relations **stimulates$_{cc}$**, **stimulates$_{cp}$**, **stimulates$_{pc}$**, and **stimulates$_{pp}$**, which we further reduced to the single relation **stimulates$_{cp}$**. However, one may argue that the relations **stimulates$_{pc}$** and **stimulates$_{pp}$** are not genuine relations in the first place. From a strict ontological point of view processes never stimulate other processes or continuants directly, but always through their outputs.

An example of this is glycogenesis[4]. Glycogen is an output of this process, but other outputs occur as well, for example uridine diphosphate (UDP), whose effects might be different that glycogen. Thus, when we have a statement that the glycogenesis stimulates glucose homeostasis, we cannot be certain whether glycogen or UDP or both are the actors unless this is stated explicitly. Nevertheless it is either glycogen or UDP (or both) that stimulate homeostasis, and not actually glycogenesis.

---

[4] Note that *glycogenesis* and the above mentioned *glyco**neo**genesis* are two different processes.

We recognize that it is a debatable issue whether processes can stimulate other processes or continuants. There seems to be evidence, however, that it is important to investigate the ontological aspects of stimulation further. Whether stimulation is among continuants or processes seems to have consequences for the inference of new knowledge, and thus the distinction should be recognized. In simple knowledge representations by graphs like in the KEGG database such observations are not accounted for. Such knowledge bases have the potential to get this representation integrated automaticaly when a semantics is agreed upon.

5.2   Future Work

With our discussions and examples we have revealed that several occurrences of regulatory relationships are characterised by vagueness or fuzziness. However, one could take it one step further by taking the characteristic fuzziness seriously and apply fuzzy logics or other logics of uncertainty to model this aspect of the regulatory relationships.

As mentioned in section 4.4 the logical framework of Description Logic is still not fully developed for representing the formal semantics of regulatory relations as we defined them in this paper. This is also a direction of future work that may tell us something about how efficient we can do automatic reasoning about regulatory relations in practice. Furthermore it may also reveal how the relations can be incorporated into for instance OWL.

Staying within the field of logic, we mentioned several possible class relations in section 4.1 and a deeper analysis of all possible class relations and there properties would also be interesting future work.

We finally suggest that the formal semantic analysis presented in section 4 can be used to define frame semantics for the verbs and verb phrases that express regulatory relations. The definition of the frame semantics is similar to the one we find in the work done in BioFrameNet [23] on other verbs. The attempt of defining frame semantics may well result in an enrichment of semantically annotated data and for instance be applied to semantic querying [24].

Acknowledgments. We would like to thank Mai Ajspur for useful comments on and discussions of an earlier version of this paper and Jørgen Fischer Nilsson for an insightful discussion of the class relations.

References

1. Caspi, R., Altman, T., Dale, J.M., Dreher, K., Fulcher, C.A., Gilham, F., Kaipa, P., Karthikeyan, A.S., Kothari, A., Krummenacker, M., Latendresse, M., Mueller, L.A., Paley, S., Popescu, L., Pujar, A., Shearer, A.G., Zhang, P., Karp, P.D.: The MetaCyc database of metabolic pathways and enzymes and the BioCyc collection of pathway/genome databases. Nucleic Acids Res. 38, D473–D479 (2010)
2. Heinrich, R., Rapoport, S.: Metabolic regulation and mathematical models. Prog. Biophys. Molec. Biol. 32 (1977)

3. Kanehisa, M., Goto, S.: KEGG: Kyoto Encyclopedia of Genes and Genomes. Nucleic Acids Res. 28, 27–30 (2000)
4. Matthews, L., Gopinath, G., Gillespie, M., Caudy, M., Croft, D., de Bono, B., Garapati, P., Hemish, J., Hermjakob, H., Jassal, B., Kanapin, A., Lewis, S., Mahajan, S., May, B., Schmidt, E., Vastrik, I., Wu, G., Birney, E., Stein, L., D'Eustachio, P.: Reactome knowledgebase of human biological pathways and processes. Nucleic Acids Res. 37, D619–D622 (2009)
5. Eker, S., Knapp, M., Laderoute, K., Meseguer, P.L.J., Sonmez, K.: Pathway logic: Symbolic analysis of biological signaling. In: Pacific Symposium on Biocomputing 2002, pp. 400–412 (2002)
6. Heidtke, K.R., Schulze-Kremer, S.: BioSim–a new qualitative simulation environment for molecular biology. Proc. Int. Conf. Intell. Syst. Mol. Biol. 6, 85–94 (1998)
7. Gene Ontology-Consortium, GO ontology relations. geneontology.org/GO.ontology-ext.relations.shtml (2009)
8. Ashburner, M., Ball, C.A., Blake, J.A., Botstein, D., Butler, H., Cherry, J.M., Davis, A.P., Dolinski, K., Dwight, S.S., Eppig, J.T., Harris, M.A., Hill, D.P., Issel-Tarver, L., Kasarskis, A., Lewis, S., Matese, J.C., Richardson, J.E., Ringwald, M., Rubin, G.M., Sherlock, G.: Gene ontology: tool for the unification of biology. The Gene Ontology Consortium. Nat. Genet. 25, 25–29 (2000)
9. Smith, B., Ashburner, M., Rosse, C., Bard, J., Bug, W., Ceusters, W., Goldberg, L.J., Eilbeck, K., Ireland, A., Mungall, C.J., Leontis, N., Rocca-Serra, P., Ruttenberg, A., Sansone, S.A., Scheuermann, R.H., Shah, N., Whetzel, P.L., Lewis, S.: The OBO Foundry: coordinated evolution of ontologies to support biomedical data integration. Nat. Biotechnol. 25, 1251–1255 (2007)
10. Blonde, W., Antezana, E., De Baets, B., Mironov, V., Kuiper, M.: Metarel: an ontology to support the inferencing of semantic web relations within biomedical ontologies. In: International Conference on Biomedical Ontology, Conference proceedings, Nature preceedings, July 2009. pp. 79–82 (2009)
11. Smith, B., Ceusters, W., Klagges, B., Köhler, J., Kumar, A., Lomax, J., Mungall, C., Neuhaus, F., Rector, A.L., Rosse, C.: Relations in biomedical ontologies. Genome Biol. 6, R46 (2005)
12. Beisswanger, E., Lee, V., Kim, J.J., Rebholz-Schuhmann, D., Splendiani, A., Dameron, O., Schulz, S., Hahn, U.: Gene Regulation Ontology (GRO): design principles and use cases. Stud. Health Technol. Inform. 136, 9–14 (2008)
13. Workman, C.T., Mak, H.C., McCuine, S., Tagne, J.B., Agarwal, M., Ozier, O., Begley, T.J., Samson, L.D., Ideker, T.: A systems approach to mapping DNA damage response pathways. Science 312, 1054–1059 (2006)
14. Smith, B., Rosse, C.: The role of foundational relations in the alignment of biomedical ontologies. MEDINFO, 444–448 (2004)
15. Blackburn, P., Benthem, J.F.A.K.v., Wolter, F.: Handbook of Modal Logic. Studies in Logic and Practical Reasoning, vol. 3. Elsevier, Amsterdam (2007)
16. Braüner, T., Ghilardi, S.: First-order modal logic. In: Blackburn, P., Benthem, J.F.A.K.v., Wolter, F. (eds.) Handbook of Modal Logic, pp. 549–620. Elsevier, Amsterdam (2007)
17. Baader, F., Calvanese, D., McGuinness, D. (eds.): The Description Logic Handbook. Cambridge University Press, Cambridge (2003)
18. W3C OWL Working Group: OWL 2 web ontology language document overview. Technical report, W3C (October 2009),
http://www.w3.org/TR/2009/REC-owl2-overview-20091027/

19. Lutz, C., Sattler, U.: Mary likes all cats. In: Baader, F., Sattler, U. (eds.) Description Logics. CEUR Workshop Proceedings, CEUR-WS.org. vol. 33, pp. 213–226 (2000)
20. Lutz, C., Sattler, U.: The complexity of reasoning with boolean modal logic. In: Proceeding of Advances in Modal Logic 2000, AiML 2000 (2000)
21. Pubmed: Medline entrez, search data base for biomedical litterature (2010), http://www.ncbi.nlm.nih.gov/sites/entrez?db=PubMed
22. Zambach, S.: A formal framework on the semantics of regulatory relations and their presence as verbs in biomedical texts. In: Proceedings of the Eigth International Conference on Flexible Query Answering Systems, pp. 443–452. Springer, Heidelberg (2009)
23. Dolbey, A., Ellsworth, M., Scheffczyk, J.: Bioframenet: A domain-specific framenet extension with links to biomedical ontologies. In: Proceedings of KR-MED, November 2007, pp. 87–94 (2006)
24. Andreasen, T., Bulskov, H., Lassen, T., Zambach, S., Jensen, P.A., Madsen, B.N., Thomsen, H.E., Nilsson, J.F., Szymczak, B.A.: SIABO - semantic information access through biomedical ontologies. In: Dietz, J.L.G. (ed.) KEOD, pp. 171–176. INSTICC Press (2009)

Smooth Introduction of Semantic Tagging in Genotyping Procedures

Alessio Bechini[1], Jacopo Viotto[1], and Riccardo Giannini[2]

[1] University of Pisa, Dept. of Information Engineering, largo Lazzarino 56126 Pisa, Italy
{a.bechini,jacopo.viotto}@iet.unipi.it
[2] University of Pisa, Dept. of Surgery, via Paradisa, 2 56124 Pisa, Italy
r.giannini@med.unipi.it

Abstract. Concepts and tools from research on the Semantic Web have found widespread application in the classification of biomedical literature works and research results. A more substantial advantage could come from the semantic classification of any kind of documents from research, or even from ordinary diagnostic test: this may pave the way to building an impressive, semantically searchable knowledge base. The use of semantic tagging at this operating level is hampered by the lack of proper tools. In this paper we present an approach to introduce semantic tagging in genotyping test procedures. A formal analysis of the process workflow is crucial to pinpoint stages where tagging might be applied. Later, an enriched Enterprise Content Management system allows the archiving of test documents, whose metadata can encompass terms from any kind of ontologies. The flexibility and the usability of the system represent key factors for an actual, widespread introduction of semantic tagging in this field.

Keywords: Document management, semantic tagging, biomedical ontologies, management of biomolecular test procedures.

1 Introduction

In recent years, research on the Semantic Web [1] has widely influenced the way biomedical results (mainly publications) are classified and searched. In the biomedical domain, the need to find common, precise terminology has lead to an impressive growth of standardized controlled vocabularies and ontologies, with no match in other research fields. A semantically annotated corpus of publications and, in general, research results can be viewed as a massive knowledge base whose full exploitation is still far to come [2]. An even more substantial advantage could come from the semantic classification of any kind of documents from research, or even from ordinary diagnostic tests: at a local level, a semantically searchable knowledge base can be established and maintained. The federation of local document bases, if a shared system of metadata would be adopted, could represent a new extraordinary source of information for both researchers and clinicians.

Semantic search can be carried out only if the documents in the knowledge base have been properly annotated with unambiguous, standard terms [3]. Standardization

S. Khuri, L. Lhotská, and N. Pisanti (Eds.): ITBAM 2010, LNCS 6266, pp. 201–214, 2010.

efforts in this direction lead to the development of controlled vocabularies as the well-known MeSH [4] in the biomedical field. Document annotation of this kind (or *tagging*) turns to be useful if it is performed in a very accurate way, so it requires both time and expertise from the tagging operators. Semantic tagging at this operating level has been deemed unpractical because of the lack of proper tools, and also because of the difficulties in selecting the correct terms within complex ontologies [5].

Genotyping tests can be considered a paradigmatic case in this setting, because they require different instruments through the progression of the test procedures, and different types of documents are produced along this path. A general way to deal with such documents may rely on an Enterprise Content Management system (ECM). The documentation archiving in the ECM can be regarded as the proper point to introduce semantic tagging. The success of these steps strictly depends on the practical feasibility of the tagging procedure, and thus the supporting software tools have to be handy, and they are asked to be as less intrusive as possible with respect to the ordinary course of the archiving activities. In other words, the supporting tools must be able to *smoothly* introduce the semantic tagging features in the used ECM. The system described hereafter has been developed to meet this kind of requirements.

In this paper an approach to introduce semantic tagging in genotyping procedures is presented. Through sections 3 and 4, a formal analysis of the process workflow is carried out to pinpoint stages where tagging might be applied. Section 5 describes how an ECM (Enterprise Content Management) can be enriched to make it suitable to support the archiving of genotyping test documents, whose metadata can encompass terms from any kind of ontologies. Conclusions are drawn in Section 6.

2 Related Works

Founding ideas of Semantic Web have received widespread interest in the biomedical research community. Approaches to data and document management in this environment have been deeply influenced by the vision of semantic searches [1] [3], and also bio-ontologies have been recognized as a key resource to organize and standardize knowledge [6] [5]. Following this mainstream in biomedical data management, comprehensive semantic models have been proposed primarily to tackle interoperability issues [7]. So far, these efforts have produced conceptual models suited to the design of new information management systems, rather than fitting the structure of existing software tools.

A typical example of the application of ontologies in a web-based tool for biological investigation is an early work on the "RiboWeb" system [8], dedicated to the study of the ribosome: it used an ontological approach to formally represent different features of the experiments that can be performed online, using computational resources over available datasets. The collaborative aspects in this kind of tools immediately come into evidence.

It is worth underlying that researchers in molecular biology, and particularly those involved in genotyping technologies, have soon recognized the need to rely on a supporting database, properly structured to ease the automation of data feeding [9]. Anyway, methods for data storage have been considered so far as mere side activities respect to the investigation goals [9], and a cross-field vision is often missing.

To the best of our knowledge, we are not aware of tools that apply the notion of ontology-related tagging to documents produced along the development of bio-molecular tests, despite the fact that a compelling need for structuring information from biomedical experiments has been clearly pinpointed and addressed [10]. Anyway, approaches similar to the one shown in this paper have been used in very different domains, for example ebXML repositories for enterprise documentation [11]. In this last case, the system has shown to be both user-friendly and effective for document archival and retrieval, although the available domain ontologies were really less abundant. The advanced state of development and standardization of bio-ontologies and the availability of semantic search engines make us confident in an ever more successful introduction of semantic tagging in the bio-molecular tests domain.

3 Procedures for Genotyping Tests

As a preliminary step, it is important to give an accurate description of the procedures actually carried out in performing a genotyping test. For this purpose, in the following we will make use of BPML [12], a formal, graphical notation suitable to model general business processes [13] (and production processes as well). A coarse-grain vision of the workflow is shown in Fig. 1. More detailed descriptions of the activities within each high-level phase can be seen in Fig. 2-5. It must be underlined that several variants to the described procedures are possible, mostly because of the nature of the specific test actually performed and the instrumentation used for it. Anyway, the process outline always keeps its validity in showing the overall approach to uncovering crucial stages where semantic tagging is recommendable.

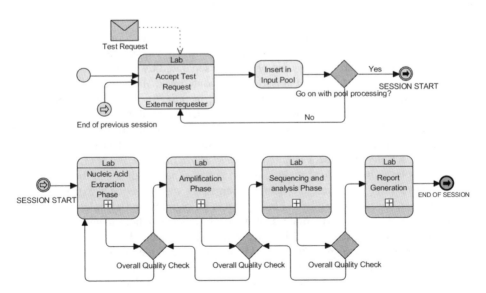

Fig. 1. A BPMN description of the overall procedure addressed in the work. Each test session is usually started upon a pool of requests, and it operates on the corresponding biological samples.

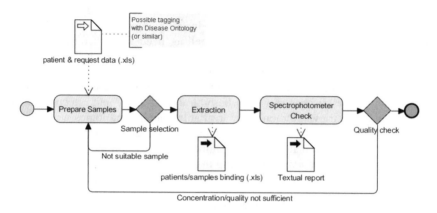

Fig. 2. Representation of the activities in the nucleic acid extraction phase

The ideal starting point for the whole workflow (Fig. 1) is the reception of a test request, which contains information on what particular kind of analysis should be performed, along with patience data. The test request comes with the corresponding biological samples. Typically, any single test procedure operates over a pool of multiple samples from several patients (not necessarily the same pool throughout the analysis path). For this reason, a preliminary buffering phase is taken into account (upper part of Fig. 1). The start of an analysis session is triggered by a decision of the laboratory supervisor upon the inspection of the pool of collected requests. It must be noted that this part of the procedure faithfully describes also what happens for investigations related to research issues, although in this case the requests are generated within the laboratory.

An *analysis session* (lower part of Fig. 1) can be thought as composed of four main phases: 1) nucleic acid extraction, 2) amplification, 3) sequencing & analysis, and finally 4) report generation. Adjacent phases are separated by an overall quality check over the results and, in case of unsatisfactory outcomes, the control flow must be redirected backward to the previous checkpoint, in order to definitely determine the point to recover the procedure. Each phase is carried out making use of specific machinery, and each instrument produces documents, aimed at describing the experiment outcomes and at characterizing the work progression throughout the experiment.

The first activity in phase 1 (i.e. *nucleic acid extraction*, see Fig. 2) is the preparation of samples, which is done making use of both the patient data and the indications in the test request. Only suitable samples can reach the subsequent extraction task. Here samples are labeled and the binding between patients and samples must be recorded. As part of an intermediate quality check, a spectrophotometer is used and a textual report of this subtask is collected from the instrument. The spectrophotometer results are used to assess the concentration and quality of the extracted nucleic acid.

Phase 2 (i.e. *amplification*, see Fig. 3) is mainly carried out by means of PCR runs. Input data for this task describe the DNA segments to be selected (and thus amplified). This information is crucial, and it depends on the test rationale from the requester: research, diagnosis, decisions on pharmacological treatments, etc.. Snapshots

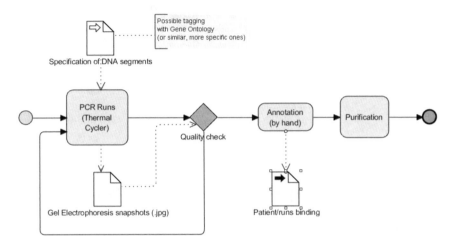

Fig. 3. Representation of the Nucleic Acid Amplification Phase

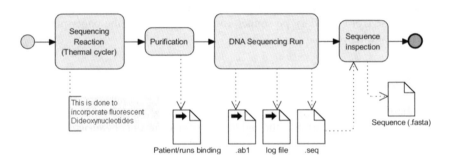

Fig. 4. Representation of the DNA Sequencing Phase

of gel electrophoreses (typically several ones in the same picture) are generated and collected to assess the outcome of the PCR runs. Also in this case, it is important to keep trace of the binding between runs and patients. The purification of the resulting samples ends up this phase. This phase is basically shaped the same way also when working with RNA (in particular with 1-step RTPCR). If cDNA has to be dealt with, an additional retrotranscription task has to be inserted.

The *sequencing* (phase 3, see Fig. 4) requires a preliminary task for the incorporation of fluorescent dideoxinucleotides and a corresponding purification. Once again, the binding between samples and patients must be recorded. The subsequent DNA sequencing run produces documentation on the read sequence diagrams (in *.abl* and *.seq* formats) and on the run progression itself, in form of a log file. The inspection of such results, which can be done in a semi-automatic way (because the human intervention is almost always necessary), leads to the determination of the target sequence, typically outlined in *fasta* format.

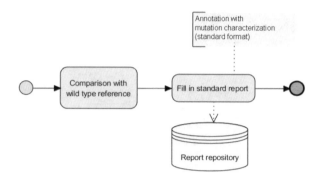

Fig. 5. Representation of the Report Generation Phase

The final phase (see Fig. 5) is aimed at formulating a precise, concise response from the analysis outcomes. This is achieved via the comparison of the retrieved sequence with the associated known wild type. Such a comparison is aimed at identifying and characterizing possible mutations. A standard report on this finding, written adopting proper standards for mutation descriptions, is filed into a repository that is also accessible from auxiliary personnel, to possibly produce the paper-printed report for the requestor as well.

4 Managing Documents

One of the most significant problems with the described workflow is that all the produced documents are scattered throughout several different, heterogeneous systems aside of the analysis instruments. As a consequence of this kind of physical distribution, it is often difficult to perform cross-platform studies and statistics involving data from multiple phases. An integrated, distributed system for the homogeneous management of the documents involved in the genotyping activity would be an ideal solution, and semantic functionalities could be built upon it.

Although integrated software suites for collecting such documents currently exist, they are not widespread at present (especially in small and medium-sized laboratories) because of cost and management issues. From a functional perspective, they can be viewed as typical Document Management Systems (DMS): at the core, a repository containing structured and non-structured documents, and an engine working on top of it and providing features like searching and versioning. Typically DMS are integral parts of Enterprise Content Management (ECM) systems, which provide all the functionalities about security and distribution that are usually required in our target environment. Moreover, integration approaches have been also studied for the development of collaborative, distributed environments in other application fields, and namely e-Business [14]. Therefore, we propose to enhance the organization of this distributed repository by leveraging a technique recently introduced in the document management field: semantic tagging.

4.1 Tagging and Semantic Tagging

The term "tagging" identifies the activity of associating words or short sentences, i.e. *tags*, to a given resource. A "resource" may be anything, from a text document to a photo, or an URL. The intended goal of a tagging system is to describe all resources in a knowledge base in a meaningful way, to ease categorization and future retrieval [15]. Tagging is currently employed also in ECM systems, and generally this service relies on an underlying relational DBMS; as this last implementation detail does not have any major impact from a functional standpoint, it will not deserve any further attention in our discussion.

In many popular social networks over the Web, tagging is carried out in a collaborative fashion [16], and any user can add tags to any resource. This eventually leads to the emergence of spontaneous bottom-up classifications, known as "folksonomies" [17]. Apart from this social facet, tags are useful even when assigned by a single individual; they are an alternative to folders, allowing multiple classifications for each object. However, the categories they introduce are flat, because ordinary tags, unlike folders, have no hierarchical structure. At least, this last statement holds for traditional tagging systems, where users can freely choose the terms to use as tags. Some variants of tagging systems restrict users' choice within a *controlled vocabulary* of some sort; moreover, this vocabulary may contain additional information, such as the relationships among terms (above all, subsumption, or "is-a", which allows the definition of hierarchies). This enhanced vocabulary is usually formalized in an ontology.

An ontology is a model aimed at describing all interesting entities within an application domain, their relationships and their properties. The most popular formalism for expressing ontologies is OWL (Web Ontology Language) [18]. As OWL is an XML grammar, it can be proficiently used in different software applications/contexts. *Semantic tagging* refers to precise annotations that can be leveraged in performing a semantic search [15]. Such precise tags can be chosen out of a given ontology, thus obtaining a twofold advantage: first, the meaning of the tag is unambiguously defined; second, relationships between terms in the ontology may be exploited in the search phase to obtain better results. E.g., trivially, if the ontology tells us that a "dog" "is-a" "mammal", we can infer that all queries involving "mammal" should also consider documents tagged with the word "dog". Ontologies are being thoroughly investigated in recent literature, and in particular bio-ontologies (i.e. related to biomedical domains) are expected to play more and more important roles in IT supports to biomedical investigations [2], and to diagnostic/therapeutic assessments as well.

4.2 Biomedical Ontologies

So far, the bioinformatics community has been particularly active in the definition and usage of ontologies [5] [19] [6]: standardized and easily interchangeable domain models are a pressing need when handling extremely large knowledge bases across multiple, closely interacting research groups. The incorporation of bio-ontologies in data annotation systems enables the integration of complex scientific data and supports the consistency of data management activities [5] [20]. The OBO initiative (Open Biological and Biomedical Ontology), for example, is a significant classification effort covering many aspects of the biomedical field [21]. It includes various popular projects, most notably the GO (Gene Ontology) [6] [22], perhaps the most famous instance of the kind. Started in 1998 with the genomic description of only three organisms, GO now encloses information about genes and gene products of a plethora of animals, plants and microorganisms. The growth of use of GO terms in scientific publications has been monitored [20], and it witnesses the more and more crucial role played by this conceptual tool in biology research.. Other significant examples of significant ontologies in the biomedical field are are Reactome, for biological pathways, Disease Ontology, for human diseases, BioCyc, for both pathways and genomes, and the recently proposed Sequence Ontology (SO), addressing biological sequences.

The importance of ontologies in this field is also witnessed by the existence of several ontology formats explicitly designed for biomedical research: e.g., the OBO format is a widespread textual representation characterized by low redundancy and high readability. BioPAX (Biological Pathway Exchange) is another example of exchange format, restricted to the domain of biological pathways. Such formats have been developed independently of the OWL standard. Although minor differences may exist in such employed formalisms, the possibility to flexibly use biomedical ontologies in a wider context of software tools has driven a widespread convergence towards OWL [23]. Hence, without loss of generality, in the following the discussion will focus on OWL ontologies.

4.3 Applying Tagging to Genotyping Test Procedures

A tagging system that supports the whole workflow for genotyping procedures can prove useful at several levels. Ordinary tagging can be used to guarantee document/data lineage retrieval in an integrated way, with no resort to a side relational system. A very basic usage of tags may consist in keeping track of all documents related to the same selected sample: in practice, there would be a one-to-one relation between samples and tags, and all documents containing results for a given sample would be associated to the related tag. This approach is intended to introduce a uniform means to bind samples (and instruments' runs over them) to the initial request and the patient's data, despite the fact that throughout the whole workflow different binding rules may be actually used in the laboratory practices. This approach can be proficiently used in all the workflow points where a "binding" document is produced (see Figures 2-5). In particular, for the initial request, document tagging with the patient ID can be complemented with a number of semantic tags that describe the actual state of the patient (e.g. diseases, habits, etc.) and/or the related biological samples. Here a recourse to terms from Disease Ontology, or akin, is recommendable. This specific annotation should also be properly propagated at the beginning of phase 1, where information on request and patient is used. The tagging tool does not necessarily have to enforce the usage of specified ontologies, but instead the laboratory manager can provide internal operating recommendations/guidelines on how to proceed with document tagging.

In the amplification phase, input documents for the PCR activities can be naturally tagged with a formal reference to the studied sequence of nucleotides. Natural target ontologies for this purpose are GO [22] and more specific ones. As usually one single laboratory may be specialized in genotyping tests in restricted domains, also "narrow" domain ontologies can be proficiently used. Generally speaking, a very specific domain ontology does not necessarily hamper the effectiveness of semantic search, because in principle external work to relate it to more generic ontologies could be exploited in semantic search. Hence, only a possible impact on information recovery performance could be expected. Similar observations apply to the classification of the gel electrophoresis snapshots (see Fig. 3), and here special care must be paid to the fact that one single document (image) groups up the outcome from multiple samples.

The output documents from the DNA sequencing runs (Fig. 4) are the description of the base-specific intensity profiles (in proprietary and/or open formats), and the log of the sequencing activity. Tags here can also be aimed at pointing out possible problems in the interpretation of the intensity profiles. Again, the obtained fasta sequence must be precisely related to the studied exact sequence (but this information can be obtained automatically from previous annotations on the samples worked out).

The final diagnosis is suitable to be tagged with standard notations for the mutations possibly found in the sample [24]. Although here no ontological information is apparently embedded, the mutation code can be related (out of the context of the used software framework) to other ontological models associated to the mutation. Even this last kind of annotation can further enable an ontology-assisted search of the collected knowledge base.

5 Actual System Implementation

As previously stated, from the information management perspective, the core of the entire process is the production of documents. Hence, we propose a solution that leverages standard document management tools (DMS) and classification techniques (tagging and semantic tagging) to enhance both quality and accessibility of information in repositories for genotyping documents.

5.1 Overall Architecture

The key component of our system is a DMS, whose repository contains all the documents that get created during analyses over samples. In the following, we will assume that from all the computers aside the instruments it is possible to upload the output documents directly into the DMS, or that some automated procedure exists to migrate those files from their output location into the repository. Obviously, a manual approach is considered as a last resort. The DMS is required to support semantic tagging, or basic tagging at the minimum (which may in turn be upgraded towards semantic awareness). To access the repository, a straightforward solution would be to directly leverage the DMS user interface. However, more complex alternatives may be required, especially in case of open knowledge bases, that should be accessible from an heterogeneous set of coworkers. This operation is not expected to be unreasonably complex, as almost every modern DMS offers APIs, or even Web Services, to easily interoperate with external applications. In this paper, we will focus on the DMS component itself, and possible special-purpose interfaces towards external machines and users may be subject for future work.

5.2 Implementation

Our prototype is based on Alfresco ECM [25], a popular Content Management system. Alfresco is an open source solution for both Document Management and Web Content Management. It is based on Java technologies and can be easily tailored to our needs. In its current basic configuration, it supports basic tagging, although not the semantic variant, so we had to implement a modification to enable ontology management. In Alfresco, documents are organized in *spaces*, a concept similar to that of folders in a web-accessible setting; spaces can be managed also in a collaborative fashion by means of web clients. Spaces are characterized by some "smart" facets: most notably, rules can be added to manage content being inserted, edited in, or removed from the folder. One of the actions a rule may trigger is the activation of a functionality, or *aspect*, for the selected documents, such as "versionable", "taggable" or "classifiable". These are the features that can be exploited to set up a simple semantic-aware environment.

As a preliminary step, two auxiliary spaces can be defined to contain the documents involved in the classification task. First of all, necessary ontologies, either in OWL or RDF (Resource Description Format, the format OWL derives from), must be uploaded to the repository. During this procedure, ontologies are treated just like any other file, and no particular action has to be performed. This upload would not be strictly necessary, because in principle ontologies might be downloaded on-the-fly from a user-provided URL, or may even be remotely navigated. A second space is reserved for contents subject to the upcoming classification activity, and it is enhanced with a rule, so that every document uploaded into that space will become "taggable" (i.e., will be extended with the "taggable" aspect). Also in this case, this second ancillary space is not essential, and the very rationale to have it in place relies on the practical need to guarantee that tagging would be always active for the documents to be classified.

The ECM web user interface heavily relies on JavaScript modules. This structural feature lets us implement a smooth, low intrusive way to modify the behavior of the tagging module and come to accommodate ontology-aware tagging. According to this low-impact philosophy, we chose a JavaScript-only approach to both ontology processing and visualization, acting only at the presentation layer of the DMS. The starting point for adding a semantic tag is the same as for traditional tagging. In the property view for a "taggable" document, an "Add a tag" link is inserted. When clicked, it reveals a new navigation interface, which lets the user choose the reference ontology by means of a combo-box filled with the contents of the ontology folder (Fig. 6). This interface might also be enhanced to allow retrieval of remote ontology descriptions as well.

After the selection of the target ontology, a graphical representation for it is shown in the web user interface, and it can be interactively explored for an easy identification of interesting concepts. To this aim, we made use of a force-directed graph layout for an animated visualization, where nodes are ontology concepts and links between nodes represent a parent-child relation (Fig. 7). Interactive navigation is performed by clicking on nodes that, once clicked, reveal direct children. Moreover, upon clicking the node, its identifying label is selected as a candidate tag, changing the text on the

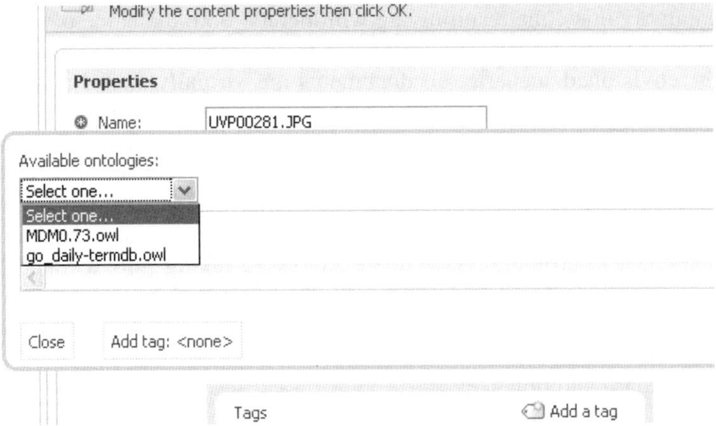

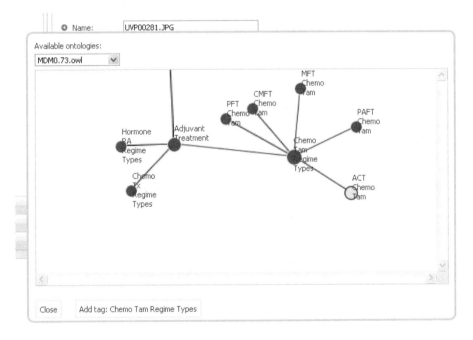

Fig. 6. Selection of a target ontology through a specific interface added into the standard ECM framework. The combo-box is automatically filled with the contents of the "Ontologies" space.

Fig. 7. Semantic tagging using a clinical ontology addressing breast cancer. The tag is selected visually on a force-directed graph representing parent-child relations.

"Add tag" button. This kind of representation lacks some expressivity when applied to ontologies; other graphic layouts may be tested for a better user experience: trees, hyperbolic trees, radial graphs and more. Finally, when the user has found the entity/concept of interest, he can add the entity name to the document's tag set. In order to avoid ambiguities, the resulting tag will include both the name of the entity and the name of the specific target ontology (in the form *<term>@<ontology_id>*).

In the envisioned scenario, all documents are virtually stored at a single site, and are therefore easily reachable and searchable. Admittedly, this is an optimistic assumption. In practice, it is far more common to deal with isolated, non interoperable systems with closed document repositories. In many cases, those repositories are not accessible because of legal constraints rather than technical ones: for instance, connecting them to the local network may void the warranty accorded by the provider. Although specific problems have to be addressed taking into account the local configurations, supposedly all technical difficulties may be overcome by building a federated infrastructure spanning the various distributed subsystems. A significant aspect that can promote the adoption of ECMs in this environment is their native support to security standard and practices.

6 Conclusions

Recently, in the biomedical domain the promises of Semantic Web have found a large potential application field, and semantic attitudes to information management are gaining wider and wider acceptance. In this paper, based on the development of a prototype system targeted to the management of genotyping-related documentation, a smooth introduction of tools for semantic tagging is proposed. Such solution leverages traditional DMSs, and this choice makes it usable and easily implementable. At the software level, it is crucial to leave the user free to choose any possible ontology (both upper- and domain ones) for selecting precise terms for document annotation. Moreover, ordinary tagging can go along with semantic one as an homogeneous way to deal with data lineage issues.

The flexibility of the tagging tool makes it usable in the context of different operating procedures adopted within a laboratory. Nonetheless, once semantic tagged documents have been obtained, they can be searched also exploiting the knowledge embedded in the used ontologies, possibly making use also of specific external reasoning engines.

Although open source systems (as the one presented here) could be inappropriate in laboratories with no people skilled in information systems to maintain them, the underlying design principles can also be exploited in customizing full-featured, specialized proprietary frameworks. We are thus confident that a smooth introduction of tools for ontology-based tagging (like the one presented here) could effectively contribute to the day-to-day operations biologists are involved in, building up an ever-growing, invaluable, semantically searchable knowledge base.

Further developments will be aimed at shaping a better interface between the ECM and the distributed machines at the instrumentation places, to tailor the system to real-world scenarios and to the actual needs of biologists involved in genotyping analysis.

Acknowledgments. The authors are grateful to Gerardo Iasparra and Francesco Santucci, for the early activity in coding the basic modules that later developed into the actual prototype applications. Special thanks for their kind collaboration are due to the personnel of the biomolecular analysis laboratory of the div. of Anatomical Pathology in Azienda Ospedaliera Pisana, in Pisa, Italy.

References

1. Berners-Lee, T., Hendler, J., Lassila, O.: The Semantic Web. Scientific American, 34–43 (May 2001)
2. Rubin, D.L., Shah, N.H., Noy, N.F.: Biomedical ontologies: a functional perspective. Briefings in Bioinformatics 9(1), 75–90 (2008)
3. Ding, L., Finin, T., Joshi, A., Peng, Y., Pan, R., Reddivari, P.: Search on the Semantic Web. Computer, 62–69 (October 2005)
4. MeSH – Medical Subject Headings. Controlled vocabulary available online at, http://www.nlm.nih.gov/mesh/ (last update: October 2009)
5. Blake, J.: Bio-ontologies-fast and furious. Nature Biotechnology 22(6), 773–774 (2004)
6. Tanabe, L., Wilbur, W.J.: Tagging gene and protein names in biomedical text. Bioinformatics 18(8), 1124–1132 (2002)
7. Deus, H.F., Stanislaus, et al.: A semantic web management model for integrative biomedical informatics. PLoS ONE 3(8), e2946 (2008)
8. Altman, R.B., Bada, M., Chai, X.J., Whirl Carillo, M., Chen, R.O., Abernethy, N.F.: RiboWeb: An Ontology-Based System for Collaborative Molecular Biology. IEEE Intelligent Systems, 68–76 (September/October 1999)
9. Le Hellard, S., Ballereau, S.J., et al.: SNP genotyping on pooled DNAs: comparison of genotyping technologies and a semi automated method for data storage and analysis. Nucleic Acids Research 30(15), e74 (2002)
10. Kothari, C.R., Wilkinson, M.: Structured Representation of Biomedical Experiments: A Bottom-Up Approach. In: Proc. of IKE 2008, pp. 199–204 (2008)
11. Bechini, A., Tomasi, A., Viotto, J.: Enabling Ontology-Based Document Classification and Management in ebXML Registries. In: Proceedings of ACM SAC 2008, pp. 1145–1150. ACM Press, New York (2008)
12. OMG: BPMN 2.0 specifications (2009), http://www.omg.org/spec/BPMN/2.0/
13. Wohed, P., van der Aalst, W.M.P., Dumas, M., ter Hofstede, A.H.M., Russell, N.: On the Suitability of BPMN for Business Process Modelling. In: Dustdar, S., Fiadeiro, J.L., Sheth, A.P. (eds.) BPM 2006. LNCS, vol. 4102, pp. 161–176. Springer, Heidelberg (2006)
14. Bechini, A., Tomasi, A., Viotto, J.: Collaborative e-Business and Document Management: Integration of Legacy DMSs with the ebXML Environment. In: Interdisciplinary Aspects of Information Systems Studies, pp. 287–293. Physica Verlag (2008)
15. Uren, V., Cimiano, P., Iria, J., Handschuh, S., Vargas-Vera, M., Motta, E., Ciravegna, F.: Semantic annotation for knowledge management: Requirements and a survey of the state of the art. Web Semantics: Science, Services and Agents on the World Wide Web 4(1), 14–28 (2006)
16. Bojars, U., Breslin, J.G., Peristeras, V., Tummarello, G., Decker, S.: Interlinking the Social Web with Semantics. IEEE Intelligent Systems 23(3), 29–40 (2008)
17. Specia, L., Motta, E.: Integrating Folksonomies with the Semantic Web. In: Franconi, E., Kifer, M., May, W. (eds.) ESWC 2007. LNCS, vol. 4519, pp. 624–639. Springer, Heidelberg (2007)
18. Bechhofer, S., van Harmelen, F., Hendler, J., et al.: OWL Web Ontology Language Reference (2002), http://www.w3.org/TR/owl-ref
19. Hadzic, M., Chang, E.: Medical ontologies to support human disease research and control. International Journal of Web and Grid Services 1(2), 139–150 (2005)
20. Jensen, L.J., Bork, P.: Ontologies in Quantitative Biology: A Basis for Comparison, Integration, and Discovery. PLoS Biology 8(5), e1000374 (2010)

21. Smith, B., Ashburner, M., et al.: The OBO Foundry: coordinated evolution of ontologies to support biomedical data integration. Nat. Biotechnol. 25(11), 1251–1255 (2007)
22. Gene Ontology Consortium: Gene ontology: tool for the unification of biology. Nature Genetics 25, 25–29 (2002)
23. Aranguren, M.E., Bechhofer, S., Lord, P., Sattler, U., Stevens, R.: Understanding and using the meaning of statements in a bio-ontology: recasting the Gene Ontology in OWL. BMC Bioinformatics 8(17) (2007)
24. Olivier, M., Petitjean, A., et al.: Somatic Mutation Databases as Tools for Molecular Epidemiology and Molecular Pathology of Cancer: Proposed Guidelines for Improving Data Collection, Distribution, and Integration. Human Mutation 30(3), 275–282 (2009)
25. Alfresco website, http://www.alfresco.com/ (last accessed: March 2010)

Laboratory Kit for Oscillometry Measurement of Blood Pressure

Jan Dvořák and Jan Havlík

Department of Circuit Theory
Faculty of Electrical Engineering, Czech Technical University in Prague
Technická 2, CZ-16627 Prague 6
dvoraj45@fel.cvut.cz, xhavlikj@fel.cvut.cz

Abstract. This paper presents a laboratory kit for oscillometry blood pressure measurement. The laboratory kit was designed for research purposes in the field of medical technology. The presented device allows to show not only the calculated results (such as systolic and diastolic blood pressure and the heart rate) as standard devices, but also the raw signals. It means there is a possibility to study the impact of set-up parameters and other factors on the measured values.

Keywords: blood pressure, oscillometry, laboratory kit.

1 Introduction

The blood pressure measurement is a commonly used method for monitoring of cardiac system condition. It is used in both hospital and home care. The most commonly used method is non-invasive oscillometry based on evaluation of amplitude envelope of the oscillations in the sphygmomanometer cuff. Today, this method is the standard method for automated blood pressure measurement.

For the full comprehension of the principle, it is necessary to study the sensing techniques, plethysmographic signal and the methods used for signal processing. Standard blood pressure meters are designed as devices able to display only the systolic (SBP) and diastolic (DBP) arterial pressure and the heart rate. Blood pressure meters built in more complex devices such as monitors of vital functions are often able to display also the plethysmographic curve and mean arterial pressure (MAP). Unfortunately, there is no chance of displaying the inner signals needed for comprehension of the function such as raw signals from the pressure sensor and signals in the processing path.

The auscultatory method based on the auscultation of Korotkoff sounds is predominant for clinical measurement. Despite all its advantages, this method is hard to automate.

Due to the described features of standard blood pressure meters, a new laboratory kit has been designed. This kit allows us to monitor all crucial signals and values in

S. Khuri, L. Lhotská, and N. Pisanti (Eds.): ITBAM 2010, LNCS 6266, pp. 215–219, 2010.

real time and records them to a PC for future processing. It is primarily designed for oscillometry measurement, but it can be a very useful tool for measurement using the auscultatory method as well. The device allows manual control of inflating and deflating, display on the board shows actual pressure in the cuff.

The designed oscillometer provides the whole pressure curve, not only the SBP and DBP values as a standard blood pressure device. From the acquired signals, it is also possible to count the hemodynamic parameters such as augmentation index (AI) or pulse wave velocity (PVW), which is very important for determination of vascular system condition.

The processing of oscillometric signals is not yet standardized. It means each blood pressure device could provide slightly different results for the same patient at the same time. Without knowledge of the whole signal (pressure curve, occurence of artifacts etc.) there is no chance to select the correct result corresponding to real values.

2   Methods

The main task is to design and to realize the laboratory kit that allows development of robust signal processing algorithms that are not susceptive to artifacts (such as moving artifacts). For easy understanding of blood pressure measurement with oscillometry method, it is important to know the mean pressure in the cuff, the corresponding amplitude of oscillations, the basic principles of measured signals processing and the calculation of required values, and finally the effect of hardware set-up parameters.

The most interesting signals are the mean pressure in the cuff and the corresponding oscillations. Monitoring of these signals is impossible when utilizing standard devices. The designed laboratory kit has to allow both direct monitoring of the signals using an oscilloscope and recording of the signals to a PC for future processing.

The process of oscillometry measurement is very simple. The control valve is closed and the cuff is inflated to a pressure in excess of the systolic arterial pressure with an air pump. Then the control valve is slightly released and the pressure reduces to values below diastolic pressure. It takes about 40 seconds.

Inflating and deflating of the cuff is controlled by a microprocessor. The processor also secures analog-to-digital conversion and calculations of required values. Firstly, measured signal is processed by peak detector. From the amplitudes of the oscillations at any point in time there is derived an envelope of maxims and minims. The point of maximum amplitude of oscillations is when the underlying pressure in the cuff corresponds to mean arterial pressure. Systolic pressure is determined from the data already acquired. SBP can be determined by selecting the underlying pressure that corresponds to the amplitude of 55% of the maximum amplitude of oscillations (MAP) before the point of MAP. Furthermore, DBP is the underlying pressure when the envelope of oscillations has decreased to 85% of the maximal amplitude as shown on the Figure 1. Finally, the processor may calculate the heart rate from average distances between the peaks of oscillations.

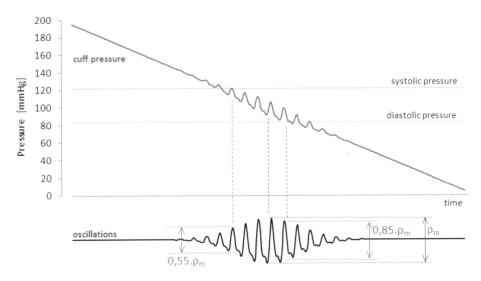

Fig. 1. Principle of calculation

3 Realization

The device is realized in form of printed circuit board with all appropriate components. The board is designed with distinctly separated function blocks, including several test pins for direct monitoring of inner raw signals with an oscilloscope. It enables to investigate all commonly inaccessible signals in detail.

The board can be controlled either via USB interface or manually. In case of remote control by computer, additional software operates the laboratory kit. However, manual control allows us to control inflating and deflating manually with a button and a potentiometer. In both operation modes, it is possible to sample signals and send them to a PC. For instance, it is possible to change the maximal pressure during inflating or the speed of deflating.

The board is equipped with an LCD display which shows the current state, the current pressure in the cuff and other detailed parameters. The PC application allows us not only to display the output values and configuration parameters but also to display the pre-processed signals and method for computing output values.

For better transparency, each block of the main board is marked with a label showing its function.

The additional software is designed to show separated signals from the cuff – absolute pressure and correspondent oscillations. It is possible to record all measured data into a file or calculate blood pressure and the other hemodynamic parameters of vascular system. The device may be also remote controlled with the software.

The main window of application for controlling oscillometer is shown in Figure 2. The upper curve is the absolute pressure in the cuff, the lower curve shows corresponding oscillations of pressure during reduction of pressure in the cuff.

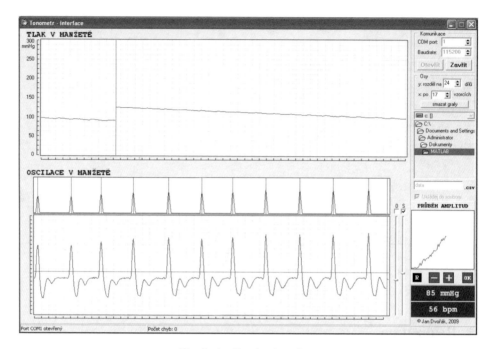

Fig. 2. Application interface

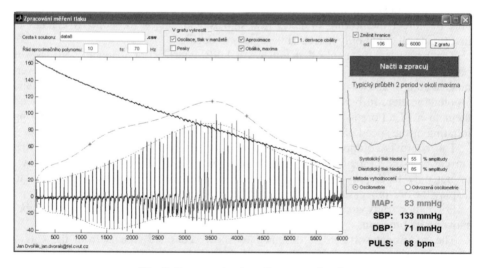

Fig. 3. Parameterization of pressure signal

After the recording of pressure signal the signal is parameterized (see Figure 3). The envelope of the signal and the amplitude of oscillations are obtained. Finally the SBP point (the amplitude of 55 % of the maximum before the point of MAP, in

Figure 3 labeled by asterisk) and the point of DBP (the amplitude of 85 % of the maximum after the point of MAP) are calculated.

Measured signals can be stored to a PC for successive processing sample by sample. It allows analysis of oscillometric signals and easy development of new methods for oscillometric signal processing (e.g. improvement of methods for calculating the SBP, DBP and MAP values and the methods for obtaining parameters of cardio-vascular system from oscillometric signal).

4 Conclusion

The presented laboratory kit is a unique requisite which allows us to develop new methods of signal processing and calculations. The kit is also a unique tool for measurement of the hemodynamic parameters of vascular system.

Values of blood pressure and the other hemodynamic parameters can often adumbrate cardiovascular problems, apoplexy or internal organs damage. Therefore it is very important to know the mentioned values. Standard devices do not allow measuring these parameters, despite the principle of oscillometry method enables it.

Furthermore, the module can be used for recording of the raw signals to a PC, which extends the possible usage. This laboratory kit can be also used for studying how artifacts, size of cuff or speed of deflating can influence signals and results.

Acknowledgement

This work has been supported by the research program Media Lab of the Czech Technical University in Prague and the research program No. MSM 6840770012 of the Czech Technical University in Prague (sponsored by the Ministry of Education, Youth and Sports of the Czech Republic).

References

1. Oliver, J.J., Webb, D.J.: Noninvasive Assessment of Arterial Stiffness and Risk of Atherosclerotic Events. Arteriosclerosis, Thrombosis and Vascular Biology 23, 554–566 (2003)
2. Wilkinson, I.B., Cockroft, J.R.: Estimation of central aortic pressure: shedding new light or clouding the issue. Clinical Science 106, 433–437 (2004)
3. Dvořák, J.: Výukový modul elektronického tonometru s možností záznamu a zpracování měřených dat. In: Proceedings of the 8th Czech-Slovak Conference "Trends in Biomedical Engineering" [CD-ROM], Bratislava (2009)
4. Webster, J.G.: Medical Instrumentation - Application and Design, 4th edn. Wiley, Chichester (2007)
5. Penhaker, M., a kol: Lékařské diagnostické přístroje - učební texty, VŠB-TU Ostrava (2004)
6. Rozman, J., a. kol: Elektronické přístroje v lékařství. Academia Praha (2006)

Initial Analysis of the EEG Signal Processing Methods for Studying Correlations between Muscle and Brain Activity

Helena Valentová and Jan Havlík

Department of Circuit Theory
Faculty of Electrical Engineering
Czech Technical University in Prague
Technická 2, CZ-16627 Prague 6
xhavlikj@fel.cvut.cz

Abstract. The paper presents an analysis of EEG signal processing methods for studying correlations between human muscle and brain activity. The main task of this work is to design the methods of EEG signal processing and to verify them on artificial and real signals. The paper introduces methods of EEG processing in time and frequency domain.

Keywords: EEG, signal processing, muscle activity.

1 Introduction

The paper presents an initial study of electroencephalographic (EEG) signal processing methods for the analysis of correlation between human muscle and brain activity.

The correlation between muscle and brain activity is one of the most interesting tasks in current biomedical engineering. As it is commonly known the muscle activity is controlled by the brain. It means the muscle activity has to correlate with brain activity. Unfortunately the brain activity is very complex and identifying of the activity respective to the muscle activity is not easy.

The correlation between brain and muscle activity was proved in many previous studies. The frequent approach is finding the coherence between brain activity and EMG (electromyogram, the record of muscle activity) signal. The brain activity is usually represented by the EEG (electroencephalogram, the electrical record of brain activity), for example [1], [2] and [3], but some studies presents the research of correlations between muscle activity and brain activity represented by MEG (magnetoencephalographic) signals [4].

The information about relationship between brain and muscle activity could help understanding how the brain controls the muscles and also could help recognizing first stages of many movement disorders (e.g. Parkinson disease and neuropathy).

Most of the previous studies concerned recognizing human body movements from EEG signals using two types of movements (e.g. the right index finger distal movement and right shoulder proximal movement [5]).

S. Khuri, L. Lhotská, and N. Pisanti (Eds.): ITBAM 2010, LNCS 6266, pp. 220–225, 2010.

The main goal of current research is to assign typical changes of EEG signals to the type of thumb motion. The thumb movements are not reduced to two types of motion for this study.

2   Experiment

Brain activity is represented by the EEG signals, the muscle activity is represented by the parameters of the thumb trajectory.

During the experiment a measured person seats in an upright position. The arm with observed thumb is supported by an armrest. The thumb moves between 3 positions – stationary states. Each movement is triggered by the synchronization pulse. The period of pulses is 6 ± 1 seconds. About 20 % of period is reserved for movement, the rest 80 % of period is the stay on the position.

The motions are sensed using a pair of standard DV camcorders. The sensed motions are recorded to a tape and stored to a PC after the experiment. The thumb trajectory is parameterized based on the processing of video sequences.

The EEG signals and video sequences are synchronized using the common synchronization signal.

3   Methods

The main task of this study is to separate blocks from EEG signal with the brain activity sensed during the finger motion and to classify the signals to the

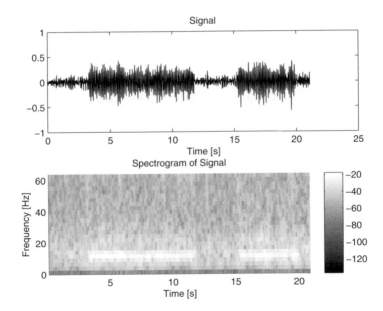

Fig. 1. Sample signal

classes – separate class for one type of motion. It is evident, that the EEG signals reflect not only intentional motions, but also all vital functions, artifacts from eye motions, spontaneous activity etc. In fact the effective signal has lower amplitude than the signal background. Unfortunately it means that it is very complicated to find the effective signal.

For these reasons the main idea is to use similar methods as methods for processing of evoked potentials. The methods are based on two main facts. The first one is that the EEG signal background is uncorrelated with the effective signal and the second one is that the effective signal is the same or very similar for each realization of motion. With this precondition the effective signal could be mined using the averaging methods. The methods assumes many realizations of each type of motion and the corresponding EEG signal.

3.1   Averaging in Time Domain

The easiest method is averaging in the time domain. Let's have N realizations of signal $s_n[t]$, where $n = 1 \ldots N$ is the index of realization, for each type of motion. The effective signal could be computed as simple average

$$\overline{s}[t] = \frac{1}{N} \sum_{n=1}^{N} s_n[t]. \tag{1}$$

This method is very simple, with very low computational demands, but the method is very sensitive to the phase of signal. It means the effective signal has to start in the same point of each processed segment.

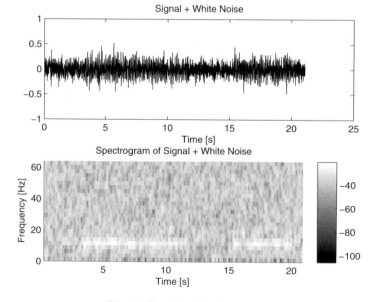

Fig. 2. Signal with white noise

3.2   Averaging in Frequency Domain

Another method is averaging the signal in the frequency domain using the Power Spectral Density (PSD). Let's have the same signal $s_n[t]$ as in the previous example divided to I segments with length J and the respective short time Fourier transform $S_n[i,j]$, where $i = 1 \ldots I$ and $j = 1 \ldots J$. The PSD matrix $P_n[i,j]$ of signal $s_n[t]$ is defined as $P_n[i,j] = |S_n[i,j]|^2$. The PSD of effective signal could be computed as the average

$$\overline{P}[i,j] = \frac{1}{N} \sum_{n=1}^{N} P_n[i,j].$$

(2)

The method is resistant to the shift of signal, but it has higher computational demands than averaging in time domain.

4   Evaluation

4.1   Evaluation on Artificial Signals

The EEG signal of eye movements with length more than 20 seconds were used for preparing artificial signal. The time behaviour and the spectrogram of the clear signal is shown in figure 1 (sample frequency $f_s = 128\,\mathrm{Hz}$).

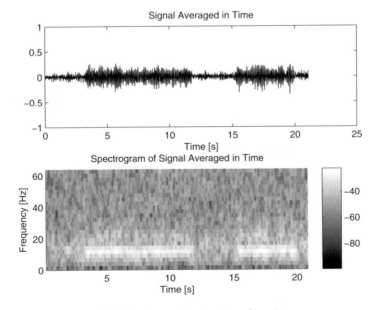

Fig. 3. Averaging in time domain

$N = 50$ realizations of the artificial signal were used for the tests. Each realization was produced by mixing of clear signal with white noise ($SNR = -5\,\mathrm{dB}$). Typical realization of signal with noise is shown in figure 2.

The averaged signal and averaged PSD are shown in figures 3 and 4. All the algorithms were implemented in the MATLAB programming environment.

4.2 Evaluation on Real Signals

The methods were also evaluated on the real dataset. The signals were acquired during two experiments. The EEG signals were measured using the 10 – 20 electrodes system with the sample frequency $f_s = 250\,\mathrm{Hz}$. The signal from sensomotoric area (electrode C3) was processed.

Each experiment had the length of about 10 min. It means that the signal database includes about 100 realizations of finger motions in one experiment. The signals were divided to the segments with respect to proper beginning of the motion. Information about the beginning of motions was obtained manually from the video sequences. Each segment was started 0.5 s before the motion start and finished 1.5 s after the motion start. It guarantees sufficient length of signal both before and after the motion.

Because the thumb moves between 3 stationary states in the experiment, the number of observed types of motions were 6 (from each position to any other in both directions). It means that the database includes about 30 realizations of each type.

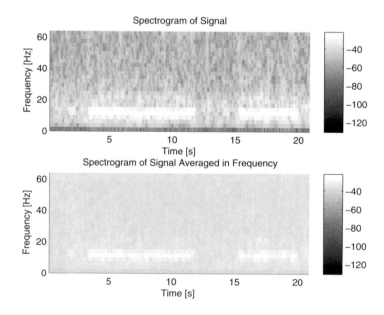

Fig. 4. Averaging in frequency domain

The results of evaluation on the real data are very preliminary. It could be supposed that the weak results have several main reasons.

The first one is very small number of realizations in database. It is necessary to make additional experiment for the proper evaluation in real conditions. The second one is uncertainty in determination of motion starts. It is principal problem, but especially for averaging in time domain it is evident that each small shift in determination of motion start could have great impact to final averaged signal.

Moreover, some previous studies showed that for some persons the coherence between brain and muscle activity is very unrecognizable. It is necessary to make the experiments with more than one measured person.

5 Conclusion

The two averaging methods were designed, implemented and evaluated during the initial study of EEG signal processing methods. The usability of the methods was evaluated both on artificial and real signals.

The test on artificial signals produced satisfactory results, but the test on real signals showed many problems. The most serious one is the requirement of great number of signal realizations. That means more experiments have to be performed for better evaluation of methods applied to real signal database.

Using the results from artificial signals it could be assumed that the methods are usable for finding the correlations between human muscle and brain activity.

Acknowledgement

This work has been supported by the research program No. MSM 6840770012 of the Czech Technical University in Prague (sponsored by the Ministry of Education, Youth and Sports of the Czech Republic).

References

1. Bortel, R., Sovka, P.: EEG–EMG coherence enhancement. Signal Processing 86, 1737–1751 (2006)
2. Salenius, S., Salmelin, R., Neuper, C., Pfurtscheller, G., Hari, R.: Human cortical 40 Hz rhytm is closely related to EMG rhythmicity. Neuroscience Letters 213(2), 75–78 (1996)
3. Tuncel, D., Dizibuyuk, A., Kiymik, M.K.: Time frequency based coherence analysis between EEG and EMG activities in fatigue duration. Journal of Medical Systems 34(2), 131–138 (2010)
4. Salenius, S., Portin, K., Kajola, M., Salmelin, R., Hari, R.: Cortical control of human motoneuron firing during isometric contraction. Journal of Neurophysiology 77(6), 3401–3405 (1997)
5. Šťastný, J., Sovka, P., Stančák, A.: EEG signals classification: Introduction to the problem. Radioengineering 12(3), 51–55 (2003)
6. Uhlíř, J., Sovka, P.: Digital Signal Processing (in Czech). Vydavatelství. ČVUT, Praha (2002)

Highlighting the Current Issues with Pride Suggestions for Improving the Performance of Real Time Cardiac Health Monitoring

Mohamed Ezzeldin A. Bashir[1], Dong Gyu Lee[1], Makki Akasha[1], Gyeong Min Yi[1], Eun-jong Cha[2], Jang-whan Bae[3], Myeong Chan Cho[3], and Keun Ho Ryu[1,*]

[1] Database/Bioinformatics Laboratory, Chungbuk National University, Korea
{mohamed,dglee,makki,min9709,khryu}@dblab.chungbuk.ac.kr
[2] Dept. of Bio. Engineering School of Medicine, Chungbuk National University, Korea
ejcha@chungbuk.ac.kr
[3] Dep. of Internal medicine, College of Medicine, Chungbuk National University, Korea
drcorazon@hanmail.net, mccho@cbnu.ac.kr

Abstract. Electrocardiogram (ECG) signal utilized by Clinicians to extract very useful information about the functional status of the heart. Of particular interest systems designed for monitoring people outdoor and detecting abnormalities on the real time. However, there are far from achieving the ideal of being able to perform adequately real time remote cardiac health monitoring in practical life. That is due to problematical challenges. In this paper we discuss all these issues, furthermore our intimations and propositions to relief such concerns are stated.

Keywords: Electrocardiogram, Arrhythmia, and Remote Cardiac Monitoring.

1 Introduction

Electrocardiogram (ECG) is a series of waves and deflections recording the cardiac's (heart) electrical activity sensed by several electrodes, known as leads. ECG signals generated by sensing the current wave sequence related to each cardiac beat. The P wave to represent the Atrial depolarization, QRS complex for ventricular depolarization and T wave for ventricular repolarization. Fig. 1 depicts the basics shape of a healthy ECG heartbeat signal.

ECG signals are very important medical instrument. That can be utilized by Clinicians to extract very useful information about the functional status of the heart. So as to detect heart arrhythmia which is the anomalous heart beat, mapped with different shape in ECG signal noticed by deflection on the P, QRS, and T waves, which acquired by some parameters. That judge against reference ones obtained through the average of normal ECG wave forms sampled from healthy people classified by age, sex, constitution and lifestyle. And then an enormous finding produced [1]. Considering the layout procedures of detecting the heart arrhythmias in real time, which begins with extracting the ECG signals, filtering, specifying the features and descriptors, selecting the training datasets, and end with constructing the classifier model to specify the types of arrhythmia in accurate manner [2].

---

* Corresponding author.

S. Khuri, L. Lhotská, and N. Pisanti (Eds.): ITBAM 2010, LNCS 6266, pp. 226–233, 2010.
© Springer-Verlag Berlin Heidelberg 2010

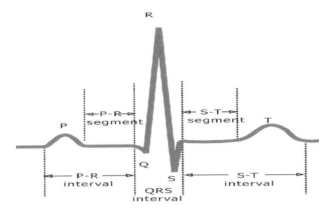

Fig. 1. Shape of a healthy ECG heartbeat signal

We specify a number of convenient challenges that stand in between monitoring the cardiac health in real time in very sufficient way. In this paper we argue these issues in details. In the rest of this paper, we give a brief background of the heart health monitoring problems, addressing the challenges for each step involved in developing real time cardiac health monitoring systems, finally the conclusion and recommendations.

2 Heart Health Monitoring Problems

Wired ECG monitoring in hospital are very crucial for saving people's life. But this kind of monitoring is inadequacy for the coronary cardiac disease's patients, who need following up in home and in the open air, those who need continues monitoring system to save their life. Generally there are three categories of systems for monitoring patients through classifying the ECG signal: 1) classification off-line 2) remote real time classification; and 3) local real time classification. Among the first group of systems, recorded ECG during continues 24 or 48 hours is going to be analyzed later, this type of systems doesn't offer a real time cardiac health monitoring. To overcome this problem, the second group of systems was developed, where remote real time classification is performed. This is can be achieved by sending the ECG data to a monitoring service center, then the ECG analysis can be made. In spite of the advantages, these kinds of systems still present number of disadvantages, such like inefficiency, that due to the high cost for transmitting the ECG data. Beside the difficulties to detect the signals when there is a limitation of networks. Moreover, troubles of compression in relation to reconstructed signal quality and coding delay are noticed. Because of the inherent drawbacks associated with the off-line and the remote real time classification of the ECG, there has been a great deal of interest in the third group of systems, those who provide real time ECG classification through intermediary local computer between the sensor and the control center [3]. It's vital for the automated system to accurately detect and classify ECG signals very fast, to provide a useful means for tracing the heart health in the right time. The effectiveness of such systems is affected by several factors, including the ECG signals, the estimated

ECG's features and descriptors, the dataset used for learning purpose and the classification model which applied. Although the local real time system are superior other systems, but there are still clear challenges, in the following sections we are going to discuss all these challenges.

2.1 The ECG Signal Extraction

The Electrocardiography is a diagnosis tool used by medical doctors to check the status of the heart. In contrast, the ECG can often be normal or nearly normal in patients with undiagnosed coronary artery disease or other forms of heart disease (false negative results.), and many "abnormalities" that appear on the ECG turn out to have no medical significance after a thorough evaluation is done (false positive results) [4].

ECG is recorded by attaching a set of electrodes on the body surface such as chest, neck, arms, and legs. The more the leads the larger the information set of data we can obtain for the heart activities. Early past, physicians used only three sensors (Right Arm RA, Left Arm LA, and Left Leg LL) in a method known as the 3-lead ECG, which suffers from the lack of information about the whole of the heart. The 12-lead ECG is the one of the hottest techniques for monitoring heart activity recording as (I, II, III, aVR, aVL, aVF, V1,V2,V3,V4,V5,V6) leads [5]. This type makes use of four limb electrodes and six chest electrodes in order to provide a comprehensive picture of the electrical activity of the heart from 12 different "viewpoints" around the surface of the body. The particular viewpoint which each lead has of the heart determines the characteristic form of the corresponding ECG signal. As a result, the morphology of the waves which make up the ECG signals for the different leads varies according to the particular lead chosen. Fig. 2 shows a single ECG waveform (heartbeat) from each of the 12 different leads. However, the costs for this enlarged amount of information are higher number of computations, more sophisticated monitoring and breakdown of large data sets, and stringent requirements on the elementary portable hardware platform.

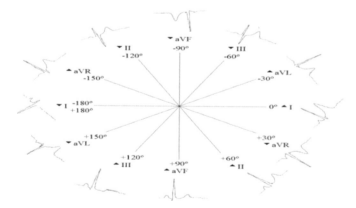

Fig. 2. Selected ECG waveforms from the 12 different leads

Unfortunately most solutions available now are based upon Massachusetts Institute of Technology-Beth Israel Hospital (MIT-BIH) arrhythmia database, where each record consists of two leads only [6]. This means, very limited information generated and discovered. As a result, we perceive only some arrhythmias, and monitoring merely the minority of the heart activity. On the other hand, there are 12 leads ECG databases mentioned in the literature just like Physikalisch-Technische Bundesanstalt (PTB), which provided by the National Metrology Institute of Germany. It composes of 16 input channels 14 for ECGs, one for respiration, and one for line voltage. But very little research and work was based on such database.

2.2 ECG Signal Quality

The filtering techniques seek in general, to specify and clarify the ECG wave elements (P, QRS complex, and T). The duration of the P wave is less than 120 milliseconds [7]. The spectral characteristic of a normal P wave is usually considered to be low frequency, below 10–15 Hz. The QRS complex lasts for about 70–110 milliseconds in a normal heartbeat, and has the largest amplitude of the ECG waveforms. Due to its steep slopes, the frequency content of the QRS complex is considerably higher than the other ECG waves, and is mostly concentrated in the interval of 10–40 Hz. The T wave reflects ventricular repolarization and extends about 300 milliseconds after the QRS complex [8]. As a result and due to the clearance of the QRS complex among the other parameters, most techniques detect the QRS complex mainly the R wave and sacrificing by the other parameters like P, T waves. QRS complex facilitates in detecting the RR interval and diagnosing many arrhythmias, such as normal heart beat, premature ventricular contractions, left and right bundled branch blocks, and paced beats. In contrast there are so many arrhythmias which couldn't be detected without considering the P and T waves [9]. Some arrhythmias, though they may have a different cause, apparent themselves in similar ways on the ECG, taking into account the main two grouping of arrhythmias the Ventricular, that occurs in the ventricles are recognized because of the abnormal QRS-morphology. And the Supraventricular arrhythmias, which occur in the atrium however, can only be predetermined because they have an effect on the ventricular rhythm. For example, prematurity is used as a parameter to detect non-sinus beats, sudden pauses as indicators of atrioventricular conduction disturbances or sinus pauses, and sometimes irregularity as a measure for the presence of atrial fibrillation or flutter. Accordingly, Supraventricular's abnormalities causing no or only gradual changes in ventricular rhythm are not observed by the current analysis programs, those who are referring only to the QRS complex for tracing the cardiac activity [10]. For that explanation, the way out of this problem would be, of course to analyze the P-wave and other elements of the ECG. Not only but also, measuring the time interval between these elements. Nevertheless, this is technically not feasible in the current remote cardiac health monitoring systems because of signal quality considerations.

2.3 QRS Descriptors

Some of the most descriptors of the QRS complex morphology are developed using pattern recognition techniques [11]. Measuring the diversity between the sequential and frequency characteristics of the QRS complex waveform is also introduced; such like Karhunen-loeve transforms [12], Hermite functions [13], and wavelet transform [14]. Recently, introduced methods of ECG signals adaptive time frequency transform and calculation of the applicable time frequency features pass on the structures of the signals [15]. The most popular approaches are based on pattern recognition techniques using morphological features, it obtained very high accuracy, but there are several disadvantages. First of all, the size of the templates that should be stored in the memory for further matching is very big. Secondly the accuracy relay on the threshold based segmentation techniques to discriminate the component of the ECG signal; these schemes are extremely receptive to the outsized morphological disparity of the ECG not only between different patients or patient cluster but also within the same patient. And finally, the limited numbers of classes of the wave form to descript specific cardiac arrhythmias, which can be extracted using such kind of features. Since there are some methods are using only the morphological descriptors of the QRS complex [16], while others are using the morphological descriptors of the P and T wave [17]. Nonetheless, we cannot use the morphological features of the P, T, and QRS waves to express cardiac patterns that do not have obvious P, T, and QRS complex. For that reason, morphological features are not fitting for describing ventricular fibrillation and some types of tachycardia. Moreover, morphological descriptors are counting a massive number of challenges in relation to computational efforts and time consuming [18]. Such computation is very complex to carry out by wireless sensors, since there are boundaries of power supply and the problem of noise; On the other hand, there are tendencies to detect the abnormality cardiac conditions using features to represent the ECG waveform through the time-frequency [19], by describing the ECG patterns through their frequencies content and time representation. Although it suffers from increasing the number of features assigned to detect different arrhythmias but still it looks much better than other methods, particularly it can be relief to some extent by utilizing the feature subset techniques.

2.4 Training Dataset

Confirming local and global dataset as the main two approaches of training dataset used to learn the classifier model. The local learning set is a customized set to specific patient, and global is built from large database [20] and [21]. The later one is preferable to build a classifier model, while it is static which means the learning process takes place through specific set of data under specific circumstances. Therefore, the model generated will be very accurate in similar situation while it doesn't in different cases. Which means it can be uses to monitor the ECG in hospital not in the open air. On the other hand, in case of the first philosophy there will be a patient adaptable local learning set. In this sense, specific strategies are adopted for local learning in some arrhythmia monitoring. Obviously, the size of the training data is very big and it is satisfy the need of monitoring just specific arrhythmia of specific patient.

The nature of ECG data in real time monitoring applications involves many changes through the time. For example, the different situations and activities of the monitored person are varying along the day, which affecting the heart activities and in usual cases it is not a bad effects but it will be detected by the ECG leads and transferred to the classifier model which is constructed by old training dataset. In case of worse condition when arrhythmias occur, the current classifier model may not detect the abnormalities or it may detect them but afterward [22]. As a result, the model constructed using the old training data no longer need to be adjusted in order to identify with the new concepts. In view of that, developing one classifier model to satisfy all patients in different situation using static training datasets is unsuccessful.

2.5 The Classification Models

Several data mining techniques were used for classifying the ECG data. Such as decision tree [23], support vector machine [24], neural networks [25], nearest neighbor [16], rule base classifier [26], fuzzy adaptive [27], and etc. The judgment upon such techniques bases on accuracy, sensitivity, speed and the reliability of the classifier. Integrating all these factors together, is essential for real time cardiac health monitoring purpose [28] and [29]. Moreover, finding out the most proper classifier model that capable for classifying arrhythmias on real time is very important issue. Even though, it is complicated process. That is due to the fact, each model was designed to detect specific kind of arrhythmias differ from one model to another, diverse arrhythmia database, unlike features extraction techniques, with dissimilarities procedures for preprocessing, and different percentages of training datasets. Although there were some efforts for comparing the performance of different classifiers model by unifying the comparison environment factors [3]. But regrettably, the comparison process takes place through few classification models, few types of arrhythmias, and slapdash to some important concerns; like memory requirement, time consumed and sensitivity. Additionally, the literature has not mentioned any assessments to these models in real life applications, such like evaluating the performance in Personal Digital Assistant (PDA), specifying the gap between the time of occurring the arrhythmia and the moment when it's detected by the model. So far, experimental results appear to indicate that various models are largely equivalent, and there is no evidence that any one model is superior to others. It will be more useful if the evaluation involve extra testing like dealing with noises. For the reason that, such applications in reality affected by so many influences for example, noise caused by surrounding environment or artifacts generated by electrode displacement, changes on the patient's body position or cardio-respiratory interactions.

3 Conclusion and Recommendations

Detecting the heart arrhythmias through ECG monitoring is mature research achievement. Research has been made, encouraging result has been obtained and cardiac health monitoring has reached a certain level of maturity when operating directly or off-line. However there are far from achieving the perfect of being able to perform adequately remote cardiac health monitoring and fulfilling the vision of providing the health care to anyone, anywhere, and any time. There are so many issues facing the current research on the area of real time heart monitoring. The number of ECG leads used to detect the heart signals are so few, limitation on arrhythmias detection quantity and quality, depending mainly upon the R wave and sacrificing by the P and T waves, which can offer better prediction in conjunction with the QRS complex wave. On the other hand, this is technically not feasible in the current remote cardiac health monitoring systems because of signal quality considerations. The computational cost of the QRS complex descriptors is very high and error-prone, which affect negatively the speed, flexibility, and the accuracy of the classifier. Also developing one classifier model to satisfy all patients in different situation using static training datasets is fruitless. Moreover, unfinished evaluations for the current general data mining classification models are listed.

Acknowledgment

This work was supported by the grant of the Korean Ministry of Education, Science and Technology (The Regional Core Research Program / Chungbuk BIT Research-Oriented University Consortium): the Basic Science Research Program through the National Research Foundation of Korea (NRF) funded by the Ministry of Education, Science and Technology (NRF No. 2010-0001732): the research grant of the Chungbuk National University in 2008.

References

1. Dale Dubin, M.D.: Rapid interpretation of EKG's, 6th edn. Cover publishing co. (2000)
2. Rajendra, U., Sankaranarayanan, M., Nayak, J., Xiang, C., Tamura, T.: Automatic Identification of cardiac health using modeling techniques: a comparative study. Inf. Science. 178, 457–4582 (2008)
3. Rodrigues, J., Goni, A., Illarramendi, A.: Real time classification of ECG on a PDA. IEEE Trans. On IT in B.med., 23–33 (2005)
4. Goldberger, A.L.: Electrocardiography: A Simplified Approach. Elsevier, Amsterdam (2006)
5. Kligfield, P.: value and limitation of 12-lead ECG monitoring. clinical window, Datex, Ohmeda (2001)
6. Mark, R., Moody, G.: MIT-BIH Arrhythmia data base directory. Massachusetts Institute of Technology, Cambridge (1988)
7. Clifford, G., Azuaje, F., McSharrg, P.: Advanced methods and tools for ECG data analysis. Artech house (2006)
8. Chritove, I., Herrero, G., Krasteva, V., Jekova, I., Gotchev, A., Egiazarian, K.: Comparative study of morphological and time frequancy ECG descriptors for heartbeat classification. Medical engineering and physics 28, 876–887 (2006)
9. Sörnmo, L., Laguna, P.: Bioelectrical Signal Processing in Cardiac and Neurological Applications. Elsevier, Amsterdam (2005)
10. de Bie, J.: P-wave trending: A valuable tool for documenting supraventricular arrhythmias and AV conduction disturbances. IEEE, 511–514 (1991)
11. Millet, J., Pkrez, M., Joseph, G., Mocholi, A., Chorro, J.: Previous identification of QRS Onset and Offset is not essential for classifying QRS complex in a single lead. Com. In: Cardiology, vol. 24, pp. 299–302 (1997)
12. Moody, G., Mark, R.: QRS Morphology Representation and Noise Estimation using the Karhunen-Loève Transform. IEEE, Comp. in Card, 269–272 (1989)
13. Lagerholm, M., Peterson, C., Braccini, G., Edenbrandt, L., Sörnmo, L.: Clustering ECG complex using Hermite Functions and selforganizing maps. Trans. on B. med. Eng. 47, 838–848 (2000)
14. Senhadii, L., Carrault, G., Bellanger, J., Passariello, G.: Comparing wavelet transforms for recognizing cardiac patterns. IEEE, Eng. Med. & Bio., 167–173 (1995)

15. Herrero, G., Gotchev, A., Christov, I., Egiazarian, K.: Heartbeat classification using independent component analysis and matching Pursuits. In: ICASSP, pp. 725–728. IEEE, Los Alamitos (2005)
16. Christov, I., Bortolan, G.: Ranking of pattern recognition parameters for premature ventricular contractions classification by neural networks. Phys. Measure 25, 1281–1290 (2004)
17. Chazal, P., Dwyer, M., Reilly, R.: Automatic classification of heartbeats using ECG morphology and heartbeat interval features. IEEE Trans. Biomed. Eng. 51, 1196–1206 (2004)
18. Jekova, I., Bortolan, G., Christov, I.: Assessment and comparison of different methods for heartbeat classification. Med. Eng. Phys. 30, 248–257 (2008)
19. Osowski, S., Linh, T.: ECG beat recognition using fuzzy hybrid neural network. IEEE Trans. Biomed. Eng. 48, 1265–1271 (2001)
20. Palreddy, H., Tompkins, W.: A patient-adaptable ECG beat classifier using a mixture of experts approach. Trans. on B. med. Eng. 44, 891–900 (1997)
21. Bortolan, G., Jekova, I., Christov, I.: Comparison of four methods for premature ventricular contractions and normal beats clustering. Comp. Card. 30, 921–924 (2005)
22. Bashir, M.E.A., Akasha, M., Lee, D.G., Yi, M., Ryu, K.H., Bae, E.J., Cho, M., Yoo, C.: Nested Ensemble Technique for Excellence Real Time Cardiac Health Monitoring. Bio-Comp., lasvegas, USA (2010)
23. Bemaid, A., Bouhouch, N., Bouhouch, R., Fellat, R., Amri, R.: Classification of ECG Patterns Using Fuzzy Rules Derived from ID3-Induced Decision Trees. In: NAFIPS, pp. 34–38. IEEE, Los Alamitos (1998)
24. Kampouraki, A., Manis, G., Nikou, C.: Heartbeat time series classification with support vector machines. Eng. in Med. and Bio. Sc. 13, 512–518 (2009)
25. Yang, T., Devine, B., Macfarlane, P.: Artificial neural networks for the diagnosis of atrial fibrillation. Med. Biol. Eng. Comp. 32, 615–619 (1994)
26. Birman, K.: Rule-Based Learning for More Accurate ECG Analysis. Tran. on Puttern analysis and Mach. Int. 4, 369–380 (1982)
27. Rajendra, U., Subbann, P., Iyengar, S., Raod, A., Dua, S.: Classification of heart rate data using artificial neural network and fuzzy equivalence relation. Pattern Recognition 36, 61–68 (2003)
28. Lee, D., Shon, Ho Ryu, K., Cho, M., Bae, J.: Clinica Database Based on Various Factors of Cardiovascular Diseases. In: International workshop on aware computing, Japan, pp. 604–609 (2009)
29. Ho Ryu, K., Kim, W., Lee, H.: A Data mining approach and framework of intelligent Diagnosis system for Coronary Artery disease Predication. In: KSES, Japan, pp. 33–34 (2008)

Author Index

Akasha, Makki   226
Aranguren, Mikel Egaña   128

Bae, Jang-whan   226
Bashir, Mohamed Ezzeldin A.   226
Bechini, Alessio   201
Berka, Petr   110
Braga, Regina   86
Breit, Timo M.   1

Campos, Fernanda   86
Cha, Eun-jong   226
Cho, Myeong Chan   226
Chudáček, Václav   57
Couto, Francisco   16, 31

Dabringer, Claus   172
Dvořák, Jan   215

Eder, Johann   172

Fernández-Breis, Jesualdo Tomás   128
Ferreira, Hugo   31
Folino, Francesco   102

García-Sánchez, Francisco   128
Georgoulas, George   57
Giannini, Riccardo   201

Hansen, Jens Ulrik   186
Ha, Sung Ho   67
Havlík, Jan   215, 220
Hirose, Osamu   158
Huptych, Michal   57

Janků, Petr   57

Karpov, Leonid   78
Khalid, Shehla   45
Koucký, Michal   57

Latiful Hoque, Abu Sayed Md.   118
Lee, Dong Gyu   226
Leunissen, Jack A.M.   1
Lexa, Matej   94

Lhotská, Lenka   57
Lopes, Luis F.   31

Mendes, Luiz Felipe   86
Miñarro-Giménez, José Antonio   128

Neagu, Daniel   45
Neerincx, Pieter   1
Nijholt, Anton   1

Ooms, Matthijs   1

Paul, Razan   118
Pizzuti, Clara   102

Ramampiaro, Heri   143
Rauch, Jan   110
Rauwerda, Han   1
Rudolfova, Ivana   94
Ryu, Keun Ho   226

Shimizu, Kentaro   158
Silva, Fabrício A.B.   16, 31
Silva, Mário J.   16, 31
Sousa, Carla   31
Spilka, Jiří   57
Stylios, Chrysostomos   57
Surr, Claire   45

Valentová, Helena   220
van der Veer, Gerrit   1
van der Vet, Paul   1
Ventura, Maria   102
Viotto, Jacopo   201

Wassink, Ingo   1

Yi, Gyeong Min   226
Yudin, Valery   78

Zambach, Sine   186
Zamite, João   16, 31
Zendulka, Jaroslav   94
Zhang, Zhen Yu   67

Printing: Mercedes-Druck, Berlin
Binding: Stein+Lehmann, Berlin